Dispatches from the Color Line

SUNY series, Negotiating Identity: Discourses, Politics, Processes, and Praxes

Ronald L. Jackson II, editor

Dispatches from the Color Line

The Press and Multiracial America

Catherine R. Squires

STATE UNIVERSITY OF NEW YORK PRESS

Published by
State University of New York Press, Albany

© 2007 State University of New York

All rights reserved

Printed in the United States of America

For information, contact State University of New York Press, Albany, NY
www.sunypress.edu

Production by Kelli Williams
Marketing by Michael Campochiaro

Library of Congress Cataloging-in-Publication Data

Squires, Catherine R., 1972–
   Dispatches from the color line : the press and multiracial America /
Catherine R. Squires.
      p. cm. — (SUNY series, negotiating identity)
   Includes bibliographical references and index.
   ISBN-13: 978-0-7914-7099-2 (hardcover : alk. paper)
   ISBN-13: 978-0-7914-7100-5 (pbk. : alk. paper)
   1. Racism in the press—United States. 2. Race relations and the press—
United States. 3. Racially mixed people—Press coverage—United States.
I. Title.

PN4888.R3S68 2007
305.8—dc22
                                                      2006021549

10 9 8 7 6 5 4 3 2 1

Contents

List of Illustrations

Tables

Preface

When my mother, a White woman, took me and my sister, two Black/White children, on walks around our neighborhood in the 1970s, well-meaning White people would often stop to look at us. My mother reports that many would ask, "Did you get them at the Cradle?" The Cradle was a local adoption agency, one of the few doing interracial placements. "No, these are home-grown," my mother would sarcastically reply as she steered the stroller away.

Fast forward to 2000: my older sister is playing in the park with her daughter, my niece. A curious White five-year-old approaches her and helps herself to my niece's snacks. She asks my sister, "Where's her mommy?" When my sister replies that she is the mommy in question, the little girl repeats her question, still snacking. Then, determined to prove my sister was not the mother of my blonde-haired niece, states as fact, "*Babysitters* are brown." And, indeed, this White child was at the park with her brown-skinned nanny. Her world was so easily divided into mothers and babysitters, each with their own color coding set in stone.

So much and yet so little has changed in the three decades between these two tales of mistaken identities, mothers and daughters, and "knowing" observers. My mother was assumed to be a charitable White woman willing to take on the "challenge" of raising Black children; my sister and I are mistaken for the hired help, assumed to be among the legions of women of color who are paid to care for White children. As a grade schooler in the 1970s, the only person—and certainly the only famous person—outside my siblings that I knew who had one Black and one White parent was Franco Harris of the Pittsburgh Steelers. I was a huge fan and loved watching the Steelers even as my classmates followed the Chicago Bears' Super Bowl Shuffle in 1985. As a kid, I never imagined that, by the time I became a mother, I'd be bombarded with images in advertisements, television shows, and newsmagazines of "mixed race" couples and "interracial families" and "multiracial celebrities." Though I took pride in both my Afro-American and German American heritage, I understood my public self to be viewed as Black, and my sense of racial identity has been framed by that experience. Even after cheekily asking my mother if I could write "Guess?" in the slot for race on the 1980 Census long form my family filled out, I never dreamed I would be writing a book about media representations of people like myself before and after Census 2000 made it possible to choose more than one race to describe oneself to government statisticians. Nor did I ever think that a "multiracial movement" would emerge to challenge binary ideologies of race. But here I am, looking back at my childhood in this new light.

I look back, and forward, with decidedly mixed feelings; appreciation for the changes that have occurred since my school days, offset by dismay at the ways in which discourses concerning people like me are being constructed for agendas I abhor. I am more than a little uneasy about the politics of multiracial identity and race relations at the dawn of the twenty-first century in the United States and abroad. I certainly don't want to go back to the days when clerks decided if your child was "yellow," "red," or "black," but nor do I think, as some commentators assert, that the growing presence of multiracial people means we have transcended race and no longer need to factor it into social, economic, educational, and health policy or statistics. I'm still occasionally referred to as "high yella" or "redbone" by catcallers on the street; one of our babysitters tells me how she's been told that she "must be White trash" by White people who find out she dates Black men.

I relate these anecdotes not to elicit sympathy or shock; rather, I hope they convey how much we still learn about and live race through anecdotes, asides, stereotype, and personal experiences (or lack thereof). In our society, most people still reside and go to school in segregated environments; despite the record numbers of interracial marriages, we still learn about other racial and ethnic groups through secondhand sources, such as the mass media, relatives' tales, or hearsay at the water cooler. We still are neither comfortable with nor do we have many opportunities to share private or intimate time with people of different races to talk about the meaning of race in our world. And, depending on one's region, school curriculum, or family history, the intellectual content of what one learns about race through educational materials or current events media varies widely. The role of multiracial people in this convoluted process of learning about other racial groups and understanding who "we" and "they" are is still quite unclear. I predict it will not follow a simple, progressive trajectory toward a world without race or racism.

Recently I was going through a box of old family records my father had kept. In the box was my grandmother's birth certificate. On the line denoting her mother's "Color," a clerk or nurse chose to describe my great-grandmother Minnie Simpson with the word "yellow." Next to "Color" for her father was "Blk." When my grandmother was born in Mississippi in 1914, there was no such term as multiracial, and no choice to list multiple races to communicate one's heritage or identity. Hospital staff and state record keepers didn't ask parents what their race was or their preference for their child; they just looked, assumed, and wrote down what was customary for their particular locality. Hence, "yellow" to describe a woman of African, Choctaw, and European descent. At that time, the Census Bureau had already discontinued its practice of having enumerators count "quadroons" separate from other "Negroes," and Jim Crow laws of the state said the same, but skin color gradation was still salient in that part of the South. I am not claiming that my grandmothers and grandfathers saw themselves as anything other than Negro or Black or African American; clearly, they knew on which side of the color line they lived and worked. I was never told, except in the context of family lore about our Choctaw heritage, that I, or my great grandmother, were "mulatto" or "quadroon." These facts concerning my grandmother's birth record illustrate how very recent the "new" multiracial identity movement is, and yet how old the practice of differentiating people of color on gradations of skin tone or parentage is in our nation.

This book maps out some of the contours of debate and understanding about multiracial identified individuals. It investigates how recent discourse about this "new" racial/ethnic group breaks from or resonates with past racial formulations and political agendas. Although news media do not provide the only information about multiracial identity and racial politics, they serve an important role in describing and chronicling controversies about race, identity, and public policy attended to by lay and elite readers. In these texts, we find prescriptions and opinions alongside "hard facts"; personal stories next to statistics; pictures of everyday people and celebrities, all connected to the same topic. As a consumer and an analyst, I see many promising and many disquieting elements, and I hope the reader finds some points of connection with my reading of multiracial identity in the news. I have an even greater hope that some of my analysis will be helpful to those navigating their way through the field of representations and narratives of people of multiple colors, and that the book can extend our conversations about race into productive new territory.

Acknowledgments

If it were not for a host of people, this book would not exist. It is a wonderful feeling to finally have the chance to thank the family members, friends, and colleagues who gave me all sorts of support as I slogged my way through piles of newspapers, wrote chapters, made revisions and more revisions. Special thanks go to all those who read the manuscript in total for a workshop organized by Dr. Kevin Gaines at the Center for Afroamerican and African Studies: Professors Robin Means Coleman, Elizabeth Cole, and Hemant Shah all gave their time and enthusiastic efforts, resulting in invaluable feedback on every chapter. I also thank George Lipsitz and the anonymous readers for SUNY Press who gave suggestions for revision that made it much easier to construct a roadmap for the final draft. Thanks to Tiya Miles and Laura Kohn for their honesty about the boring working title (jettisoned, finally, after brainstorming with my husband, Bryan, for two weeks in the car! Hope you like the new one!), and for their support as colleagues and friends at key times over cups of tea and brunches on the run.

My colleague and chair, Susan Douglas, was an unbelievable resource helping me navigate the ins and outs (and ups and downs) of securing a publisher, and provided insightful comments on the project at various stages, including early feedback during department collquia. Bambi Haggins (holla back!) and I determined to prop each other up in the summer of 2005 and read each other's writing diligently, and I cannot thank her enough for the coffee and sympathy over those long months of uncertainty and angst. I must thank Lisa Chesnel and Ron Jacobs for their confidence in the project from the first read of the prospectus, and for their competent, professional advice throughout the stages of publication. Mike Traugott and Nick Valentino said valuable words about seeking funding and articulating "the big why," respectively, as I crafted the studies and the text. Reg Daniel's periodic e-mails kept me encouraged, and readers in Lori Brooks's Black Studies Group (are we going to start up again?) convinced me to keep a positive mental attitude about the prospects of the manuscript. Brad Mosher designed my wonderful book cover. Daniel Brouwer remained my close friend, intellectual comrade, and meticulous reader throughout the project and beyond, sending immensely helpful messages and support from the Arizona desert.

Parts of the research for this book were funded generously by three University of Michigan institutions: the Rackham School of Graduate Studies; the Marsh Center for Journalistic Excellence at the Department of Communications; and the Undergraduate Research Opportunity Program. I cannot thank my research assistants enough, especially Ian Douglas, TaKeshia Brooks, Nikki Stanton, and Allison Zaleski for their untiring work on the data collection, coding, and editing. Parts of chapter 2 were first published in the journal *Critical Studies in Media Communication* in 2002. Some segments of the analysis on the Black press in chapter 5 appeared in the *Journal of Intergroup Relations* in 2003. Chapters 3 and 4 were presented, respectively, at the International Communication Association conference in 2005 and National Communication Association conference in 2004, where I gained valuable feedback from respondents and audience members. I am sure there are plenty of other people to thank, and my apologies to those I have not named.

Here I must pause to say how much I appreciate the love, support, and hard-nosed editing my mother, Helen Gagel, contributed to this book. Since grade school, she's helped me shape my writings into better vehicles for my (often nutty) ideas with patience and a no-nonsense approach to the beauty of grammar. (All comma splices that may exist in this book, though, are my fault.) To my sisters Theresa Collins and Leah Squires, thanks for having my back, for long late-night conversations where you picked me up when I was struggling to get motivated, and for letting me know when I was getting a bit too serious. And to my dad, Robert Squires, who didn't live to see me finish it, but whose devotion to solving racial problems was often on my mind as I wrote.

There exists no sufficient vocabulary to express my appreciation for my husband, Bryan Mosher, and our twins, Will Franklin and Helena Rose, who were so generous with me as I worked on this book. Bryan, thanks for taking the kids on numerous adventures while I was chained to my laptop; for having broad shoulders for weepy moments; and for bolstering my confidence when I wasn't sure I could finish this book. You have no idea how much your enthusiasm about the book and my ideas means to me. I hope I can return all the love and good will you provided as you pursue your work. Will and Helena, your patience with Mommy when she had to "go work upstairs" exhibited fortitude uncharacteristic for toddlers. Thank you for understanding when it wasn't time to "play with the numbers and letters" on Mommy's keyboard, and thanks for giving me good reason to take breaks to dance around the living room with my favorite partners. I'll be writing something else soon, but now that it's spring again, let's go play outside.

Introduction

Remember: identification, not identities. Once you've got an identification, you can decide which identities are working this week.

—Stuart Hall, "Subjects in History: Making Diasporic Identities"

How did it come to be that, after two hundred years of abject status, restrictive public policy, and negative stereotypes, multiracial identity has emerged as a favorite child of American racial politics? What transpired in the four decades since the Supreme Court struck down the last laws prohibiting interracial marriage to make mixed race couples chic? Why are multiracial children now key figures in politicians' pleas for "colorblindness"? Once deemed signs of racial chaos and corruption, interracial couples and their families are today celebrated as proof of racial harmony and the declining significance of race. The "last taboo" of race relations—sex and marriage—has been overcome. Or has it? Is interracial intimacy really the key to solving racial tensions and inequalities, or has this particular social phenomenon become popular with politicians and the media because it further displaces discussion of intransigent racial problems?

As mainstream journalists disseminate optimistic pronouncements and statistics concerning race mixing, public opinion polls show a continued gulf between Whites and people of color in views on racial policy and climate; social statistics on wealth, income, education, and other key indicators of economic, political, and social equality reveal continued racial discrepancies.[1] At the same time, high-profile White politicians book speaking engagements at Bob Jones University, which had an anti–interracial dating policy in effect throughout the 1990s. After his death in December 2003, Senator Strom Thurmond's secret biracial daughter finally spoke the truth of her parentage and the pain of her father's racism, which he (and his adopted Republican Party) used to great advantage throughout his long career. How did these events and trends in discourse coincide?

1

Some answers to these questions can be found by exploring how our society discusses race in the post–civil rights movement era. This book is particularly concerned with one facet of this discourse: the news media's framing of multiracial identity. Comparing cases across time and types of news media, I argue that news coverage of multiracial individuals and issues hews close to dominant ideologies of race and race relations in general, and that multiracial individuals and organizations provide opportunities for political actors to channel their preferences about race and public policy. Contrary to the hopes of some activists and academics who focus on the progressive possibilities of multiracial identity, official acknowledgment of hybrid racial identities has not, thus far, inspired significant progressive changes in the ways that race is discussed in the dominant public sphere. Rather, in most mainstream media accounts, multiracial identity is yet another vehicle for denying the social import of race and reinforcing the dominant notion that race is matter of individual tastes and psychology, not structural inequalities. Indeed, as has happened sporadically with Asian Americans, multiracial people seem to be moving into a "model minority"[2] niche in mainstream news media accounts of their rise to visibility and demographic critical mass.

Media coverage of conflicts surrounding multiracial identity are, as Stuart Hall would say, defining a portion of the "horizon of possibilities" for how we discuss race in the United States. Of course, in defining the scope of this horizon, the media are not determining the outcomes completely. Indeed, the concept of a distinct, government-recognized multiracial identity is so new that there is certainly time to question and, possibly, contest dominant interpretations of this "new" racial identity in mass media and public policy. Discourses of a "new" multiracial identity are part of society's attempts to understand the meaning of race at the beginning of the twenty-first century, in a world changed by immigration, globalism, and increasing calls for tolerance of diversity. How multiracial people are talked about is indicative of society's general state of race relations. In the past, interracial intimacy and multiracial children have been (and in some spheres, continue to be) symbols of the ultimate race problem; and only in a few rare cases were they seen as a solution. From the fear of amalgamation and racial impurity of the nineteenth century to the twenty-first century hope that rising interracial marriage rates will engender racial harmony, and everything in between, debates concerning race mixing reflect, reinforce, and in some cases challenge, social norms. This book examines how news media are shaping the current role of multiracial identity in how we explain race in America. As such, I chart a shift that has occurred over the last twenty years, wherein multiracial people have been discursively transformed from objects of curiosity and pity, to symbols of the racist past and, today, hopeful portents for the future. These discourses are not merely descriptive, but also contain and promote prescriptions advocated by political and social actors seeking an advantage for their particular racial projects.

Framing Racial Realities:
News Media and Racial Formation

Public life in the United States is punctuated by events wherein the public is asked to consider the question, "Does race (still) matter?" Since the 1980s, Americans have, in the main, been encouraged to answer "no." Whether egged on by neoconservative or liberal visions of "color-blindness," poll data showing decreasing racist attitudes, or backlash against affirmative action policies, the idea that race is no longer a significant part of American life is now hegemonic. This new hegemony is energized by the political successes of the neoconservative movement, as well as particular readings of postmodern and scientific studies that argue race doesn't exist as a biological, essential reality of humankind. In the words of historians, sociologists, and others, race is a part of the social world whose meanings are constructed, not fixed; in the speech of scientists, there is more diversity within allegedly discrete racial groups than across those groups. Despite the "unreality" of race, though, it still asserts a very real set of parameters on how we interpret the social world and our fellow human beings. As Michael Omi and Howard Winant explain, "we should see race as a dimension of human representation rather than an illusion."[3] As such, the main engines of representation, the mass media, provide important sites to investigate when considering current trajectories of racial discourse in the United States.

As institutions of ideological production, the news media are part of the process of racial formation and racial projects. Omi and Winant define racial formation as a "sociohistorical process by which racial categories are created, inhabited, transformed, and destroyed."[4] A racial project is "simultaneously an interpretation, representation, or explanation of racial dynamics, and an effort to reorganize and redistribute resources along particular racial lines."[5] Racial projects, then, rest upon particular conceptualizations of racial identities and how these identities and the meaning of race itself are communicated. For example, African Americans have continually sought to transform or destroy dominant definitions of African American identity as part of the struggle against legal and social oppression in America. Dominant social institutions, including mainstream news media, upheld, reinforced, and disseminated oppressive characterizations, stereotyping African Americans as unfit for citizenship in order to justify White hegemony. Latina/os, Native Americans, Asian Americans, and other groups have acted similarly, finding much fault with the news media's role in stereotyping, marginalizing, or even erasing people of color. From the Kerner Commission to the Christopher Commission mainstream news media have been named as important sites of representation of racialized publics and their problems, as well as conveying the possible solutions to those problems. As such, they play a crucial role in portraying what race and racial groups are—or should be—at a given moment; news representations of racial groups and racial controversies can reflect current trends in racial thinking and, at times, can reject them, contributing to the process of racial formation by supporting or challenging dominant ideas about our racial reality. When people of color mount strong challenges to hegemonic racial ideology, news media may dispatch their protests to broader publics. As multiracial people became visible players in newsworthy racial events—such as the federal government's restructuring of race and ethnicity categories for the 2000 Census—the press became involved in communicating their racial identities and agendas to the public.

Following Jane Rhodes, I view press coverage of social movements and marginalized racial groups as a

> *dialogic relationship* between media subjects, media producers, and consumers in a rich mix of communication, ideology, and history. These interlocking components—the mode and substance of news stories, the political and cultural beliefs underlying the stories, and the national histories that made these stories newsworthy— form what Mikhail Bakhtin called a heteroglot of language. . . . Woven together, they produce the fabric of news. Each group ha[s] an agenda and an ideological framework within which it operate[s].[6]

Through the dialogic model, we can view the coverage of multiracial identity as power-imbued negotiations over the meaning of race, nation, and public policy between journalists, minority organizations, politicians, and government officials. Although multiracial organizations and individuals have tried to foster alternative ways of seeing multiracial identity, stories about multiracial identity reflect and are influenced by the organizational practices of journalists, the history and tenor of race relations in the United States, and the way news organizations imagine the identities and preferences of their audiences. These factors set the stage for particular renderings, or *framing*, of multiracial people, their histories, allies, and opponents, and other racial groups.

News producers contribute to racial projects and racial formation through the process of framing. Framing, according to Robert Entman, is the process of "selecting some aspects of a perceived reality and mak[ing] them more salient in a communicating text . . . to promote a particular problem definition, causal interpretation, moral evaluation, and/or treatment recommendation."[7] Individual journalists, editors, photographers, sources, and institutions consulted by newsmakers all contribute to the framing process by selecting and providing particular views of an issue, its causes, remedies, and repercussions. Drawing not only from outside sources but also from their own predispositions and cultural conditioning, we can expect that there would not be a perfect match between the narratives about multiracial identity produced by journalists and the ideas promoted by all individuals or organizations within the multiracial identity movement. Rather, multiracial individuals and organizations are portrayed in relation to broader racial contexts and ongoing projects of the time as well as significant elements from the racial past.

In the case of racial controversies, oftentimes this process results in a dominance of White viewpoints in mainstream news. In the dominant press, the majority of practitioners are White and male; so too are the majority of their sources and contacts, including politicians, civil servants, and businesspeople. When issues of race arise, then, the mainstream media can act as an echo chamber as news-gathering routines—which privilege government sources—and assumptions about the majority (White) audience steer reporters to frame racial events from the standpoint of White Americans. Consciously or unconsciously, most mainstream journalism reinforces the racial status quo and dominant understandings of racial categories. Thus, framing is a process by which journalists—as individuals and as a profession—in concert with (or in opposition to) dominant institutions and political actors, help shape the perception of racial reality in society. This perception influences public opinion and policy by delimiting the discussion of racial issues. If, for example, the colorblind perspective dominates framing of racial issues, news coverage will likely privilege specific remedies consonant with neoconservative policies and goals. That same coverage will also likely suggest that people of color who assert that race still matters and racism still operates in society are outside the norms of public opinion.

Through the framing process, news media influence the public's sense of the salience of racial issues. Too often, many scholars have noted, coverage of these problems ebbs and flows with little or "no relationship to actual changes in the status of those problems."[8] Thus, the press's lack of consistent attention to particular ongoing racial controversies may hinder its own and the public's ability to gauge the severity of racial conflicts, their causes, and the range of workable solutions. Specifically for racial issues, the dominant news values that steer mainstream journalists to cover extraordinary and deviant events often results in dependence upon stereotypes and readily available frameworks that reinforce hegemonic views of racial minorities.[9] As Robert Entman and Andrew Rojecki remind us, we most often hear about racial conflict and violence, perhaps skewing our sense of racial tensions in the United States. In addition, sporadic coverage of racial issues does not allow for sustained attention to the complex web of history, culture, politics, and institutions that underlies even the most sensational race conflict stories. Thus, Iyengar explains, as journalists focus on the "facts" of immediate events, they rarely include the role of institutions and structures in a given conflict. As a result, they tend to emphasize the faults of individuals on the contemporary scene and ignore the role of institutions, historical patterns, and other societal influences.[10] As I will discuss in later chapters, given how mainstream news media covered the results of Census 2000's experiment with a multiracial option, this tendency to individualize stories looms even larger because the biographies of individual mixed-race people are often the focus of stories. This reinforces the prevailing ideology that race and racial attitudes are matters of personal choice, not structural or legal.

Although scholars take care to point out that individual journalists may not be consciously creating racial frames, framing is not happenstance. In addition to the prevalence of official sources in mainstream news, one side in a racial controversy may attract an "issue sponsor," an individual or organization with access to media elites who helps shape the story in the interests of particular constituents.[11] For example, certain organizations in the multiracial movement allied themselves with Newt Gingrich and like-minded Republican congressmen as they lobbied for a multiracial category on Census 2000. This assured the involvement of neoconservative issue sponsors, who were able to activate their extensive media networks to deliver their opinions on the subject in prominent media outlets and public places.

More subtly, because of their overdependence on official sources, mainstream journalists may inadvertently participate in "political rituals" with racial consequences. In James Ettema's study of political repositioning after the death of Harold Washington, the first Black mayor of Chicago, he explains how the press became a player in the struggle between White and Black politicians. Here, the ouster of certain Black officials was framed as a necessary "cleansing ritual" to "heal" the city and return it to its rightful state of harmony, all but erasing the role of decades of racist Democratic machine politics in the crisis.[12] The preference some elites seem to be showing for multiracial individuals versus traditionally defined people of color may be shaping a similar "cleansing ritual," as conservatives argue that multiracial individuals symbolize colorblindness and that Blacks and Latina/os must cease "playing the race card" to selfish, divisive ends.

Similarly, although the news media currently attempt to present a "multicultural America," this multicultural reporting does not automatically translate into more consistent and comprehensive coverage of racial groups. Studies of news coverage of the post–Rodney King upheavals and "new" immigrants reveal troubling patterns wherein Latina/os, Blacks, and Asian Americans are pitted against each other in a race to assimilate to a White/American norm. Immigrants of color are still mainly depicted as threats to U.S. culture, and stories exploring "Black-Brown" or "Black-Yellow" relations often end up reifying stereotypes and positioning Latina/o Americans and Asian Americans as "model minorities" in comparison to Blacks.[13]

Despite their obvious market dominance and audience reach, mainstream news media do not enjoy a complete monopoly over framing racial realities for audiences. The United States has a rich history of ethnic and racial group–oriented news media, including the development of an independent Black press during the early nineteenth century. These alternative news media have provided important counterpoints to mainstream definitions and understandings of racial and ethnic identities and the political projects affecting them. This is not to say that they do not hold their own particular biases; rather, news media created by and for racialized groups present views and cover events that rarely appear in mainstream news, despite attempts to integrate dominant news organizations. Thus, it is crucial to seek out the contributions of minority media practitioners when investigating matters of racial identity. We should expect that minority media will produce, at times, counterhegemonic racial discourses and projects. Because mainstream newsroom staffs are largely White and often ambivalent about the task of diversifying their ranks, and because they often imagine their readers to be predominantly White and/or uninterested in racial issues, mainstream news media rarely introduce alternative frames on race. For minority media, in contrast, owners and practitioners know that their primary audience expects them to present different or counter points to mainstream news in concert with projects of racial reform.[14] Thus, reading minority media often provides important insights and correctives to mainstream news sources.

However, minority news media practitioners do not always produce innovative or radical content.[15] Indeed, because of their (usually) more precarious position in the economic marketplace, many ethnic or racial group–oriented media may not have the ability to compete with large, established mainstream news media. For example, in the case of Black-owned radio and television outlets, market imperatives have largely eliminated news divisions at leading Black-owned stations.[16] Relatedly, those minority-owned media that seek advertising revenues from general market businesses may feel pressures to conform to dominant norms or avoid certain political topics due to fear of losing commercial sponsors.

This leads to the question, What can prompt journalists in dominant or minority news media to abandon or alter their normal routines and assumptions when reporting on race? Crises that challenge racial norms or expose flaws in racial logic present opportunities to reassess race. Racial groups asserting counterhegemonic discourses and racial projects certainly challenge status quo renderings of race, even if news practitioners struggle to contain them.[17] Indeed, many social movement theorists have credited the dramatic mainstream television news coverage of White violence against Black civil rights protestors as a contributor to a shift in White public opinion against legalized segregation, even when the coverage contained negative opinions about Blacks or Black leaders.[18] The appearance of "new" ethnic and racial groups in the public sphere certainly can shake the foundational categories of race and ethnicity our society has taken for granted for centuries. In these ways, people of multiracial descent present all three of these challenges to normal racial routines: they present themselves as figures who do not fit traditional modes of racial classification; they reject systems that elevate one racial group over another; and their renaming of themselves—as multiracial, mixed, métis, Cablinasian, or Hapa[19]—introduces new ways of being raced into the public sphere. However, the originators of these forms of resistance to dominant understandings of race cannot completely control how they are interpreted and incorporated into other racial projects. And, indeed, this book argues that the potential for these challenges to bring about substantive change in news routines and discourses has been hampered by the ascendancy and successes of conservative racial projects in the public sphere, including their success utilizing the mainstream press as a conduit for their views.

Most mainstream media coverage of multiracial identity reinforces what some scholars have identified as a "conservative consensus" on race in the United States.[20] This consensus, referred to by other scholars as "modern racism," "new racism," "subtle racism," or "respectable racism," rejects the notion that race has any meaningful influence over life outcomes or group inequalities.[21] Advocates argue that since the victories of the civil rights movement, any lingering of chronic differences between Whites and people of color can be explained by the individual or cultural failings of Blacks, Latina/os, or Native Americans, not structural or institutional factors. Furthermore, they define racism as the behaviors, opinions, and beliefs of a small (and implied declining) number of individuals who no longer have enough social capital to harm minorities in any significant way. People of color are accused of "crying racism" or "playing the race card" in order to benefit from government largesse rather than pull themselves up by their bootstraps on the allegedly level playing field created by the civil rights acts and Supreme Court decisions of the 1950s and '60s. Politicians and pundits thrive on the work of conservative think tanks that showcase conservative Black scholars—such as Shelby Steele—and the circulation of commentary from Black conservative pundits—such as Ken Hamblin—who advocate "colorblindness" or an end to race-based policies.

Researchers of race and media have consistently found that, particularly since the 1980s, mainstream media portrayals of racial groups, racial policy issues, and racial crises reinforce both racial stereotypes and conservative views on race. In both news and entertainment media, scholars find that post–civil rights media discourses continue to position Whites at the top of the racial hierarchy in subtle and not-so-subtle ways. African Americans and other racialized groups are portrayed as outsiders who need to earn their way into the American Dream as individuals. Affirmative action is decried as a handout and "reverse discrimination," or at best a temporary way to assuage White guilt and do some good for a few minorities. Latina/o and Asian Americans are more likely to be portrayed as new immigrants or illegal aliens, if not nearly absent from the mainstream media. The racial past of slavery, conquest of Native American lands, xenophobic immigration policies, and state-sanctioned violence against people of color are rarely part of the narratives of mainstream media's explanations of the racial present or future.[22]

Much of the scholarship on race and news media concentrates on African Americans and Whites, due in part to the focus on these two groups in U.S. media and the historical dominance of Black/White conflict being the main "race problem" in public discourse since the days of slavery.[23] This work endeavors to unearth the ways in which media makers and political actors frame racial issues in the public sphere, how particular frames affect public opinion, or how racially coded messages spark negative associations for White audiences. In content analyses, effects studies, and audience research, scholars have found that mainstream media frames mirror hegemonic discourse and promote negative perceptions of people of color and policies meant to remedy racial inequalities. Researchers have demonstrated how politicians and political interest groups hoping to garner White votes use racial cues in political advertising and other materials targeted at the electorate.[24] Throughout television and

print news media, race-neutral terms such as *welfare* and *crime* have come
to signify Blackness for many Whites.[25] News media are most likely to
portray racial conflict and differences between racialized groups and rarely
represent the areas where Whites and people of color are in agreement
or share interests.[26] Furthermore, the concerns of people of color are
often overlooked, minimized, or framed as shallow complaints with little
basis in fact or validity.[27]

In a dominant media environment where race is portrayed as a
negative yet dwindling aspect of social life, the issue of multiracial identity has gained immense popularity. If, as Stuart Hall suggests, identity is
the taking up of a particular position within the larger culture that recognizes one in a historical context, how did news media that usually
emphasize racial conflict come to recognize multiracial-identified individuals as positive symbols of racial harmony? More specifically, after
centuries of portraying biracial people as exotic misfits and degenerates,
how did mainstream media come to embrace a "new" multiracial identity
so quickly? In the space of a few decades, this transformation has taken
place due in part to the identity entrepreneurship of organized multiracial
groups. I take the term *identity entrepreneurs* from Stephen Reicher, whose
work on social identity suggests that we see social identity as an ongoing
process or project, and that social groups that occupy subordinate positions in society actively recreate identities as part of efforts to change
their position. Importantly, Reicher asserts that "those who aspire to direct the masses need to become entrepreneurs of identity before they can
become leaders of people"[28] because they must project a new, compelling
identity to attract followers and imagine a better future. Multiracial-
identified people have engaged in such a racial project, and in so doing
have built up an impressive set of texts, theories, organizations, and political projects aimed at reconceptualizing mixed race identity, interracial
family life, interracial adoption, and state-sanctioned racial terminology
to combat and debunk racist myths and practices that oppress multiracial
people. Mass media have been important arenas for this project of redefinition. Through publications targeted at multiracial families and individuals, Web sites, best-selling autobiographies, talk show interviews, press
conferences, public testimony at government hearings, and "outing" of
multiracial celebrities,[29] multiracial people have used media to disseminate new images and descriptions of their identities and experiences in
the American racial landscape, carving out an important niche and presence in the public sphere.

But multiracial people are not alone in their entrepreneurial reshap-
ing of their identity in the media. As previous scholars have demonstrated, new social movements do not have total control over news framing

of their identities, goals, and processes. Indeed, mainstream media are more apt to highlight only those facts and individuals who fit into previously available hegemonic frames and demonize those who challenge those frames.[30] Part of this process includes the information journalists gather from dominant political and economic actors who seek to frame identity and movements for their own ends. The "new" multiracial identity that became highly visible in the mid-1990s has commonly been articulated with neoconservative racial projects. Dominant political actors seized upon particular themes and goals promoted by multiracial organizations and used them to reinforce their own racial policy preferences and ideology, weaving mixed-race identities into a conservative consensus on race.[31]

From Public to Private Issue: Transformations in Racial Discourse in the United States

During the nineteenth and early twentieth centuries, in the law and in all aspects of everyday life, White superiority and segregation of the races was common sense for the great majority of Whites. Part of this common sense was the "one-drop" rule, defining anyone with any trace of African, Asian, Latino, or Native American heritage as a non-White person. Until the civil rights movement shook the foundations of this common sense, it was rare for anyone to challenge this definition, although a long tradition of protest against its effects is clearly visible in the historical record. It is fitting that historian Manning Marable referred to the 1950s as "the second reconstruction," for it not only makes reference to the long gap between the end of slavery and effective legal reform of the racist American system, but also it emphasizes the need to remake an entire *system*—reconstructing laws, culture, social practices, institutions, and other structures of civil society in order to make racial equality a real possibility. When the protests of African American and other racialized groups became too frequent, visible, and disruptive to be ignored or answered only with state-sanctioned violence, Whites had to consider the question of how to address inequalities and how to answer for centuries of racist dominance. For an all too brief decade, the public was focused on the wrongs of institutionalized racism in law, education, commerce, and the public sphere. Although most of the scrutiny centered on White Southerners and Southern states, White culpability and public policy as well as personal beliefs were vigorously debated. But as the civil rights movement looked North and began to question entrenched economic and social inequalities as well as legal strictures, things began to change. Very soon after the major legal victories of the movement, many Whites began to question whether more reforms were necessary.[32]

If we could sound bite the debates over race relations and racial public policy since the late 1960s, it could be boiled down to those who believe in the "declining significance of race" and the preeminent role of personal responsibility in achievement, and those who contend that "race matters" in both personal beliefs and through the role of social structures in maintaining racial inequality. Supporters of the former argument maintain that any residual inequalities can best be explained by the individual or cultural failings of minority groups, particularly Blacks. Advocates of the latter strain of debate insist that racial reform barely got started with the de jure reforms of the 1950s and 60s, and that continued political, cultural, and economic reforms are necessary to create a true level playing field. Moreover, they argue, continued patterns of discrimination and inequality are due in part to race and racism, and that these lingering inequities stand as proof that legal and policy reforms have not gone far enough.

One could describe the discursive and political turn away from race-based policy as (at the very least) a dual phenomenon: the liberal "retreat from race" on the Left, and the conservative backlash on the Right. As progressive thinkers and activists began to discuss the need for social and economic reforms to realize the promise of the legal rights won by racial minority groups in the courts and Congress, Whites on both sides of the aisle reacted with displeasure. Stephen Steinberg's history of the liberal retreat from racial policy locates the first cracks in the coalition between liberal whites and people of color in the mid-1960s, cracks that widened and found expression in opposition to "racial preferences" and a turn away from analyses of institutional racism and toward the "pathologies" of Black culture.[33] Indeed, in President Lyndon Baines Johnson's famous Howard Address in 1965, he outlined the conceptual framework utilizing the research of Daniel Patrick Moynihan to describe the problems facing poor Blacks. Thus, "the focus would no longer be on white racism, but rather on the deficiencies of blacks themselves."[34] The press latched onto LBJ's speech and interpreted it, as did a *Washington Post* reporter, as proof that "the time had come for [Negroes] to come to grips with their own worst problem: 'the breakdown of Negro family life.' "[35] This theme has carried on and gained strength throughout the last three decades, and is a key pillar of opposition to color-conscious policy.

As this shift took place, many Democrats were worried about the growing advantage Republicans gained in White votes in the South. Nixon's "Southern strategy" was viewed as evidence that linking the Democratic Party and liberal policies to race would cause more defections of White voters. In the wake of the defeat of the Great Society initiatives (a defeat many believed was partly due to racial issues), a new strategy emerged: present social uplift policies for "everybody" that will gradually lift Blacks and other Americans out of poverty. The idea that Whites will not vote for public projects of policies that are explicitly targeted at racial groups was reinforced both by political strategists and academics, who assert that there exists no political constituency for Black-specific policies, an assumption that guides the "New Democrat" approach to racial inequalities.[36] Many on the Left believe that turning to class-based, rather than race-based, policies will ameliorate racial inequalities since Blacks and Latina/os are dispropor-tionately represented in lower economic strata. Others believe eliminating or qualifying references to racial groups, particularly Blacks, to make poli-cies sound "colorblind" can garner more White support, and in the process lift the boats of poor Blacks and Whites.[37]

Scholars who are critical of the "colorblind" stance have argued that policies must explicitly account for both race and class (not to mention gender or sexuality) to achieve true equality of opportunity in employ-ment, housing, and education.[38] Furthermore, excluding race from the set of acceptable categories for political discourse and policy hinders efforts to consider, understand, and ultimately begin to solve the continued racial inequalities we observe in the United States. These investigators contend that, despite some important civil rights advances, we are far from a fully equitable and integrated society; indeed, many fear that the conservative social and political backlash of the 1980s and 1990s has hindered our society's ability to further racial progress. One measure of the continued impact of race in society is housing segregation. While analysis of recent Census data shows a consistent overall decrease in residential segregation, large metropolitan areas in the Northeast and Midwest continue to be defined by starkly segregated neighborhoods. Authors of a Brookings Institute report on housing segregation advised policymakers to be cau-tiously optimistic about the overall trend, and described the process of desegregation as one guided by economic *and* political change.

> We think that the contemporary decline in segregation shows the effectiveness of the civil rights revolution in this country between 1940 and 1970. [But] there are still large metropolitan areas with substantial amounts of segregation. Moreover, the past 30 years have brought the least amount of change to these areas.[39]

The authors conclude that desegregation progress reflects "both rising black incomes and government action against discrimination." Far from advocating a "color-blind" market approach housing policy, the report recognizes the need for continued vigilance and monitoring of the hous-ing market and for political actors to contribute to the process of solving hyper-segregation in older cities.[40] Similarly, class-based policies may not break the patterns of residential segregation that continue across America, because without attention to the race of housing seekers, banks, realtors, and landlords could easily continue to steer people of color away from White neighborhoods.[41]

Black workers experience difficulties due to the interactions of residential and occupational segregation, and the effects of racial and gender stereotypes create a job market where Black women and men are massed in lower-wage and lower-status jobs than both White men and White women.[42] Recent studies by William Julius Wilson and others demonstrate that, despite regulations against employer discrimination, racial stereotypes, segregated information and social networks, as well as the suburbanization of many industries still serve as barriers to Black employment.[43] One of the most striking findings published in Wilson's book *When Work Disappears* is that 74 percent of the Chicago-area employers interviewed for the study asserted that "inner-city black workers—especially black males—bring to the workplace traits . . . that negatively affect job performance."[44] Unfortunately, Wilson's 1996 book hasn't drawn the attention that the title of his first book, *The Declining Significance of Race*, did in the 1980s. Many who applauded the provocative title then (but failed to read the analysis itself, which pointed to the necessity of examining the effects of race and class simultaneously) have largely ignored Professor Wilson's recent research on the continued discrimination Black people face in the job market.[45]

Although many critics find the liberal retreat from race exasperating, one redeeming element is that many Democrats and constituents on the Left still believe that public, government-sponsored solutions are valid and necessary to combat socioeconomic inequalities. On the Right, however, the backlash against race-based policy is linked to the belief that individuals, not government or other institutions, are responsible for any and all changes in social, political, or economic status of members of a particular racial group. Although liberal and conservative arguments against race-based policy certainly dovetail with each other, since the 1980s the conservative side has been louder and more widespread in mainstream media than the liberal. By the 1990s, many observers concur, a new conservative racial consensus among (mostly) White Americans has emerged. The ideological basis for this new conservatism on race is found in the work and words of scholars who endorse "racial realism." Racial realism rests on three interrelated claims.[46] First, that great progress has been made in race relations and that liberals and Blacks ignore this in favor of race-baiting tactics to win support from people of color and guilty whites. Since the civil rights legislation of the 1960s, they argue, there is no need for race-based policy. Second, persistent inequalities between Whites and minorities are best explained by "the moral and cultural failure of African Americans" and liberals are holding Blacks to a lower standard and refuse to see, as they would in a colorblind society, that Blacks are hurting themselves. Third, contemporary civil rights leaders are corrupt and manipulative, and trade on the gullibility of guilt-ridden white liberals and separatist people of color looking for government largesse. The overarching principle lauded by racial realists and neoconservatives is that the government and society should be colorblind, producing "a particular kind of social order, one where racial identity is irrelevant."[47] As I will argue in later chapters, the belief that race can be rendered irrelevant and usher in a society where all are judged as individuals, is a large reason why the multiracial movement became so attractive to conservatives.

There are at least two faults in the logic of this new racial consensus and the scholarship and ideology upon which it gained legitimacy in the public sphere. First, the proof offered by racial realists that race is no longer an impediment to the progress of people of color is most often based in public opinion poll data and rests on false dichotomies. Because they maintain individual behavior is the most important factor, they rarely consider group-level phenomena (save for indictments of Black culture, for example). Instead, they use trends in White public opinion about Blacks and other minorities to prove that White racism has abated. However, they do not examine the disjuncture between what Whites say they believe about Blacks and real-world behavior and racial outcomes. For example, one favorite poll result of racial realists is that Whites say they are willing to live in integrated neighborhoods; however, very few do, and very few say they would support policies that would allow greater housing integration. Additionally, racial realists leave out unpleasant poll results, such as those that show that a large majority of Whites still believe that Blacks are more prone to violence and laziness than other groups.[48]

The racial realist position can be summed up by the following dichotomous reasoning: either there is White racism, or Blacks are not performing well due to individual or cultural deficiencies. And, since their evidence says the former is not true, then it must be the latter that is driving racial inequality. This dichotomy, however, positions individual intent as the preeminent causal agent in race relations and inequality. Overt, interpersonal acts of racial stereotyping or discrimination do not encompass the whole of racial oppression; bigoted behavior is only one aspect of a racist system, which depends upon racially neutral policies and institutions and a historical legacy of practices that have created racial stratification that is hard to overcome without attention to race.[49] The individual perspective ignores the three centuries of government action, institutional cultures, *alongside* individual attitudes that provided privileged access and dominance of resources and power to Whites. The insistence that Blacks individually pull themselves up ignores the group benefits reaped by Whites historically and currently through government policies. Thus, "Conservatives incorrectly assume that the civil rights laws were confined to abolishing racial classifications and that the meaning of discrimination was limited to bigoted behavior."[50] But, arguably, civil rights laws overturned *institutional racial practices* and acknowledged a system of *group-based privileges and discrimination*; as such, public policies that explicitly reference racial groups are needed to remedy the historical damage and accelerate the move to equality.[51] This requires attention not only to attitudes, but socioeconomic inequality and imbalances in political representation, not just individual-level "equal opportunity."

But the hegemonic racial discourse depends on a bifurcation of group and individual identity. It is difficult at best, as critical legal scholars have noted, to distinguish between individual and group rights, since an individual's rights are dependendent in large part on how his or her group is treated.[52] Craig Calhoun reminds us that identity is both private and public; both elements contribute to our sense of who we are, how others see us, and how multiple social actors consider and mold identities in the public sphere.[53] To focus only on matters of individual choice misses important aspects of identity as well as sources of inequality. This is why I argue in later chapters that conservatives who charge civil rights groups with applying the one-drop rule when they oppose multiracial identifiers are cynically twisting the history of the one-drop rule. Their charge, that the NAACP is now using the rule to prevent multiracial people from exercising their individual rights, misremembers the intent and effects of the one-drop rule. The rule was created to maintain a system of White dominance and political exclusion of people of color. True, it may be unfair for the Mexican American Legal Defense Fund or the NAACP to oppose the government's endorsement of a multiracial designation, but this opposition does not exclude multiracial people from access to jobs, votes, or housing as the one-drop rule did for hundreds of years. The multiracial movement entered the public's consciousness after the ascent of racial realist/neoconservative discourse. Thus, it not surprising, as I will argue, that mainstream media practitioners and sources fit multiracial identity into frames consonant with the dominant trend.

Multiracial Identity in the News Today: Organization of the Book

Each chapter in this book explores how, at different points in time and in response to different racial crises, mainstream and ethnic media framed the identities and interests of people of multiracial descent. The cases examined in this book all involve the explicit use of racial categories by institutions to determine individual and group identities, and to distribute formal and informal, real and imagined benefits and privileges. It is rare, in our allegedly color-blind society, to have frank discussions or explanations of how, when and why racial categories are applied or deployed. In the cases of multiracial individuals or groups that cause controversy, at least some explanation of why they do not fit easily into—or have not chosen—a socially recognized racial category is necessary. Thus, the unveiling of a multiracial identity may produce opportunities to question and destabilize dominant understandings of racial categories and their functions in society. However, this opportunity is not guaranteed; while there is much optimism in many theoretical considerations of the power of hybridity to break open hegemonic identity frameworks that bolster the White status quo, thus far there is little evidence describing the conditions under which liberatory discourses and/or courses of action will emerge from confrontations with individuals of multiracial descent. From the mid-1980s to the present, these case studies reveal that as the conservative consensus on race was forming and becoming hegemonic, the presence of multiracial people in the news rarely inspired mainstream reporters and their sources to reconceptualize racial identities or discuss the continued workings of racial hierarchy in the United States. So far, dominant newspapers and magazines have not often exercised the opportunity to decenter Whiteness; rather, the "hybrid" racial and ethnic difference represented by multiracial people is co-opted to uphold a linear narrative of racial progress and the futility of race-based remedies in public policy.

The book demonstrates how hard it can be, particularly in dominant mass media, to break racial conventions. Even with the presence of people who deny or collapse conventional systems of racial identification and signification, mainstream news media recirculate hegemonic understandings of race, nation, and identity that stifle transgressive or radical interpretations of multiracial identity. Specifically, the work multiracial identities could do to destabilize whiteness is usually stifled by conventional media framing practices and newsgathering routines. So we must ask, what are the conditions under which multiracial identity news can disrupt assumptions of white normativity and dominance? Under what conditions do multiracial identities create space for novel or challenging discussions of race in society?

The third chapter suggests that controversy over multiracial identity can "out" whiteness through exposure of White complicity in and control over the assignment of racial categories within institutional settings. Chapter 3, "Not as Black as the Next Guy," examines press coverage of the blonde, blue-eyed Malone twins, two aspiring firefighters with "white skin" who claimed White identity the first time they took and failed a civil service exam in 1975, and then claimed Black identity when they retook the test two years later to qualify for jobs in the Boston Fire Department under new affirmative action guidelines. In 1988, personnel officials accused them of lying about having a Black ancestor. Eventually, the State Supreme Court of Massachusetts ruled that the Boston Fire Department was correct to conclude that the Malone brothers had no valid claim to Black identity. Their saga presented a challenge to news media accustomed to framing Whites as innocent victims of affirmative action politics. In this case study, White deviance was so stark, reporters—particularly those of African American descent—could hardly ignore the power and privileges enjoyed by Whites in the situation. This opened up space for critiques of racial inequity in hiring.

Importantly, the case brought into question the criteria used by the state to determine minority racial identity. Reporters and commentators wrestled with the reality of people with mixed racial heritage, but were unable to propose alternative solutions to monoracial categories. The novelty of the case presented an opportunity for the press to create new frames to cover the story, particularly in terms of describing Whiteness. The result was a novel mix of frames that had to incorporate explicit references to Whites—usually not done in news reports—due to the specifics of the case. However, despite the emergence of some alternative frames, coverage reinforced the dominant norm that race and affirmative action are Black-White issues, even though there were opportunities to make the case that racial politics involve other groups.

In contrast, in the fourth chapter the power of White-dominated institutions to assign racial categories and varying benefits to those so named was obscured by the focus of news media on "troublemaking" people of color. Chapter 4, "Descended from Whom?," presents the case of law professor Maria Consuelo O'Brien Hylton. Maria Hylton's parents are a Black Cuban woman and a White Australian man. When Northwestern University considered her for a position at the law school as part of a retention package for her husband, feminist, Black, and Latino student groups protested her candidacy. Each group claimed that she would not represent or meet their needs because of her background and theoretical interests. In addition, the school's first Black law professor, Joyce Hughes, told her fellow faculty members that she would not support the hire, and declared in a lengthy memo that Maria Hylton was not Black "in a United States context."

When the press reported on this case, reporters and commentators gravitated toward the perceived irony of Blacks declaring other Blacks "not Black enough." This, I will argue, fit in with two recurrent themes that emerged in the mainstream media during the 1990s: judging which black people "deserve" affirmative action, and an interest in Black intraracial conflicts. Media coverage of the Thomas-Hill case, "black-on-black crime," and the "failure" of the Black middle class and Black celebrities to give back to and uplift the "Black underclass" are part of this trend. Maria Hylton's case, unlike the Malones' case, was not so much about the role of institutions in determining Black identity, but about the "discovery" of (dysfunctional) heterogeneity in the Black public sphere. Thus, journalists framed the story in the terms of conservative approaches to race, transforming the story into a cautionary tale of black organizations clinging to defunct, irrational racial politics.

Another place to find news media narratives and practices that destabilize the conservative consensus on race is in news media made by and/or for people of color. I first explore this venue for counterdiscourses in chapter 2, "The In/discernible Body of Susie Phipps" (written with Daniel Brouwer). The chapter analyzes news media coverage of the case of Susie Phipps, who sued the state of Louisiana to have her birth certificate changed from "colored" to "white." The state argued that the record could not be changed and marshaled evidence to "prove" that she had knowledge of her" black ancestry." In the eyes of the state and many commentators, Phipps had "passed" across racial lines from Black to White. Analysis of the dominant (mainstream) press and news discourses produced by and/or addressed to Blacks reveals prominent frames through which news consumers are invited to perceive these events. In particular, the portrayal of Phipps, who was arguably a multiracial woman, as "tragic," "marginal," and/or "passing" remained a guiding principle for many dominant journalists. In contrast, African American writers framed racial passing within broader cultural and historical contexts than dominant media. The study exposes the similarities—including community consternation about the passer—and differences—including disparate focus on civil rights rather than identity issues—between Black and White coverage of Phipps's case.

Comparing mainstream and minority news media reveals other counterdiscourses in the fifth and sixth chapters, each of which focus on the 2000 Census. Chapter 5, "Counting Race, Counting Controversy," analyzes news media coverage of the experimentation with and creation of Census 2000's new race and ethnicity system. The chapter compares coverage by African American–owned and oriented, Asian American–owned and oriented (English-language), and dominant print media. The three-way comparison was done for three main reasons. First, I join with other scholars and activists who urge us to shift away from a Black-White paradigm, without underestimating the power of that binary, to a multifaceted look at race. By comparing more than Black and White responses, we are reminded of how the Black/White divide affects other racialized minorities. Second, examining discourses about race produced by Asian Americans forces us to reexamine racial binarism through the critical lenses and experiences of those who fall outside the prevailing binary model. Their insights can provide resources to rethink racial issues and expose dynamics of racial projects within and outside the Black/White binary. Finally, I chose to look at Asian American news particularly because demographers predicted that allowing multiracial identification would impact Asian Americans more than other racial groups.

Chapter 6, "After the Census," continues the comparison of different news media coverage of the multiracial category after the release of Census 2000 data. Although many multiracial activists and academics hope that the acknowledgment of multiracial people will generate progressive, challenging narratives about race, coverage of the race and ethnicity data released by the Census Bureau was not as innovative as they may have hoped. In dominant media, two themes stood out: (1) multiracial people are part of a demographic trend that will lead to the end of race as we know it; and (2) multiracial individuals have a right to a personal choice of identity that should not be superseded by other civil rights concerns. The Black press produced three main themes in the post-2000 articles. First, there were more discussions of how and why to include multiracial people and other people of color in political coalitions with Blacks. Second, there were broader discussions of how the concept of Blackness is changing overall, and what that means in terms of the future of civil rights battles. Third, as with the White-dominated press, the issue of whether or not Hispanics outnumber Blacks—and whether people can be simultaneously Hispanics and Black—surfaced with the numbers and reaction to the political hype around the possible Hispanic "usurpation" of Black political clout. Two major themes emerged in Asian American reports on the 2000 Census data: (1) concerns about political ramifications of multiracial Asian counts; and (2) Hapa experiences with White racism, including resistance to being granted "honorary Whiteness."

Through examinations of how the Asian American and African American presses reported on the controversy surrounding Census 2000, I find multiple spaces for critique of Whiteness vis-à-vis multiracial identities. In the Asian American press specifically, feature stories about individuals of multiracial descent, which in the mainstream press serve to mask the institutional aspects of racial hierarchy, function as explicit attacks on White supremacy, White racial practices of looking at racialized others, specifically Hapas, and challenge lukewarm multicultural readings of mixed race identity as exotic, new, or hip. In the African American press, attention to traumas of race mixing, such as rape and colorism, reject the color-blind ethos of mainstream narratives of multiracial identity as a symbol of unquestionable racial progress or maturity in the United States. However, in the Black press, ambivalence toward the idea of a separate multiracial identity for people of Black descent serves at times to distract from the overarching or implied critiques of white domination and emphasize tensions between mono- and multiracially identified Blacks.

The Conclusion reviews the chapters and then turns to considerations of how multiracial identity will be understood and deployed politically in the future. Beginning with a meditation on the immense popularity of golfer Tiger Woods and biracial senator Barack Obama's breakout performance at the Democratic National Convention, I speculate about the media's role in communicating the meaning and utility of multiracial identities and the prospects for a transformative impact on society's understandings of race. If the visibility of multiracial individuals and work of multiracial social movements is going to dismantle racial hierarchies, much political and discursive work needs to be done. In mainstream media, multiracial people are being used to support problematic discourses of "diversity." They are presented as symbols of a racially and ethnically sophisticated society, where cross-racial relationships are no longer constrained by power imbalances or oppressive social norms. Rather, they personify citizen-consumers' embrace of and desire for difference, and signal that racial strife and inequalities are things of the past. To end this chapter, I present an alternate framework for reporting on race that would ideally go against the trends summarized in the conclusion, and focus on some promising developments in journalism education and practice that could inject new frameworks for understanding race in the news.

In one sense, this book provides a series of snapshots of how racial discourse has been altered by the presence of multiracial people since the mid-1980s, and asserts that media discourses of race mixing are a gauge of race relations broadly. In decades not so long past, talk of race mixing reflected the conventional wisdom of preventing intermixture of supposedly pure races. Thus, to begin the book, chapter 1 provides an overview for readers of the history of discourses of race mixing in the United States. The ideologies embedded in the stereotypes of the tragic mulatto, the marginal man, and the amalgamated fiends found in news, film, and novels throughout the nineteenth and twentieth centuries supported (and in some cases, protested) a system of White supremacy and institutionalized racial inequality. Today's headlines featuring Tiger Woods and popular films such as *Guess Who?*—the twenty-first-century comic remake of *Guess Who's Coming to Dinner*—might make a time traveler from the

1900s believe that race mixing has become an unchallenged norm in our society, and that racial hierarchies have been eliminated. However, this assumption would be wrong, for the rehabilitation of the image of mixed-race individuals has neither been fully accomplished, nor has racial hierarchy been dismantled in the United States. Rather, a more complicated set of shifts has occurred both in the discourses and practices of race in our society. Looking back at past discussions of race mixing helps us to appreciate both how far these discussions have come from White fears of amalgamation, but also show us how deeply embedded "old" conceptions of race are in today's world. Indeed, this book argues that as we read dispatches from the color line, we must continue to look back to see if the demarcations of our racial past continue to influence us, molding the future visions of a multicultural world even as we try to shake off the binary traps of yesteryear.

A Word On Methods

This book contains case studies that were researched and completed at different times. They draw upon both qualitative and quantitative methodologies for analyzing news content. Below is a brief description of how I went about finding and dissecting the multiracial discourses presented in each case.

Finding the Stories

Contemporary news research has been made easier and faster due to database technologies that eliminate much eye-wearing work in microfilm and fiche files. I found the majority of articles analyzed in this book through these databases, although I and my research assistants still spent plenty of time in the microfilm and periodicals stacks of the library to gain copies of African American news articles, as well as to grab prints of photos in articles where computer searches did not provide access to images. Articles were found through searches of Reader's Digest, LEXIS/NEXIS, GenderWatch, ProQuest, EthnicNewsWatch, and the Index to Black Periodicals. Once I had copies of all the articles, I looked for notes regarding photographs and other graphics. Where possible, (especially with magazine articles available on ProQuest) I downloaded the photos along with the articles as PDF files, which mimic the original print. Where no photos were available online, my research assistant pursued the photos and graphics on microfilm or in bound copies of magazines. Through this process, moving back and forth between electronic and paper/film resources, I was able to amass nearly all the accompanying photos and other graphics for the stories found in the database searches.

Chapters 2, 3, and 4

The amount of coverage these stories attracted varied. Phipps, due in part to the length of her legal battles, garnered the most articles about her case; Hylton the least. However, in each case, national news media included these stories as newsworthy, distributing these tales of passing and mixed race to audiences that number in the millions. From the leading print news outlet, the *New York Times*, to general interest magazines such as *Time* and *People*, journalists and editors found these stories compelling for their readership. As such, these cases represent a compelling subset of what newsmakers deemed "newsworthy" about race in the post–civil rights era that reached a broad public, contributing to ongoing discourses of the role of race in law, society, economics, and politics.

Qualitative analysis of media texts goes by several names, many of which employ overlapping techniques and approaches to the idea of analyzing discourse. Textual analysis, discourse analysis, ethnographic content analysis, and semiotics all represent ways of understanding texts and their meanings within particular contexts. My approach to qualitative content analysis of news media texts is influenced by *grounded theory*.[54] Grounded theory is based in the idea that a researcher must be guided, as much as is possible, by the meanings available in the data themselves rather than shoehorning data into preexisting theoretical models. Although practitioners of grounded theory realize that no researcher can empty her mind of preexisting ideas about a project, the goal is to be as true to the data as possible. This is a crucial task for discourse analysts, who are already dealing with a mediated form of experience: mass media representations of events, opinions, and people at a particular time in history. Indeed, Lindlof and Taylor suggest that it is hard for any communications researcher to avoid using a grounded theory approach when dealing with qualitative data.[55]

Understanding a grounded approach to textual analysis and doing it are different things of course, and qualitative researchers (rhetoricians, ethnographers, semioticians) often use different processes and routines to elicit meaning from data. Some researchers utilize computer programs such as N*Vivo or AtlasTi to find patterns across masses of text. Others, like me, use pen and paper, and homemade spreadsheets. This heterogeneity of process, however, does not mean that qualitative analysis of media content is not rigorous, but rather that the nature of the method lends itself to different approaches. My own process has been informed by

Miles and Huberman's and Altheide's advice on how to organize and analyze textual data.[56] These authors instruct researchers to immerse themselves in the data, organize it in categories, and ask other researchers and readers to look over the findings and gauge the validity of any analyses. Through this intense interaction with the texts and checking in with other scholars, one can achieve confidence that her analyses make sense and go beyond mere opinion.

To begin my analysis, I read through the articles multiple times. In the first read-through, I began a running commentary sheet for each piece, noting potentially interesting or contradictory remarks, themes, or questions. This process is often referred to as "open coding," whereby the researcher tries on ideas for categories and codes. With each successive reading, I tried to make lists of possible categories and concepts that could be applied to all of the stories, as well as novel or unexpected themes that may only occur in a subset. Then I started to look for overlap in the codes and tried to streamline the set of codes created in the earlier readings. In so doing, I created a set of ad hoc codes, which are tested by repeated readings. To keep track, I followed Miles and Huberman's advice and created "data displays" (charts, lists, and other graphic renderings of data) to visualize comparisons across texts and groups of texts.

Cycling through the data and creating displays, I was able to see similarities and differences in the articles and keep track of thematic elements that were more or less important to each type of periodical. As the differences and similarities emerged, I connected them to contexts provided by the individual articles, journalistic conventions and practices, and historical, political, and cultural information. In this way, I can tell a story about both the individual articles and types of periodicals and about how they relate to each other. At various stages of the process, I presented parts of the analysis to colleagues in formal and informal settings, gaining invaluable insight and direction for further deliberation about the meanings of individual texts, the group of texts as a whole, and broader cultural and historical contexts.

Chapters 5 and 6

Chapters 5 and 6 differ from the first three in that the census-related research was done using both quantitative and qualitative content analysis. These chapters present analysis of news reports about the potential Census changes from January 1995 to May 1, 2000 (Chapter 5) and January 2001 to July 30, 2004 (Chapter 6). These periods represent news coverage written before and after the Office of Management and Budget (OMB) made its final decision about how to recognize multiracial individuals in census data collection, and reports from after racial data were released to the public. To find the articles, we used the databases described above and used search terms such as "multiracial and Census," "biracial and Census" and "interracial and Census." All articles from periodicals that contained mention of both the Census and multiracial groups' or individuals' desire to change its system of race classification were included in the analysis. Only English-language periodicals were analyzed.[57]

Quantitative content analysis is used to determine explicit, countable elements of a media text. For many, the "hard" data of this type of content analysis is very persuasive, especially when large differences or discrepancies can be detected through comparison across time, cases, or types of media. In theory, other researchers could use the coding scheme to produce similar results with the same sample of articles. Thus, one's codes need to be recognizable and understandable to a broad audience and must focus on elements of a text that can be easily discerned and transformed into numerical data. However, the impetus to create coding schemes that produce results that can be replicated by others means that only the most obvious kinds of content can be included in quantitative coding measures.

Oftentimes, researchers use a set of codes created through review of literature and theoretical models and apply them to a sample of texts. However, as one interacts with texts, unexpected issues and themes unaccounted for by the preset codes can emerge. For this project, I used both predetermined and emergent codes to create the content analysis protocol for the chapters on the 2000 Census. The predetermined codes grew out of three major sources. First, I created and drew upon the substantial (and still growing) body of scholarly and policy publications related to multiracial identity and government categorization of citizens. This body of work produced many of the basic codes for the content analysis. Second, I conducted an exhaustive review of work on the main literary, scientific, and popular culture representations of multiracial people in U.S. history, and used these tropes and stereotypes to create codes to see if the historical representations emerged in contemporary descriptions. The other codes in the protocol emerged from my reading of a small subsample of the articles my research team collected for the analysis. Before we began testing the codes, I read through this subset of articles, taking notes in a running commentary to find issues and themes I hadn't anticipated with the predetermined codes. This reading process, for instance, alerted me to the need to include multiracial celebrities in the coding structure, and the need to create more nuanced rules for determining the race of individuals mentioned in articles. Below are examples from the codebook.

CELILUS

Mark "1" for this code if a multiracial celebrity mentioned to illustrate multiracial identity issue (*NOT Tiger Woods*. He has his own code. Halle Berry, Derek Jeter, Vin Diesel, Lenny Kravits and others all fall under this code). EX: "Hapa actors like Jennifer Moon and Keanu Reeves are hot in Hollywood because they appeal to multiple audiences" both stated that they think "the multiracial category makes little sense" would be coded CELILUS.

CENOFFICIAL

Mark "1" for this code if a government official from the OMB, Census Bureau, or other Census-related department is quoted or paraphrased in the article. EX: "Jennifer Stevens, an OMB statistician, expressed concern that the new system would make it difficult to compare 2000 data with 1990 data" would be coded CENOFFICIAL.

Three research assistants recruited from the Undergraduate Research Opportunity Program (UROP) coded the articles collected for chapter 5, and I and two graduate research assistants coded the articles for chapter 6. Coders were trained using articles from outside the time period of data collection (pre-1995) due to the fact that there was such a small set of articles and I did not want to lose any to precoding. Once the coders had sufficient simple agreement with each other, and we eliminated confusing codes and rules, they began coding all the articles. We calculated intercoder reliability separately for stories in each time period, since a few codes were added for the second time period. Reported results reached at least 85 percent agreement among the coders.[58]

As my research assistants coded news stories independently, I took copies of all the articles and pictures and began close readings of all the pieces, looking for more subtle themes and to capture the tone, emphases, and nuances that are often missed in quantitative content analysis. This process followed the procedures described for the first three chapters and extended well beyond the quantitative coding period. Once descriptive statistics were available from the coded stories, I compared frequencies of codes, both within each type of press and across. I then laid this numerical data side by side with my qualitative reading summaries and data displays, comparing the qualitative and quantitative information.

Combining quantitative and qualitative textual analysis is a useful approach to understanding complex sets of discourse, particularly when dealing with a topic such as racial identity. While quantitative content analysis is the preferred method for taking account of explicit textual information, qualitative analysis of texts allows a researcher to access and evaluate implied meanings as well as take into account the cultural and historical context of a text. Qualitative analysis of the texts, then, helps the researcher explore how and why certain themes show up more frequently than others, or are shown more prominently in news texts. A combination of quantitative and qualitative analysis is satisfying to many researchers because it allows for both numerical information about the quantity and frequency of themes and exploration of the nuances of how information is contextualized for the audience.

Chapter One

"Hybrid Degenerates" to "Multiracial Families"

Discourses of Race Mixing in America

The Filipino tends to interbreed with near-moron white girls. The resulting hybrid is almost invariably undesirable.

—C. M. Goethe, "Filipino Immigration Viewed As a Peril"

Ordinarily, the marginal man is a mixed blood, like the mulatto in the United States or the Eurasian in Asia, but that is apparently because the man of mixed blood is one who lives between two worlds, in both of which he is more or less a stranger.

—Robert E. Park, "Human Migration and the Marginal Man"

Particularly since the nineteenth century, mixed-race people have been included in discussions of how to define who is an American. As the nation grew spatially west and southwest, slavery, immigration, Native American and Mexican sovereignty over lands were tied to questions of race and citizenship. In the battles over territory and status, race was a crucial element of Manifest Destiny discourse that proclaimed Anglo-Americans to be the rightful occupants and rulers of lands west of the Mississippi as well as superior to former slaves, new immigrants from Asia, and already-present populations of Mexican and Native Americans.

In the last two hundred years, two main theories dominated hegemonic discourses of miscegenation and mixed race people: the theory of "hybrid degeneracy" and the "marginal man" thesis. The former emerged out of slavery, colonialism, and emerging biological sciences in the eighteenth and nineteenth centuries and conceptualized "half-breeds" as the inferior offspring of separate races (sometimes referred to as separate

29

species).[1] The marginal man idea was conceived in the rise of the social sciences in the first decades of the twentieth century, rescripting the inferiority of mixed-race people as a product of social tensions and psychological trauma rather than the biological incompatibility of the parents.

Much of the recent boom in scholarly literature on passing, multiracial people, and miscegenation focuses on Black/White race mixing, but dominant discourses were not limited to that particular interaction.[2] Although some argue that the opposition of Black and White is the bedrock of and affects the dynamics of all race relations in the United States,[3] dominant discourses included specific antimiscegenation references to any group deemed Other or threatening to White hegemony through purity. Thus, although I do not have the space to provide a full census of the literature available, in this introduction I have endeavored to include an array of sources to introduce the reader to examples of antimiscegenation narratives involving people of Asian-, African-, Hispanic-, and Native American ancestry.[4] Whether or not the Black/White divide serves as the basis for all other iterations of antimiscegenation discourses, the hegemonic response to race mixing included and adversely affected all people of color. Additionally, I include examples from various media and genres to show how prevalent and popular narratives of mixed race were, and how, whichever the group, racially mixed individuals or interracial couples were almost always rendered with suspicion, condescension, disgust, exoticism, or some mixture of these. In a later section, I also provide readers with a section illustrating how Black journalists and authors have approached race mixing, to provide contrast and to foreshadow the conflicts and controversies encountered later in the case studies. This section emphasizes the importance of the counterhegemonic narratives produced in the Black press, and demonstrates further how widespread and contentious issues of miscegenation were within the Black public sphere.

Hybrid Degenerates

The hegemonic view of mixed-race people in the nineteenth century was that persons from different racial groups were nearly (or for some, actually) different species. Thus, a sexual "amalgamation" of two races would produce defective hybrid offspring, similar to hybrid pairings in the animal world. Theorists of "hybrid degeneracy" were part of the mainstream scientific community, and published work well into the twentieth century.[5] These scholars believed that mulattos, mestizos, and Eurasians lacked physical, mental, and moral strength. Merging superstition, theology, and Darwin's theory of evolution, scientists of amalgamation and eugenicists measured heads, sex organs, and other body parts to prove the superiority of Whites over people of color.[6] In addition to reinforcing their theories that "full-blood" Africans, Asians, and Native Americans were mentally and/or physically inferior to "Nordics" and "Aryans," these scholars aimed to demonstrate scientifically "the disharmonic phenomena in half-breeds."[7] Beyond academia, this (pseudo)science reinforced antimiscegenation laws and racist social sentiments, and was used to justify everything from the enslavement of Blacks, to annexation of Mexican territory, to legislation barring Chinese and Japanese immigration. As such, discourses of multiracial people have been used to protect not only White identity, but White property and political privileges. In delimiting who could be included under the label "White," both law and custom reinforced White hegemony.[8]

Demonstrating racial difference and White superiority became key strategies in the debates over slavery, westward expansion, and other imperial projects. Historians and cultural critics have documented how Whites deployed theories of uncontrollable Black sexuality to conceal and excuse their sexual exploitation of enslaved women, brutalization of enslaved men and lynching of free Blacks.[9] In order to justify the one-drop rule, which made any child of one White and one Black enslaved parent a slave, theologians, scientists, and politicians drew upon various bodies of "evidence" to prove these offspring did not have the capacity for full citizenship as their "pure" White siblings did.[10]

Cynthia Nakashima describes how hybrid degeneracy theory was used to argue that "mestizo" Mexicans were unfit to govern themselves, justifying White confiscation of Mexican-held territories and denial of full citizenship to certain people of Mexican descent.[11] Nakashima notes that "[t]he connection between the scientific and theological aspects of hybrid degeneracy comes from the idea that what is 'unnatural' is also against God's wishes," thus the hegemonic wisdom concerning mixed-race people supported the evangelical nature of Manifest Destiny: Whites were not only destined to rule the West, but also were naturally more fit and morally bound to rule over those people of color who existed there. In the wake of the Mexican American War, this logic played out in the newly annexed territories of the United States, operating to exclude people of partial Mexican and/or African descent from citizenship.[12] The new southwestern U.S. states rejected Mexico's inclusion of *mestizos* and *afromestizos* in its citizenry, and denied non-White Mexicans living in U.S. territory citizenship, while granting U.S. citizenship to many White Mexicans who remained in newly annexed lands.[13]

In a similar vein, the allegedly inferior moral and physical faculties of Eurasians were integrated into discussions and policies for curtailing Asian immigration. Americans borrowed theories from English and French colonists who wrote treatises on the inferiority of children born of White and Asian parents. White politicians warned that male Asian immigrant laborers would marry White women or bring in a "horde" of brides that would have higher birthrates than Whites, increasing competition for jobs and land. Hysteria over population growth rates and racial inter-breeding informed much of the "Yellow Peril" rhetoric. Madison Grant's popular book, *The Passing of the Great Race*,[14] advocated extending the one-drop rule beyond Blacks to all other "inferior races," including "Hindus, Asians in general, Jews, Italians, and other Southern and Eastern European peoples."[15] Congressmen used Grant's arguments to argue for laws barring "inferior" immigrants, such as Asians.[16] In a 1921 essay for *Good Housekeeping*, Vice-President Calvin Coolidge declared that the laws were necessary be-cause "[t]he hybrid is clearly both a diseased entity that could only perpetuate that illness and a sign of a monstrous union" of different races.[17] Mixing with the wrong kind of immigrants, he and many others believed, would "dilute" superior White American blood beyond reckoning.

The "half-breed" status of certain Native Americans was another topic of discussion for the federal government. Depending on the government's goal, mixed-blood Native Americans were defined differ-ently. If "mixed-bloods" had ties to White communities and were sympa-thetic to government policies, they were often portrayed as superior to their "full-blood" counterparts. If they were allied with their tribe, they were usually excoriated as degenerates. "At best," Terry Wilson relates, "these children were 'marginal people of minor significance'; individuals who excelled as leaders were 'renegades' or 'designing half-breeds.' "[18] By stereotyping mixed-race Native Americans as "degenerates" less worthy of land or status than "full-bloods," Karren Baird-Olson describes how the government used the blood-quota system to undermine indigenous definitions of family and tribal status. In contrast to the blood quantum used by the Bureau of Indian Affairs (BIA) and other government agencies, many Native American tribes understood tribal status as determined "by family lineage, marriage, adoption, or . . . long-term membership and com-mitment to the various communities." Thus, enforcing blood-quantum rules had the dual effect of decreasing population counts and assimilating Native Americans into the hegemonic racial structure of hypodescent.[19]

The Marginal Man

In the decades between the world wars, the Anglo-American foreign policy establishment, along with select few domestic politicians, predicted that racial problems could destabilize their international hegemony.[20] In European-held colonies as well as in America's Deep South and northern industrialized cities, tensions around color, caste, and class were deemed a liability. This concern supported the development of a new line of inquiry in the social sciences: race relations research. Frank Furedi stresses that the impetus of this research was to minimize damage to the national and world systems shaped by Whites; therefore, the main "problems" analyzed in much race relations research were people of color's "adjustments" to White rule. Although many in the new field of race relations supported the expansion of legal rights for people of color, the overwhelming majority believed that "social equality" was out of the question.[21] Through this research, "mixed-bloods" were offered (again) as scientific justification for continued social segregation and other restrictive policies and practices. In the new social science, however, the mulatto was not described in terms of biological deficiency, but in terms of psychological and social maladjustment.

According to sociologists, biracial people were "marginal" because they were incapable of settling into a role in society. Indeed, it was impossible for them to find an acceptable role, because their dual racial heritage warred both within their psyches and also between their parents' racial groups. In the quest to manage race relations without upsetting Whites, social scientists and elites found the marginal man thesis a more than adequate (and palatable) substitute for the racist theories of moral and physical degeneracy based in biology championed by the prior generation of scientists. Although as late as 1944, some scientists still published work on the degeneracy of "mixed bloods," theories of the maladjusted or "marginal" man had largely displaced the older research.[22]

Despite the substitution of psychological and social, rather than biological, reasons for the tragic condition of mixed-bloods, the marginal man hypothesis was no less racist in its implications for people of color. "This perspective readily lent itself to an apologetic interpretation, where the maladjusted mind rather than the problems of colonial domination or racial oppression, became the problem."[23] Thus, emerging nationalisms and racial consciousness of people of color around the globe were explained as the products of dissatisfied "native intellectuals" and "halfbreeds." Some Whites hypothesized (and feared) that this group of marginal men would be more likely to lead insurgencies as a result of their inability to accept their subordinate place in the Anglo-American social matrix; others didn't predict organized resistance, but rather violent, isolated outbursts of frustration emanating from the mixed-blood's tragic placement in a race/class limbo. No matter the social result, the mixed-blood person was theorized in social science as a problem, and one to be avoided by retaining existing social and legal restrictions on race mixing.[24]

Tragic Romance, Shifty Immigrants, and Passers: Race Mixing in Popular Media

Throughout the nineteenth and twentieth centuries, the mulatto, mestizo, half-breed, and miscegenation were important topics in multiple discursive domains. The burgeoning popular media drew upon scholarly theories of race mixing to create narratives and stereotypes that continue to resonate into the twenty-first century. Scientific theories were dramatized and disseminated widely in popular culture. Dramas centered around the horrors of race mixing were commonplace in works by authors, filmmakers, playwrights, and journalists. Although these texts emphasized different issues, four common themes are clear in media concerning race mixing: (1) miscegenation and mixed-race people are a source of pollution of "pure" Whiteness and/or a pure nation; (2) miscegenation and mixed-race people are tragic, unnatural phenomena; (3) mixed-race people are psychologically damaged outcasts, angry at both parents' racial groups; and, (4) miscegenation and mixed-race people are exotic and desirable, yet ultimately forbidden to Whites.[25]

The Passer

The fear that an unmarked person of African descent—someone passing—would infiltrate White society was a regular feature in popular books, films, and the news. The ability to "read" blackness in a person whose physical attributes were not clearly "African" was a popular theme and plot device in American novels.[26] One of the most prolific writers who used miscegenation as a key theme was Thomas Dixon, author of *The Clansman*,[27] the story that was transformed in 1915 by D. W. Griffith into the first blockbuster film, *Birth of a Nation*.[28] In Dixon's work, White-looking mulatto characters revealed their inferiority through violence, wanton sexual desire for White women, and deficient character. Cathy Boeckmann explains that even though Dixon and other authors conceded that "black blood" is not always physically visible, they believed that the "degeneracy" of mixed-race people would be expressed in their faulty character. Thus, "looking white" would never translate to truly "acting white" or having the essence of whiteness in one's soul.[29]

Beyond Dixon's tales, the plots of many sentimental novels turned on whether the White hero or heroine would realize that his/her beloved was passing for white before it was too late.[30] Passing characters expressed fears that their children would be born with dark skin or some other telltale mark of Blackness, ruining their charade; the families of their duped fiancés investigated their backgrounds tirelessly to test their suspicions. Many plots turned on a White hero or heroine's ability to "see" the mark of Blackness somewhere on the mulatta fiancee's body, often in the "bluish tinge" underneath the suspect's fingernails.[31] In other dramatic scenarios, tragedy ensues for mixed-blood women, who had been reared as Whites. Inevitably they discover on the eve of marriage or motherhood that they have the "taint" of Black blood. This discovery often leads to public shame, exile, or death, either from a tragic illness, suicide, or murder.[32]

Accounts of passing and miscegenation appeared frequently in the news as well, providing lurid scandals of betrayal and shame for readers. One of the most infamous was the *Rhinelander v. Rhinelander* case of 1925. Attorneys for White heir Leonard Rhinelander claimed that his wife, Alice, had failed to disclose her Black ancestry before their marriage, thus "passing" and fraudulently marrying into his blueblood family.[33] Attorneys for Alice Rhinelander countered that her physiology obviously revealed her Black identity. As argued by her lawyers, proof of Alice's innocence resided, ironically, in the preternatural ability of Whites to "see" through her white-looking skin.[34] Newspapers from New York to Des Moines had a field day with the case, publishing excerpts from love letters read in the courtroom as evidence.[35] Sensational cases such as the Rhinelanders' kept the issues of miscegenation and passing in the public eye across the nation.[36]

Tragic and/or duplicitous characteristics were not uniquely assigned to those of Black/White descent in popular media. Nakashima asserts that "by the time of the Civil War and the Mexican American War, the American public had already become familiar with the tormented, pathetic, and often dangerous multi-racial Black-White and Indian-White, and to some extent the Mexican-White, all of whom were favorite character types in mainstream fictional literature."[37] Unlike depictions of African-descended mixed bloods, artists typically did not imagine Eurasians who could pass for White. "Yellow Peril" narratives depicted biracial characters with clear "oriental" or "Mongoloid" physical features. Concerns about Asian immigration and how it threatened the United States' purity as a nation of White Americans dominated these tales; contamination—of individual bodies and the soul of the country—was the main fear. As with mulatto/a-White pairings, White-Eurasian love affairs almost always ended tragically for both the White and Asian partner, in death or disease. "But before his or her untimely demise, the Eurasian . . . is an especially persuasive witness to the racial and cultural superiority of Whites over Asians, and of the 'unassimilability' of Asians into mainstream America."[38]

The 1904 opera *Madame Butterfly* is, perhaps, the best-known template for doomed Asian-White lovers and the danger of possible offspring.[39] Cio-cio San (Madame Butterfly) falls in love with a philandering White U.S. naval officer. She bears his child after he abandons her and remains loyal to him against her father's wishes and cultural expectations. When her husband returns three years later with a new White wife, Cio-cio San kills herself, hoping that her son (nicknamed "Trouble") will be able to live a respectable life without the shame of his abandoned mother. Butterfly's wish for her Asian-White son, however, was not realized in later tales of mixed-race Asians. The central Japanese-European character in the 1921 novel *Kimono* was, notably, described in terms consonant with the marginal man thesis: "A butterfly body with this cosmic war shaking it incessantly. Poor child! No wonder she seems always tired!"[40] This "butterfly" daughter of a Chinese criminal, who murdered her White mother, is literally killed by her Asian heritage: her evil Chinese father dispatches her before she can expose him to the police. The same novel also contains a "psychotic Eurasian character, Yae Smith, who is described as a 'bundle of nerves' . . . doomed to a life astray between light and darkness."[41] A similar character appeared in the 1936 film serial "Shadow of Chinatown." Portrayed by horror-film actor Bela Lugosi, this insane Eurasian chemist blamed and hated both Whites and Chinese for his pariah status.[42]

In contrast to narratives of Black/White and Asian/White miscegenation, Native American/White pairings were sometimes portrayed "positively." To be sure, many pulp novels and Westerns contained plots with lustful Indians kidnapping White women; however, the status of Native Americans as original inhabitants of the land elicited specific anxieties about citizenship and belonging. In her analysis of silent Westerns, Joanna Hearne illustrates how the bodies of Native American characters in movies such as *Squaw Man* and *Maya, Just an Indian*, become vehicles for Whites to legitimately take hold of natural resources and land previously owned by tribes.[43] Cross-racial romances still fail in these narratives, but White characters do not uniformly reject the children born of these unions as in much of the tragic mulatto and passing literature. Hearne explains that "these early Westerns . . . provide a composite narrative that depicts the white 'family' on the land emerging from the 'broken home' of a previous mixed-race marriage, and that equates children, land, and gold as the spoils of failed romance, not of war."[44] The painful results of White conquest were reimagined as failed romance, papering over the violence and injustices Native Americans experienced in this relationship. These fantasies, then, substituted individual relationships for institutional policies. Unlike many narratives of Black/White children, in Westerns half-breeds could gain the acceptance through proper cultural behavior, dress, and other intimate knowledge of how to act in White society.[45] These plots echoed government policies for assimilating Native Americans, such as taking children from their families to be fostered at White-run schools or in White homes, and other acts of coercion. Through cultural changes, intermarriage, and "gentle" displacement by White settlers, these films suggested, Native Americans would vanish from the landscape, making way for White Americans to prosper.[46]

These popular media narratives reveal different degrees of refusal to integrate or accept people of color in the American sociopolitical body. With the exception of Native Americans, complete rejection of interracial intimacy was the advice conveyed to readers in most tales. Even though a handful of silent westerns often portrayed Native heroines and half-breed heroes with sympathy, like the Eurasian and the mulatto, there was no space for these people to coexist with Whites as equals; they must return to "their people," perish, or shed the remaining cultural markers and behaviors of people of color in order to achieve compatibility with the dominant group. Racial separation and hierarchy were depicted as necessary elements of the nation in these media texts. This pattern did not change significantly until the mid-twentieth century, when a handful of "progressive" race narratives emerged in dominant mass media.

Black Media on Passing and Miscegenation

The first part of this chapter summarized dominant narratives of passing and miscegenation in mass media of the late nineteenth and early twentieth centuries. Black media makers also produced narratives of race mixing, albeit they were often quite different than those created by their White counterparts. Rather than viewing mixed-race people and interracial sex from the hegemonic stance of White supremacy, Black authors of the nineteenth and early twentieth centuries were engaged in protest against slavery, racist stereotypes, and anti-Black violence. In their fight against racist discourse and practices, they attacked those elements of the dominant ideology that assigned deviance to all Black sexuality, outlawed miscegenation, and demonized mixed-race people. However, rejection of racist stereotypes and laws did not necessarily lead to acceptance of miscegenation, passing, or mixed-race people. Indeed, ambivalence and discomfort could be offered as the best descriptors for attitudes toward people of African descent who crossed—temporarily or permanently—the color line.

Interracial Sexual Exploitation

> The Lynching record for a quarter of a century merits the thoughtful study of the American people. It presents three salient facts:
>
> *First: Lynching is a color-line murder*
>
> *Second: Crimes against women is the excuse, not the cause*
>
> *Third: It is a national crime and requires a national remedy.*
>
> —Ida B. Wells, "Lynching, Our National Crime"

Before the end of slavery, abolitionist and Black-owned newspapers criticized White slaveholders' sexual exploitation of Black women, calling out the hypocrisy and barbarity of rape and the enslavement of their own flesh and blood.[47] After slavery, sexual exploitation and brutality continued under slightly different circumstances. Black journalists covered these issues, most famously with Ida B.Wells's antilynching investigations. Publishing first in her own paper, the Memphis *Free Speech*, and later the *New York Age*, Wells was determined to refute the prevailing White discourse of violent black sexuality. She deconstructed the sacred myth of lynching: that it was done to protect the honor of white women. She described this excuse famously in a May 1892 editorial as "a threadbare lie." Soon after, a White mob descended on the offices of *Free Speech* and destroyed the building, promising to kill her if she returned. The destruction of her paper and threats on her life only strengthened her resolve. T. Thomas Fortune, owner of the *New York Age*, offered her a job as soon as word of the mob violence hit New York City. After the first issue of the *Age* including Wells's investigations came out, Fortune had to print an extra edition of ten thousand to meet the demand of Black readers.[48] It is clear from her success as a writer that her portrayals of lynching and interracial sex resonated with a large number of African Americans. In her pamphlet, "Southern Horrors," Wells attacked the double standard in rape prosecutions: White women were granted protection of their virtue, while Black women's virtue was not even recognized. She also reported multiple instances where White women admitted to and continued consensual relationships with Black men, and how some of these women helped their lovers escape mob violence.[49] Wells's publications served as templates for future black journalists' accounts of lynching, miscegenation, and other aspects of race mixing. Confronted with a new wave of racist violence at the end of World War I, the Black press continued to speak out against sexual stereotypes.

The golden age of the Black press began in the years leading to World War I, as circulation reached into the hundreds of thousands.[50] The *Chicago Defender*, cited by many historians as one of the most influential Black papers, contained many articles about miscegenation and racial violence.[51] A fast-growing Black audience rewarded papers such as the *Defender* for calling Whites on their sexual hypocrisies, and for encouraging Blacks to practice self-defense. In 1915, a *Defender* editorial described the "Negro of Conquest," a figure juxtaposed with Negroes who were "happy" living in the South. This man of conquest did "not believe in raising his family in a section of the country where the law allows the white man to live in open adultery with a black woman and is looked upon with favor by the Negroes, and lynch a colored man if he is seen talking to a white woman."[52] The paper was full of stories of race men and women combating White sexual violence. Headlines such as, "Must not insult women of the race: Lawyer Carter gives uppercut to white brute," proclaimed Blacks' right to fight back against sexual exploitation of Black women.[53] Similarly, in this excerpt from a 1916 edition, women were encouraged to use physical force if necessary:

> In numerous instances over the country reports are different now. Women have become tired of white men treating them like inhumans [*sic*] and instead of the women being beaten up, the white men are taken to hospitals.[54]

During the months of race riots and lynchings in 1919, dubbed "Red Summer," the topics of lynching and rape myths were prominent in Black newspaper headlines nationwide. An article in the October 18, 1919, edition of the *Louisville News* condemned the lynching of a Black soldier rumored to have a White girlfriend and made the claim, "If white men were to be lynched for insulting and seeking to thrust their attentions on colored women here there would be lynchings daily."[55] A week later, a dispatch from the Associated Negro Press declared that Southern White men possessed a "dual character" when it came to Blacks with the headline: "Is Both Negro Hater and Keeper of Colored Mistresses."[56] In the view of Black journalists and editors, the stereotype of Black predatory sexuality was clearly a cover for White sexual urges to cross the color line. The *Chicago Defender* summed up this view in an article titled "Attacks on White Women" in the September 20, 1920, issue:

> It is the same old excuse—"attacks on white women." What the nature of these attacks have been is left to inference. . . . If the press of this country were honest in their statements concerning

such matters race rioting would be robbed of its chief inspiration. If the men of our group were to make reprisals upon the white people for the wrongs done the women of our race, America would see a red day. During the period of slavery the lecherous white master consorted with the slave women of his plantation and filled the South with his tawny offspring. The white sons of this master class are today passing laws to segregate their yellow kinsmen, but, if all reports are true, the separatist measures are only intended for daylight.[57]

Romance across the Color Line in the Black Press

Although the most common stories of interracial sex in Black papers involved violence, consensual relationships were also covered, particularly when members of high society were involved.[58] Usually, the newspapers portrayed these unions as destined for trouble, due to an imminent violent response from White men or the duplicity of a White woman. In an article titled "Actress Wanted Color, Not Husband's Love," the *Defender* reported how a White actress filed for divorce after discovering that her husband was "not a full-blooded white man." Another report focused on White entertainer Ruby Clark, the lover of a Black actor, Bob Anderson. Anderson was married to an African American woman, and also allegedly dating another Black woman, referred to as Cleo. When Clark accompanied him to see his Black mistress, a fight ensued over his two-timing, and Cleo shot him. Anderson's wife, the paper noted, blamed his White lover, Miss Clark, for instigating the attack.[59] Other articles depicted White women tricking their husbands into thinking that Black male employees or local businessmen had become their paramours.[60] Although papers didn't explicitly discourage interracial romance, it was clear from the stories that it was foolhardy for a Black man to attempt a consensual relationship with a White woman.

Black newspapers spoke out against antimiscegenation law, but this did not translate into wholehearted support for interracial marriage or intimacy. Rather, editors qualified these protests by proclaiming that most Blacks didn't want to "socialize" with Whites or marry them.[61] They declared that it was unjust and racist to legislate against miscegenation because the laws rested upon foul stereotypes of Black inferiority and White hypocrisy. Indeed, writers often suggested that it was White male desire that generated the most interracial sex, and the laws were merely vehicles for racist ideology.

Most people outside the penitentiary have the privilege of selecting their friends and associates. This fact should tend to allay the fears of those who are imbued with the idea that it is our aim to break into their "exclusive" social circles. . . . American history records the fact that from the very beginning the white man sought us. How intimately he has been associated with us can best be judged by a casual survey of the millions of mulattoes in this country.[62]

In the same vein, articles concerning Black women and White men almost always depicted Black men protecting Black women from White sexual aggressors. One of the largest front page headlines for the October 9, 1920, *Defender* read, "Life of White Man Threatened for Insulting a Woman." The story related how "the trouble started when Harry Roeger (white) . . . knocked down a women of our Race" Afterward, a group of Black men proceeded to beat Mr. Roeger and his friends. Another *Defender* article applauded the fighting spirit of two race men who refused to allow a White man to accost a Black woman. The *Wisconsin Weekly Blade* relayed the story of a Black man who killed a White man in order to protect two young girls from him.[63] These articles charged race men with the duty of protecting race women at all costs, even one's life.

But some Black women were portrayed as deserving neither the chivalry nor the vengeance of race men. Black women who chose consensual cross-racial liaisons were treated with disdain and suspicion. The papers accused them of lacking morals and race pride. This set up a double standard in regard to interracial sex. Unlike the sympathetic men who escaped violence with the help of White female lovers chronicled in the work of Ida B. Wells, Black women who consented to relations with White men were targets for ridicule and shaming, as indicated by the following story, headlined "Southern Afro-American Girl Parades Her White Paramour at Fiske University Reception."

> A merry waltz was in progress when in paraded a southern white brute and lyncher and his *mulatto* lover. Right here in Chicago and in the very midst of those who denounce the way the white men treat our women in the South. . . . [T]hey came in and sat UNMOLESTED. All day Friday the Chicago Defender received calls over the phone asking us to please make mention that this wench had dared to flaunt her low southern brute before the faces of decent mothers and sisters.[64]

This excerpt reflects many common stereotypes about mulattas. Notice that in the headline, the offending woman is referred to as "Afro-American," but by the middle of the first paragraph she is referred to as "mulatto." This shift in language suggests that mulattas are attracted to Whites and/or draw the attention of White men because of their blood mixture and desire to be like Whites.[65] The article continues with more negative descriptions of mulattas:

> There are lots more here in Chicago . . . mulatto girls who care only for certain jobs because they have white blood, and are forced to sell their bodies to hold a job. . . . Recently at a popular dance a certain young girl was ignored by a set of young, manly fellows who are well-known in this city. Her reputation for loving white men came and was known before she arrived. She was made to feel uncomfortable and she left.

The *Defender* suggested that, even if they try to socialize with Blacks again, mulattas who cross the color line are to be socially ostracized. "Real" race men are encouraged to criticize and embarrass Black women who choose White partners.[66] In the same vein, completely crossing over to the White side of the color line was cause for alarm, shame, and dismay. Interracial romance was one thing; passing quite another.

Passing in the Black Press: Ridicule and Redemption

> How can you tell who is a Negro?
>
> —*Chicago Whip*, September 13, 1919.

Periodically, stories of lighter-skinned Blacks passing for White appeared in the pages of Black newspapers. Multiracial Blacks who chose to pass were represented in a variety of ways. Some who passed were called race traitors in some accounts, as tricksters who "get over" on the White man, or as stealth "race spies," bringing back secrets from White society, in others.[67] Some writers justified passing as a means of subversion, as in this article from the *Chicago Whip's* September 13, 1919, edition:

> In the United States to-day [*sic*] there are over 1,000,000 mulattoes, octoroons, and quadroons, that are so Caucasian in appearance that science is baffled. . . . Ninety-five percent of these hybrid people have gone over to the other side. They look like White people, they talk like White people . . . *but they always think as Negroes . . . the memory of old insults, and the knowledge that his fellows are still suffering, keep his mind forever colored and the spark of loyalty for his colored progenitors from ever dying.*[68]

In the New Negro era, this imagination of race solidarity made sense. Papers such as the *Whip* and the *New York Age* strove to present a united front of Negroes, striving toward excellence and resistance to White supremacy. Attributing race loyalty to an unknown (but large) number of passing Blacks functioned both to refute the White supremacist assumption that White blood and society were better and to project a solid coalition of Americans of African descent.

Not all stories of passing Blacks characterized them in such a positive light. Passers were often chastised for abandoning the race. Kathleen Hauke's essay on Elsie Roxborough provides an example of this trend.[69] Roxborough was the daughter of the first Black state senator in Michigan and the first African American woman to live in student housing at the University of Michigan, where she attended theater classes with future star playwright Arthur Miller.[70] Unlike her White male classmate, race and gender barriers squelched Roxborough's dreams of success as a writer. Reborn as New York fashion maven Mona Manet, however, she wrote for magazines and produced fashion events, successfully passing as White among her closest co-workers.[71]

However, the Black press knew about her new life, and writers commented with humor and derision on the disappearance of the young woman who had once regularly graced their society pages. A 1937 column by William Smallwood in the *Baltimore Afro-American* spread the following word to the wise:

> Though none of the metropolitan lads who pound typewriters for a living know it, Elsie Roxborough . . . has been living in Gotham for the past few months as Nordic—much to her family's undisguised disgust. You can imagine poor La Roxborough shuddering each time she slips into an uptown subway train.[72]

The writer's displeasure with Roxborough is clear. Not only is her family's disapproval (both her immediate and the implied family of the Black public) clear, but also the writer takes time to imagine her fear of being outed by Blacks living uptown (i.e., Harlem), because he assumes they would be able to see through her pass. Roxborough's pass was not total; she sporadically made contact with her friend, the venerated writer Langston Hughes, in her life as Mona Manet. Although the poet's feelings on passing were negative, Hughes did not expose her secret. Similarly, after her death when her uncle came to claim her body in New York, he made no mention of her past and told her New York acquaintances that the funeral would be private. He himself was light enough to pass, and thus, he did not expose her secret at death through his presence.[73] Her uncle's silence is indicative of the ambivalent relationship many Blacks had and continue to have with passing; it is hard not to sympathize on some level with the passer's desire to masquerade and enjoy the privileges of whiteness, or to snicker at the duped Whites who could not "see" the Blacks among them. But the sympathy or pleasure felt when confronted with passing is always haunted by the realities of racism and continued oppression suffered by those without the privileges of light skin pigmentation.

While stories of "getting over" on Whites through passing probably provided some pleasures for readers of Black newspapers, newswriters did not sanction passing as a normative behavior or response to racism. The urge to pass, as in the *Whip's* fantasy of legions of ex-colored men, is a function of a racist system; light-skinned Blacks should remember their roots rather than attempt a complete transformation like Elsie Roxborough. In this way, the newspapers echoed the sentiments of many Black novelists and filmmakers that featured passing in their work. Giulia Fabi asserts that African American authors of the nineteenth and early twentieth centuries used passing to depict the evils of slavery, racism, and prejudice.[74] Similarly, Boeckmann's chapter on James Weldon Johnson's work notes that his passing character recognizes and describes the presence and effects of White racism as part of his journey.[75] Like the *Whip*, Johnson's *Ex-Colored Man* is, in some ways, always "thinking like a Negro" even as he enjoys the benefits of his light skin. Indeed, at the novel's conclusion the main character expresses his frustration at his inability to use his musical talents to demonstrate the genius of the Black race.

Jennifer DeVere Brody's analysis of Nella Larsen's *Passing* highlights the passing Clare Kendry's refusal to frame her Black working-class roots as deviant/Other; she desires the company and memories of Black people and jokes with her semi-passing friend, Irene Redfield, about Whites.[76] Lauren Berlant's reading of the same novel emphasizes Irene's yearning to inhabit a body that is not stigmatized by color and gender conventions.[77] In contrast to White narratives, where White supremacy was reasserted and justified, Black authors used passing to expose and wrestle with the double standards of racial identities and expose injustices and traumas experienced by Blacks of all hues. Likewise, Oscar Micheaux's filmed depictions of mulattoes and mulattas often contained an inversion of the White-authored passing novel; discovering one's Black identity led to a happy ending and closure, not exposure and death.

The idea that people who passed would (and should) ultimately "embrace the race" returned at the advent of the civil rights movement of the 1950s. *Ebony, Color,* and *Jet* magazines all produced articles featuring former passers who had recently decided to refuse the opportunity to pass. Gayle Wald analyzed this set of features and found that they followed the themes of middle-class advancement of Blacks popular in the press of the postwar period.[78] Structured this way, stories of individuals rejecting passing and embracing Blackness called into question "the exclusion or selective inclusion of Blacks in the public sphere" by manipulating the usual framing of passing "to imagine a world in which 'White' skin would no longer be a prerequisite to equality."[79] The "reformed" passers were used to illustrate not only race pride, but the idea that individual social mobility was more accessible to Blacks due to reforms of the war years that opened new opportunities in certain industries and government service.[80]

Given this history of Black authors' approaches to passing, it is not surprising that the Black press, when confronted with Susie Phipps's story[81] in the 1980s, emphasized race pride and the hypocrisies of white supremacy. As with Elsie Roxborough and the passers of the past, her case was met with a mixture of bitter humor, memories, and political agendas that highlighted the continued effects of racism in Black lives and national culture.

Mainstream Media Portrayals of Race Mixing after World War II

In the years before and during World War II, filmmakers and radio producers were encouraged to produce programs to defuse racial and ethnic tensions, which the federal government feared might damage the war effort. The target groups for many of these media messages were Blacks and working-class European ethnic groups.[82] Hollywood's "message films," many of which lauded the contributions of Black soldiers, created a popular space for a new liberal race relations discourse. After World War II, Hollywood continued to experiment with liberal "message films," meant to encourage the masses to aspire to particular cultural traits and goals and to reject prejudice. Gayle Wald examines two such films that revolved around passing, Alfred Welker's *Lost Boundaries* and Elia Kazan's *Pinky*, which contained different, less tragic, outcomes for their miscegenated protagonists than the passing tales of the nineteenth and early twentieth centuries.[83]

While these biracial characters—all portrayed by Anglo actors—are exposed as fraudulent "passers," they have already achieved and performed bourgeois respectability that distinguishes them from other stereotypical Blacks. Additionally, Wald argues, "both films represent racial discrimination and exclusion as inducements to pass" but "the real heroes of the films are sympathetic whites" who allow passers to participate in a limited engagement with white middle-class society.[84] For example, the mulatta

Pinky decides to end her engagement to a White fiancé. She is later rewarded by a windfall inheritance that allows her to open a hospital— for black children—that solidifies her position as a lady and member of the middle class. Thus, Pinky is placed above other Blacks, but still distanced from White public and private spheres. In *Lost Boundaries*, after the passing parents reveal to their son that they are part Black, he runs away from their White middle-class enclave to see "real Blacks." His harrowing trip through a stereotypical Harlem highlights the deviant behavior of other Blacks who display none of the middle-class behaviors of the protagonists and their White neighbors.[85] Thus, Wald concludes, race and class are intertwined in passing narratives; distancing oneself from the lower class (and race) is crucial for the passer/multiracial character who wishes to remain in or near the White public sphere, however tenuous his or her position may be.

Interracial romance films of the 1950s and '60s often emphasized the roles of heroic, forward-thinking Whites. In *Sayonara*, for example, Marlon Brando's main character and his White buddy both protest the U.S. armed forces' attempts to keep GIs from marrying local Asian women. In contrast, Brando's Japanese love interest is the one who pessimistically insists to her lover that their marriage would never survive. In that climactic scene, she is the one to cry the question, "What about the children?" He answers, "They'll be half-American and half-Japanese; half yellow and half white." In this and other romances between White male soldiers and Asian women, the presence of the American military is played down as a mere plot device to join star-crossed lovers. Relatedly, male Asian characters who pursued White women were usually sinister or slapstick caricatures, never serious rivals to White men.[86]

Similar to *Pinky* and *Lost Boundaries*, interracial romance films reinforced the importance of class and geographic distance from other people of color to make limited interracial intimacy work. The most famous American interracial romance film, *Guess Who's Coming to Dinner*, features a solidly middle-class Black man, played by Sidney Poitier. A doctor, an eloquent speaker and sharp dresser, Poitier's character was the perfect prospective son-in-law—except for the color of his skin. Susan Courtney's analysis of the film and other 1960s films that featured mixed-race couplings reveals that, save for small moments of tension, these movies reinforced racial divisions and did not challenge White patriarchal authority.[87] Likewise, in many other films and TV shows that featured Black actors in the 1960s (e.g., *I Spy*, *Julia*), the Blacks allowed into the circle of White society are "exceptional" in every way. As Robin Means Coleman explains in her history of Black sitcoms, in the 1960s and '70s Black actors were either isolated from all other Blacks or particular expressions of culture or behavior identified as Black, or segregated in all-Black casts with little or no contact with Whites.[88]

Despite these small steps toward "positive" portrayals of interracial contact, in other arenas of mid-century popular culture, race mixing was still viewed as a looming threat to White status and control. The incredible popularity of Black performers of rhythm and blues music with White youth sparked consternation, censorship, harsh rhetoric, and physical violence across the country. As the civil rights movement built momentum and crossover Black artists and their White adherents and imitators increased, uglier descriptions of miscegenation resurfaced as part of the massive resistance campaign and in more genteel circles. Politicians, parents, and music industry officials worried (and periodically continue to worry) about the effects of Black music on White teens. Musicians who played "race music" were harassed, attacked, and in some cases, chased out of the business by Whites who feared amalgamation.

Brian Ward recounts the trial of the "wholesome" Black doo wop group, the Platters, who were arrested for entertaining three White women and one Black woman in a Cincinnati hotel. Although the group was acquitted of the charges of aiding and abetting prostitution, the judge in the case took the opportunity "to deliver a lengthy rebuke, encapsulating white fears of rampant black sexuality: 'You have taken that which can be the core of reproductive life and turned it into a socially abhorrent, tawdry indulgence in lust.' "[89] Some segregationists were so sure that Black music had the power to turn White girls and women into sexual partners of Black men, they bullied and intimidated radio programmers and record store owners in addition to Black musicians. Members of the Ku Klux Klan vandalized the transmitter of WEDR-Birmingham, one of the most popular stations playing Black music.[90] Louisiana and other states passed laws against interracial dancing, musical performances, and the like, all of which were assumed to incite miscegenation.

Patterson relates how, in the wake of *Brown v. Board of Education*, segregationists used fears of miscegenation in public campaigns against school integration.[91] Responding to the *Brown* ruling, many Whites felt free to publicly insist that "black men lusted after white women and that mixing would pollute the purity of the white race."[92] From state legislatures to the pages of leading newspapers and magazines, segregationists insisted that mixed schools would result in mixed blood. In the *Atlantic Monthly*, one South Carolinian wrote that school integration would mean "mixed matings would become commonplace and a greatly enlarged mixed-blood population would result."[93] The specter of mixed-bloods was used to justify the intense violence and legal intransigence that Black students and their parents faced as they courageously tried to desegregate schools.

Despite the scholarly turn to more liberal consideration of race relations and a rejection of biological conceptions of race by many scientists, segregationists were comfortable with using the language of amalgamation and blood pollution to support their violent opposition to Black freedom movements and cultural influence.

By the time the Supreme Court overturned the last antimiscegenation laws in *Loving v. Virginia* in 1967,[94] no clearly new profile of mixed-race people had emerged from scholarship, law, or popular culture, although some stabs had been made at portraying interracial romance in a positive light.[95] Whether based on biological assumptions or social psychology, people of mixed race were still seen as misfits by the dominant society. The marginal man theory still reigned, and interracial parents were encouraged to teach their children to associate themselves with a single race. Even with the emergence of "children of the movement"—born to interracial couples who met through civil rights activism—the overriding ideology concerning race mixing was that it would harm families and/or society by creating a set of people with no natural or definable racial home. Not until the emergence of a new group of multiracial scholars and activists was this conventional wisdom vigorously challenged.

Reimagining Race Mixing: New Multiracial Scholarship and the Mixed Race Movement

In the 1970s, groups of mixed-race families and their children began to form to support formal networks. Founded in 1978, I-Pride (Interracial Pride) is recognized as the first large-scale organization dedicated solely to advocacy for multiracial people. According to most accounts, these groups functioned as safe havens for multiracial people and their families, providing social contacts and fora for people to share experiences and dispel stereotypes about interracial marriage and mixed-race identities. In 1988, the Association of MultiEthnic Americans (AMEA) was created to serve as a national umbrella organization for the growing number of state and local organizations for multiracial families, to give those groups a national presence. Thus, by the 1990s, many of them had grown beyond consciousness-raising and family picnics; they had become social movement organizations with offices and boards of directors. Through organizations such as AMEA, they were able to plan strategies locally and nationally as a new social movement.

Simultaneously, a body of scholarship emerged. A new generation of social scientists proclaimed the presence of a new multiracial identity that directly challenged the hegemonic stereotypes of tragic mulattos and hybrids. Gloria Anzaldúa's *Borderlands/La Frontera: The New Mestiza* and

Maria P. P. Root's edited collection *Racially Mixed People in America* are considered landmark texts in this scholarship.[96] Anzaldúa asserted that the borderlands are spaces where mestizas can access a rich, complex vision of society and power relations in order to deconstruct hierarchy and foment struggle. Root and colleagues argued against dominant psychological and historical approaches that depict people of multiracial identity as inherently damaged and doomed to ostracism. Rather, these authors emphasized the role of racism in subjecting multiracial people to shaming, violence, and isolation. These books and their descendants present a multiracial identity that privileges intersectionality, and proclaims that a both/and identity and perspective on race can be achieved, and that racial dichotomies are rooted in White supremacy, imperialism, and sexism.

In the last thirty years, this growing group of activists and scholars has made efforts to reclaim multiracial identity as a positive quality, to be celebrated and deployed in order to expose and undermine the fictions of racial hierarchy and racism. Similar to other new social movements, constructing a positive, generative identity is central to this movement, if not its defining aspect. Through conferences, marches, scholarly and popular writing, multiracial people and their allies have rejected the stereotypes of the "tragic mulatto" and the idea of distinct racial groups, advocating instead for psychological and sociological approaches to race that recognize that bi- and multiracial people can indeed adopt a both/and sense of racial identity rather than being torn apart (or rejected) by two social groups, or choosing one over the other. One main goal articulated by many multiracial organizations has been to change how the state classifies multiracial people. Parents, particularly, have articulated their children's need to have the choice to identify the races of both parents on school and health care data forms. Breaking from the school of thought that one had to bond with a single racial group to have a healthy self-concept, parents of multiracial children and psychologists argue that multiracial children would be healthier if they were not forced to choose between their parents, a choice that could imply a hierarchy of races in the household and the wider society.[97] Indeed, the original mission of I-Pride was to lobby the Berkeley, California, school system to include a multiracial option on school forms.[98] By 1995, multiracial activists were successful in changing school forms in Ohio, Michigan, Florida, Illinois, and Indiana.[99]

As these individuals and organizations endeavored to reframe multiracial identity in the public sphere, the most visible aspect of their project became the campaign to add a multiracial category to the U.S. Census. In 1989, AMEA contacted members of Congress about changing the Census Bureau's racial categories to include a multiracial option, and were later invited to testify to the House Subcommittee on the Census in

1993.[100] Thus, the first multiracial issue to gain national publicity was the fight for a new census category. This nationally visible campaign, spearheaded mainly by AMEA and Project RACE (Reclassify All Children Equally) has drawn the most attention among the news media, following sparse interest in multiracial identity since the mid-century. Indeed, despite sporadic attempts in entertainment media in the1980s and 1990s to portray interracial love stories or biracial characters, the notion that tens of thousands, if not hundreds of thousands, of individuals and families in the United States were in the process of forging new multiracial identities was lost on mainstream media.[101] However, bolstered by the census campaign and the popularity of young multiracial celebrities, such as Tiger Woods, who publicly described and celebrated their multiracial heritage in the 1990s, news media latched onto the story of multiracial people. Certainly in contrast to earlier depictions, contemporary mainstream media have put multiracial identity in a better light.[102] However, just as the burgeoning mixed-race literature and multiracial-identified populace flew under the radar for years before gaining media attention, specific aspects of the movement and its varied philosophies and goals concerning race have been lost in the glare of subsequent publicity. Namely, mainstream media have avoided the challenges to Whiteness and racial hierarchy that many multiracial scholars and activists emphasize in their work.

The successful campaigns to include a multiracial category on school forms followed by the push to make similar changes to the Census put multiracial organizations directly in conflict with many well-established civil rights organizations, including the NAACP, MALDEF, and National Council of La Raza. When the OMB solicited public comment on changing Directive 15, the rules that created the five racial designations used and officially recognized by the federal government, AMEA, Project RACE, and other groups took the opportunity in hand. In the eyes of other civil rights groups, however, multiracial activists were heading in the wrong direction. The liberation movements for people of color in the 1960s and '70s ushered in an era of racial and ethnic pride and an investment in one's right to choose and claim a particular, nonpejorative identity label. Thus, as Kim Williams argues, the multiracial movement is connected to other movements for people of color in the quest to determine for themselves how they are named in society. However, because Directive 15 and many pieces of civil rights legislation were implicitly referring to inequalities between Blacks and Whites, the categories created in 1977 were problematic from the start. Williams writes, "[T]he policy outcomes associated with the civil rights movement focused exclusively on racism, discrimination, and equality, leaving aside (a) the question of race itself and (b) the possibility of ongoing and considerable changes in racial demographics."[103]

This part of the bureaucratic apparatus that made many aspects of civil rights oversight and prosecution possible—the collection of racial data—has become the target of the multiracial movement. Kimberly McClain DaCosta notes, however, that the multiracial movement differs from earlier movements' assertions of racial identity and self-determination of racial labels in that multiracial activists have "used the codes of liberal individualism" to claim racial and ethnic identification as an individual right.[104] This individualist ideology and rhetoric can be contrasted to the nationalistic claims made by Blacks, Chicanos, and Native Americans in earlier fights for representation. Hence, the approach and aims of some multiracial activists toward racial categorization are greeted with suspicion by established civil rights organizations that view the government's racial categories primarily as a tool for racial justice, not a vehicle for an individual right to self-realization or validation.[105]

Nancy Brown and Ramona Douglas emphasize that many participants in the movement, particularly members of AMEA, have been simultaneously concerned with questions of social justice and equality for people of all races in addition to the more visible issue of government racial categories. The work of Maria Root, Teresa DeLeon and Cynthia Nakashima, and G. Reginald Daniel, among others, reflects the concern that antiracism and resistance to White supremacy should be integral to the movement and conceptions of multiracial identity. Other chroniclers of the movement, such as Dalmage, emphasize that many White members of interracial families were initially drawn to these groups because they had felt "for the first time, the hurtfulness of racism" through their experiences with spouses and children; however, many then adopted the idea that multiracial identity and involvement in cross-racial intimacy are the means to transcending race, rather than arguing that society needs "to transcend the biased meanings associated with race."[106] As I demonstrate in chapters 5 and 6, however, the groups and scholars that endorse this latter view are not the ones normally consulted by the mainstream press.[107]

Some observers of the multiracial movement are suspicious about the role of White parents, many of whom have been quite visible at congressional hearings and other media events concerning the 2000 Census. These adults who claim to speak for the rights of their bi- and multiracial children are often viewed as disconnected from the communities and concerns of people of color. The large numbers and visible presence of White mothers in multiracial organizations have generated the suspicion that multiracial activists want to distance their children and themselves from other minority groups. One person who has inspired this interpretation in particular is Susan Graham, head of Project RACE, who testified during congressional hearings on the Census racial categories. Graham publicly embraced Newt Gingrich for his endorsement of the stand-alone multiracial identifier, and expressed outrage when a stand-alone multiracial identifier was rejected in favor of the multiple check-off system supported by established civil rights organizations such as the NAACP and MALDEF.[108] Indeed, her reaction and the desires of others to have stand-alone multiracial identifiers frustrated civil rights groups, who argued that the most important issue with the Census was avoiding minority undercounts that would effect many important policies crafted to monitor racial progress and sanction those who discriminate against minorities. In her study of the movement, McClain DaCosta notes that members of AMEA were self-conscious about the fact that the majority of their representatives were from Black/White couples and families, and made efforts to diversify their public image as they negotiated with the OMB and Congress. "In particular, the support of Asian multiracials eased the suspicion of some that those in favor of multiracial classification were actually interested in being a little less Black."[109] Despite the outreach to multiracial people who are not Black/White, many traditional civil rights groups and laypeople still harbor concerns that the multiracial movement aims to achieve a higher "whiter" racial status for its constituents than for monoracially identified Blacks, Asians, and Hispanics.

White members of multiracial organizations and families are not the only ones viewed critically for pursuing a separate identifier for multiracial people. A vocal group of multiracial-identified political activists have wholeheartedly adopted the "color-blind" rhetoric and political positions espoused by neoconservatives. For example, Charles Byrd, editor of the e-zine *Interracial Voice*, has thrown his support behind conservative University of California Regent Ward Connerly, sponsor of the anti–affirmative action Proposition 209. Like Graham, Byrd was angered by the OMB decision to use a multiple check system without a stand-alone multiracial category and blames civil rights groups for "denying" multiracial people their own unique category. Because of his position as an editor and his connections to major multiracial organizations, Byrd has been a favorite contact for journalists. Connerly—who has recently become eager to explain his White, Native American, and Black ancestry to the media—has launched another racial ballot proposal named the "Racial Privacy Initiative" (RPI). The RPI calls for an end to government collection and use of racial categories; Byrd and others have come out in support of the measure.

As I discuss in both chapter 6 and the Conclusion, Connerly and other neoconservatives use the growing multiracial population and a number of interracial marriages as "proof" that race no longer matters in our society. Byrd and others have supported Connerly's latest "solution" to racial issues, arguing that racial labels themselves must be eliminated to achieve a "color-blind" society. This link between the emergence and increase of the multiracial population and the elimination of all racial categories does not necessarily hold sway with the majority of mixed-race individuals; however, many newsmakers have been quick to predict that the demographic phenomena that have engendered multiracial identity will, in the not-too-distant future, usher in racial harmony for the nation. In addition, many commentators have lambasted civil rights groups that have been critical of a separate multiracial identity for adhering to an outdated way of thinking about race to further their political agendas. Thus, the multiracial movement's drive to rehabilitate and formally acknowledge multiracial identities has been meshed with the imperatives and ideology of neoconservative racial politics.

The next three chapters consist of case studies that predate the contemporary multiracial movement and the changes to Census 2000. Each in its own way illustrates the difficulties of the state and society in coming to terms with people of multiracial descent even decades after the Supreme Court struck down the last antimiscegenation laws. These cases provide an important contrast to and serve as prehistory for the new multiracial identities circulating in media today. These chapters help us remember that, not so long ago, the dominant understanding of race mixing was that it meant confusion. They also help us see that the bureaucratic decisions surrounding racial labels certainly matter, not only to people of color but also to Whites, the state, and other institutions that hold the power to name and change the names of racial groups. These cases also remind us that, more often than not, news coverage about race mixing and multiracial people reflects current thinking about race and race relations broadly, not just the specific identities of the actors in a particular story. Finally, the opening three cases took place in the last two decades, prompting us to recall how recently society has been introduced to Cablinasians, Hapas, and the other new names for racially mixed people in the United States.

Chapter Two

The In/discernible Body of Susie Phipps

With Daniel C. Brouwer

Who is the state of Louisiana to tell me I'm colored? What gives them that right?

—Susie Guillory Phipps

She stopped suddenly and lifted her hand, staring with wildly dilated eyes at the nails of her finely shaped fingers to find if the telltale marks of negro blood were there...

—Thomas Dixon, *Sins of the Father*

As scholars of passing have detailed, in the nineteenth and early twentieth centuries, people who passed for White were subject to social, physical, and legal repercussions if Whites discovered their masquerade. One could reasonably assume, however, that the end of Jim Crow and many other legal barriers to equality in the 1950s and '60s eliminated most of the incentives for people of African descent to pass for White. In the years following the civil rights movement and *Loving*, one might surprised to find "passers" crouching in fear of anything more than social embarrassment or family disappointment. One might ask the question: Is the concept of race passing still salient in a post–civil rights world, where politicians laud the goal of "colorblindness" and large numbers of non-Whites have achieved access to formerly segregated institutions and arenas of life? Would a person who lived life on the "White side" of the color line but who "belonged" on the other (at least according to Jim Crow–era laws) be treated the same if she were "outed" after the 1960s?

55

Consider the case of Susie Guillory Phipps: according to Louisiana state records, her parents were born "colored" but died "white." She herself claimed, "I'm white. I'm going to be white. I've been white all my life and that's just it,"[1] but discovered in 1977 that the state of Louisiana had designated her "colored" on her birth certificate. When for more than a year the state of Louisiana refused to change her birth certificate to read "white," Phipps filed suit against the state, thus instigating public controversy over the standards and criteria for determining racial designations. Despite the progress in race relations in the two decades preceding her lawsuit, the courts and the press were far from colorblind in regard to her case.

The most obvious obstacle to Phipps's effort to be designated as White was a Louisiana law. In 1970, Louisiana changed its racial designation codes and instituted the one thirty-second rule, whereby anyone with one thirty-second Black ancestry was considered legally Black.[2] In 1981, Phipps's lawyer, Brian Begue, filed suit to have the racial designation on her birth certificate changed and to rescind the state's one thirty-second formula of racial designation. Three days of testimony in 1982 included potentially damning narratives by some of Phipps's elderly relatives who told the court that at least parts of the family had always considered themselves "colored." Although the state legislature quickly overturned the blood quota law in response to public outrage and embarrassment, during the prosecution of her case, attorneys representing the state of Louisiana did not budge on the birth certificate. The state marshaled genealogical evidence that Phipps's great-great-great-great grandmother had been a freed slave named Margarita. With this and other evidence, the state's genealogist concluded that Susie Phipps had three thirty-second "Negro ancestry." A geneticist testified on Phipps's behalf that there was a good chance she had inherited *no* genetic material from her ancestress, Margarita. Even in the face of solid scientific evidence that Phipps had no "black blood," the court denied her request to have the document changed. Phipps appealed to higher courts, arguing that the state had no right to block a person from choosing their own racial designation on official records.[3] Her appeals failed at every level up to the United States Supreme Court, where the justices refused to hear her case in 1986. This dismissal ended her legal battle and reinforced the legitimacy of the "colored" designation on her birth certificate.

Throughout her march through the courts, the national and international media[4] followed her story, creating headlines and editorials about race in the United States. This chapter compares dominant and Black interpretations of Phipps's case in the U.S. news. Throughout this chapter and the book, the terms *dominant media* or *dominant discourse* indicate the relative position of power that those media and discourses occupy. Although some scholars prefer the term *mainstream media*, and some prefer the term *White media*, "dominant media" more precisely exposes the power of mainstream media to shape mainstream tastes and values. Further, "dominant" is used here instead of "White" because not all producers or consumers of this media are White, although the majority of actors involved in the dominant press are White, and its producers often imagine that Whites are their main audience.[5] The terms *Black media* and *Black discourse* here refer to media produced by and/or for a Black audience.

Through this comparison of dominant and Black media, the chapter explores how journalists and commentators portrayed the criteria different constituencies advocated for the proper identification of Susie Phipps, and for "Black" and "White" people generally. Three main questions guided the study: (1) What kinds of creative, critical, or other types of interventions did journalists or their sources make in conveying the case of Phipps to readers? (2) What themes about people of mixed race, if any, emerged in the telling of Phipps's story? And, (3) What did these themes tell readers about race and media as practiced and theorized in the late twentieth century in the United States? These questions guided a qualitative content analysis of the news articles about Susie Phipps.[6]

Passing for White

When people speak of passing, they may be referring to women passing as men or homosexuals passing as heterosexual. The focus of this chapter is the practice of light-skinned people of color taking on White identities for themselves in the dominant public sphere. Race passing, thus, holds the potential to destabilize the regime of White privilege by undermining the validity of racial categories. When passers are "discovered," though, they expose the fact that despite the inability to use visible physical and behavioral differences to tell us who is White and who is not, such failure is not sufficient to destroy the legitimacy of racial categories. Rather, the failure calls into action actors who rely on racial categories. In this process, multiple methods of determining racial difference are made visible: legal, social, and "scientific" norms and evidence are used to put the passer back into the right category and quell anxieties over blurred boundaries. Upon discovery of a pass, many actors have much at stake. On the one hand, these "scandals" threaten a backlash by the state and dominant populations against identity groups with whom they have complicated legal, political, and social histories. On the other hand, marginalized racial groups are confronted with the seeming necessity of identity maintenance that is critical to both a politics of difference and a politics of justice. The conflict between personal identity, state entities (such as law enforcement and courts of law), and social expectations was dramatized in news coverage of Phipps's case.

Passing and catching someone in a pass make clearly visible the web of individual, state, society, and culture involved in maintaining identities. Passing is a transgression that inspires fear in the state and dominant social groups. Dominant groups and institutions desire the ability to survey and evaluate all subordinates with ease, thereby ensuring knowledge and readiness. As Elaine Ginsberg argues, "When 'race' is no longer visible, it is no longer intelligible: if 'white' can be 'black,' what is white? Race passing not only creates, to use Garber's term, a *category crisis* but also destabilizes the grounds of privilege founded on racial identity."[7] However, the fact of destabilization does not neutralize the power of the dominant group, or dictate a particular response: when a passer is revealed, the result can be scandal, interrogation, punitive legal procedures, violence, or even murder.

Communication scholars have examined passing along lines of class,[8] sex,[9] sexual orientation,[10] and race.[11] Of particular relevance to this chapter, Marouf Hasian and Thomas Nakayama examine the legal and rhetorical dimensions of "Whiteness." In their analysis of courtroom argumentation and dominant press coverage of the Susie Phipps case, the authors draw attention to the fictional and provisional nature of racial classifications, and they argue that efforts to refine and improve racial classifications for purposes of judgment actually perpetuate racial problems.[12] Like Hasian and Nakayama, this chapter also examines news coverage of Susie Phipps's alleged passing, but adds analysis of African American news coverage of the case.

A comparison between marginal and dominant media coverage is justified on several accounts. First, the majority of media studies concerning race focus on dominant constructions of marginal identities.[13] Such scholarship is important in articulating the obstacles that marginal peoples face; however, it only tells part of the story. Identity construction is not a unidirectional process, and scholarship must reflect the importance and impact of marginal groups' narratives of identity or selfhood. Second, including marginal media production alongside dominant media texts reminds us that although the dominant media have great influence and reach in our society, the influence and reach of dominant media are not total.[14] Media resources produced by and for marginal peoples provide interpretations of events and identities that may run counter to dominant representations.[15] Third, the comparison between marginal and dominant media discourses yields a richer account of the processes of interpretation, presentation, and representation of marginal and dominant identities. Exposed through this juxtaposition are competing histories, cultural memories, and understandings of power. Moreover, the comparison between Black and dominant media reveals the strength of particular ways of thinking about race in the early 1980s that resonate with past and present dilemmas about people of multiracial descent.

Given the history recounted in chapter 1 of Black newspapers' accounts of Blacks passing as White, it is not surprising that the Black press was ambivalent at best regarding Phipps's goal to attain a White birth certificate. As with Elsie Roxborough, her case was met with a mixture of bitter humor, memories, and political agendas that emphasized the continued effects of racism in Black lives and in our national culture. In the dominant, White media, however, the notion that racism was still a major factor in the lives of dark- and light-skinned Blacks was not a central theme. In the next two sections, the reactions of the dominant press and the Black press are compared, producing telling differences as well as some similarities in how a modern-day passer is portrayed.

Framing Susie Phipps in Dominant Media

As Phipps's case made its way through the Louisiana court system, the dominant press did not consult or gather opinions or information from Blacks or mixed-race individuals in any meaningful way. As a result, the news frames were constructed mainly from the views of the central actors in the case, the state, and residues of past understandings about mixed-race or "mulatto" people. Three main frames emerged in the forty-five stories in dominant news: (1) the case was a local, archaic anachronism; (2) the case was a bureaucratic and legal, not civil, issue; and (3) there exists a shadow world between races where people such as Susie Phipps reside. Overall, the framing of the story suggests that Susie Phipps and others like her are "marginal" individuals, ever reaching for acceptance in a social group (White) they cannot attain. These frames will be discussed below using evidence from the texts to illuminate the organization of the stories. Alternative frames from Black authors and publications will be discussed afterward to show how dominant newspapers limited discussion of the complexities of the case.

Frame 1: Localizing Race and Miscegenation Laws

Journalists repeatedly highlighted the fact that this case was "caused" by a 1970 Louisiana law. Some writers erroneously declared that Louisiana was the last state in the United States to have an "equation for determining a person's race."[16] Consistent iteration of the uniqueness of the Louisiana law served to contain the story of Susie Phipps firmly within the boundaries of her home state. One story included a map of the state of Louisiana with an inset of the area where Susie Guillory's family came from, pinpointing the problem safely within state lines.[17] In the headline of a *People* magazine article, Phipps was described as a "Louisiana Belle," invoking a chivalric heritage unique to the Southern region and implying that that quirky heritage inflected the character of the court case.[18] The emphasis on the "unique" heritage of Louisiana and the South reinforced the dominant trends in the history of racial inequality in the United States: the South was (and remains) the main locale of racism and racist laws, while the North was innocent of racial oppression.

Other stories characterized Louisiana as "a state of many distinctions,"[19] and spoke of "a little local color."[20] In *The New Yorker*, writer Calvin Trillin reminded readers that "from its earliest days as a French and Spanish colony, Louisiana has had a substantial number of residents who are not easily categorized racially by their appearance."[21] "The story," wrote Gregory Jaynes in the *New York Times*, "has elements of anthropology and sociology special to this region."[22] The uniqueness of Louisiana's racial system was also reinforced by the fact that few other people of mixed race were mentioned; the only two people of mixed racial heritage quoted other than Phipps were also from the region. In addition, only one story hinted that a favorable court ruling might have national impact, but what sort of effect was not discussed.[23] In summary, writers for dominant media did much to contain the significance of the Phipps case to the state of Louisiana or the region of the South, omitting its parallels in other states and minimizing its significance to a national conversation about race and law. On December 8, 1986, the U.S. Supreme Court refused to hear Phipps's case, further minimizing the potential for an extensive national conversation on racial identity.

Along with the written framing of Phipps's case as a Southern anomaly, the graphics themselves and the interplay between words and graphics served to reinforce the idea that race was a problem of the deep South and to encourage readers to judge for themselves how White or Black Phipps was. The photos in the newspapers were almost always full frontal shots of Phipps containing no obstacles to a view of her face and skin. She was totally available to scrutiny, with no shielding attorney, no protective husband to block the lens of the camera. The reader could easily peruse her photos without obstructions to visual "evidence" on her face or skin. In a piece that ran in the *New York Times*, Phipps was directly linked to the phrase "local color" by a headline that ran right above a large picture of her, suggesting that the locale of Louisiana is the only place that offers up faces such as hers.[24]

People magazine chose to present multiple pictures of the woman they referred to as a "Southern Belle" in the headline.[25] A large close-up of Phipps opened the article, and subsequent pages featured her side-by-side with her White husband or White attorney, allowing the reader to compare their "authentic" skin to her questionable skin. Photos in popular magazines such as *People* are meant to invite the reader to imagine herself in intimate contact, up close and personal, with the celebrity featured in the photo.[26] In this case, readers were not invited to measure her beauty or star power, but her Whiteness and/or Blackness. Would they be able to tell her ancestry from a close look like the one provided by the main photo? Could they imagine—as jurors in the Rhinelander case were asked to imagine—how her husband, working with her daily side-by-side in their business and having intimate relations after work, could not know the "truth" of her blood ancestry? The pictures and the accompanying headlines and captions reinforce the idea that race is in the blood or other biological matter, and can be discovered through examination of bodies.

The Phipps case was further isolated by the omission of other recent challenges to Louisiana's one thirty-second law. Despite the focus on the region's special issues with race, the reporters failed to discover or note that the state of Louisiana had been dealing with the shortcomings of its one thirty-second law off and on since it had passed. Only a large feature in *The New Yorker* highlighted the fact that up until 1976—the year before Phipps attempted to change her birth certificate—clerks in many records departments had continued to "investigate" people who they believed might have a Black ancestor. None of the articles, however, related to readers that, in addition to Phipps, at least two other plaintiffs had demanded that the Bureau of Vital Statistics change birth certificates from "colored" to "White" in the mid-1970s.[27] In 1974 in the case *Messina v. Ciaccio*, Judge Samuel Lemmon of the Fourth Circuit decided that the Bureau of Vital Statistics had to change a birth certificate to read "white" instead of "colored" because the Bureau had not met "the requirement for exactness established by the legislature in providing the one thirty-second Negro ancestry test." The court stated that designations such as "mulatto" or "quadroon" as recorded by the Census and other agencies prior to the one thirty-second law were not governed by strict blood percentage rules, but rather by inexact, socially generated criteria. Therefore, the judges ruled that the state's genealogical evidence—similar to that used against Phipps—was *not* sufficient to make a determination of how much Negro blood the plaintiffs had. This ruling was certainly a contrast to the rulings in the Phipps case, where the court did not challenge the genealogical evidence. Overlooking or omitting cases so similar to Phipps's, particularly cases where plaintiffs won what one newspaper called "the fight to be white," made Phipps and people like Phipps seem even more anomalous and detracted from the legitimacy of her suit.

Frame 2: Maintaining Integrity of State Records versus Moral Integrity of State Laws

In the dominant media, reporters emphasized the legal, bureaucratic processes that both gave rise to the case and promised to solve it. Head-lines such as "Written Arguments Attack Racial Classification Law"[28] and "Appeal Filed on Blood Law"[29] focused on various steps in the legal process. As discussed above, reporters paid much attention to the state's evidence that "proved" that it had accurately recorded and tracked the racial composition of the Guillory family. Thus, the burden was placed on attorney Brian Begue—in the papers and the courtroom—to prove why the state should change its time-honored record-keeping practices. Only Phipps, her husband, Begue, and a few other commentators spoke to the civil rights issues raised by the case, or expressed the idea that states should allow citizens to name, and thus control, their personal identity. Quotations from Begue threatened the legal-bureaucratic framing of the story when he defended the right of the individual to self-designate and invoked the racist past of the designation laws. In one dramatic court-room moment documented by the New Orleans *Times-Picayune*, Begue held out a photo album for the appellate court judges:

> "I mean, look at these people," he said. "They were victims of the times. People were getting lynched out in the country for trying to pass as white. They had no choice" but to put black on Phipps' birth certificate.[30]

Invoking the racist past, Begue claimed that the forced choices under Jim Crow terror should not be legitimized in a post–civil rights world. Begue also decried the seemingly stubborn decision of the court of appeals to refuse Phipps the right to change her racial designation, even though the legislature overturned the law and Phipps was born before its existence.

> Mr. Begue said that, "in the absences of a legitimate standard" for determining race, repeal [of the one thirty-second statute] "creates a vacuum into which 'traceable amount' is drawn. . . . "Preponderance of evidence looks good," Mr. Begue said, "but there's no way out if you look white and all your records say you're colored . . . . Because we don't know what makes a person colored" [anymore].[31]

Begue's court adversary, Jack Westholz, also admitted frustration that that neither the judges nor the legislature had created a standard of evidence regarding Blackness.

> "If we can't define what constitutes a Negro, how can we decide this case," said Jack Westholz, attorney for the state Health and Human Resources Department. "If there are no standards, how can I argue this case? We need some help. We need some courage from this court."[32]

In depicting the drama of the courtroom, therefore, the legal question of whether or not the state's records are "accurate" was complicated from time to time with the question of whether it is right that the state can label an individual without her consent. Despite Westholz's spoken desire for standards, his pursuit of Phipps and his ardent defenses of his office's records were much more prominent in news reports. For example, he told Calvin Trillin that he considered birth certificates historical documents that could not be changed. No matter that he personally believed Susie Phipps "looked white," Westholz said she should "[l]et it be. We can't go back and change history."[33] In the majority of the articles, the state's evidence against Phipps was piled high: in twenty-seven out of forty-five stories her slave ancestor was mentioned, and eleven quoted testimony from her relatives that they considered themselves "colored."

> Mr. Westholz also took depositions from some of Mrs. Phipps' realtives, who consider themselves "colored," meaning black. An aunt, Virginia Fretty, said . . . "Well, I always followed the colored." Another aunt, Alicia Jordan, said, "I was raised colored."[34]

In addition to discrediting Phipps's account of her upbringing, the previous quote (from a *New York Times* article) is notable because of the way the journalist interpreted the meaning of "colored" for Susie's family members as "black." This interpretation is misguided in the context of the case and the region because as Phipps herself acknowledged, her family was placed between the Whites and the Blacks in public places. Thus, the reporter rewrote the racial designation of the Phipps family to fit into the contemporary dichotomy of Black and White rather than the obvious grey areas and multiple social statuses for people of color generated by centuries of racial and cultural mixing in Louisiana.

Although it is clear that many reporters found the idea of blood percentages wrong, only three of the forty-five stories presented the opinions of geneticists and other scholars who insisted that neither scientific nor genealogical methods could prove that Phipps had inherited genetic material from her slave ancestor, and only one included remarks from the geneticist who testified on her behalf.[35] None of the reporters ever posed the question: What evidence is necessary or legitimate in a case such as this? There was no description of what evidence could have proved Phipps was "White" to the state, but the judges (and implicitly the journalists) decided that she did not have a sufficient amount of whatever it would be. Witness testimony quoted from the trial affirmed that those who are the products of interracial unions are perhaps not Black but colored, which was described in one witness's quote as still "never white."[36] Again, the absence of the criteria to prove someone White—and the assumption of white purity—privileged evidence of Black ancestry as legitimate grounds to challenging Phipps's visual and behavioral presentations of whiteness. Opportunities to explore whiteness opened up by this case, particularly commentary from scholars that up to 5 percent of "Whites" probably have some Black ancestors, were not pursued by the dominant press.

Frame 3: Trapped in a "Shadow World" in the South

Dominant coverage of the Phipps case between 1982 and 1986 rarely acknowledged the existence of interracial people other than the plaintiff. When they did, the results were less than flattering. The quotations and descriptions reporters chose to include resonated with the long-standing stereotype that multiracial individuals will never fit into society. As G. Reginald Daniel notes in his recent book on multiracial identity in the United States, eugenicists, psychologists, and sociologists from the late nineteenth and twentieth centuries hypothesized that people of Black and White heritage would always experience a sense of being "betwixt and between" in a way that would translate into marginality and related pathologies of social dislocation and personal alienation.[37] And, as noted in the introduction, well into the twentieth century sociologists theorized that marginal men such as mulattoes would live frustrated lives, forever unsatisfied because the taint of Blackness would never fade to allow their acceptance in the White world.[38]

Phipps's own conduct and reaction, as described in her interviews with the press, suggest that she, too, felt it would be tragic to be seen as part Black rather than as purely White. In several articles, reporters repeated her assertion that the racial designation on her birth certificate made her physically ill for three days; her initial refusal to reveal her ancestry to her second husband also echoes passing literature of the nineteenth and twentieth centuries; reiterating her frantic, secret quest to erase race from her birth certificate, the journalists reconstruct a passing drama for the 1980s. She lived, they related, in fear of what her husband would do. The family members who initially joined her suit also reenacted the passing narrative as relayed by the press. After the first phase of Phipps's legal fight ended in defeat, her siblings withdrew from the lawsuit because, we are told by writers, "[t]heir children had white birth certificates, and they decided to leave well enough alone."[39] Thus, it was implied that her family members continued the practice of suppressing "evidence" of their one drop of "black blood," similar to previous generations of passers.

One of the two women with White and Black heritage featured in a *New York Times* article was presented with a statement from her personal writings that conveyed the idea that multiracial people will never fit in: "My mother says I am Creole. My teacher says I am Negro. . . . Who am I?"[40] Even quotations from Phipps's attorney fit this mold. One reporter quoted Begue's description of Phipps as "emotionally white and legally black,"[41] a description that reflects previous psychological theories that multiracial people would never be able to mentally or socially reconcile their racial identities. The description also recalls the tragic mulatto who yearns to elevate herself to White society but is constantly undermined by her ties to a Black world. In what registers as a concession to Phipps, Louisiana state attorney Westholz was quoted saying that "it is true that Susie is more white than black."[42] However, Westholz was quoted in another article saying that Phipps was born as one of those "unfortunate people in between" Blacks and Whites.[43] These elements of the articles reinforce the notion that mixed-race people don't fit into acceptable social categories and, by extension, are bound to experience problems fitting into society at large.

The nebulousness of this in-between world is not entirely tragic, however, for individuals can exploit the ambiguities of interracial identity to improve their lot in life. Indeed, in addition to the narrative of Susie Phipps escaping and denying the colored identity shared by many of her family members, another story of escaping her roots emerged in the press: her rise from cousin-marrying rural poverty to small business affluence. *Time* magazine noted that Phipps was "married to a wealthy white crawfish merchant."[44] Likewise, a *New York Times* reporter stated that Susie Phipps was "the wife of a well-to-do white businessman in Sulphur, La."[45] Phipps's marriage to her second husband was often mentioned with an accompanying phrase about his wealth, despite the fact that she was an equal partner in the business. Even those authors who did note her participation in the business intimated in other ways that she intended to climb the social ladder. Trillin noted that for "colored Creoles" as light as the Guillory family, "it would not have been difficult to convince some of them of the advantage of simply marrying a white person and melting into the privileged caste. It's a process that is still going on."[46] In Trillin's accusation, Phipps exploited the indiscernability of her body in order to improve her economic and social status. By stating that the process continued, he suggested that other "colored Creoles" were circulating in White society unnoticed and reaping the benefits of Whiteness.[47] Thus, in the public sphere presented in this article, passing still exists, although Trillin was more ambivalent as to whether this type of racial and class social climbing is a valid strategy in the post–civil rights era. However, at the end of his feature, Trillin concluded that "[i]t's difficult, though, to imagine what Susie Guillory Phipps could come away with that would satisfy her" desire to be recognized by the state as White.[48] Trapped between the courts' decisions that she is not White and her own view of the matter, Susie is perpetually unsatisfied, striving for what she cannot attain, similar to the marginal man's frustration for lack of a real opportunity to climb the social ladder.

Before turning to the Black press' response to Phipps's dilemma, the lone masthead editorial about the Phipps case, a piece in the *New York Times* titled "Black and White," merits discussion. In this piece, the editors argued strongly that the Louisiana one thirty-second law was unjust and racist. However, the remedies suggested are unsatisfactory on many fronts and for many participants involved in the case. The editorial supported, in general, the government's use of racial designation as a tool to "eradicate the harmful effects of discrimination," but asserted that Louisiana's law expresses an "extreme bias in favor of whites." However, the editorial presented the quandary of mixed-race people as a matter of choice: "Some of the descendants of the interracial unions choose to live as whites; others live as blacks. Indeed, some of Mrs. Phipps's relatives say they are black, though they are as light-skinned as she is." This reduction of the lived experiences of mixed-race people ignores the difficulties involved. In the case of those "choosing" to live White, the simplicity of the *Times'* description papers over the deception and pain that is often required to leave Black community ties behind in order to gain full acceptance in White society, let alone the potential social embarrassment or ostracism possible if Whites discover one's "true" race. Indeed, this fear drove Susie Phipps to keep her birth certificate a secret from her husband for a year and convinced her siblings to abandon the lawsuit to protect their children's White status.

For those who "choose" life on the other side of the color line, the "choice" to be Black is hardly completely of their own making; in Louisiana in particular, a cadre of state employees as well as long-held social customs and cultural assumptions guide the "choice" of Blackness for even the "whitest-looking" person of African descent. This makes the *Times'* final comment, a remedy of sorts for Phipps' dilemma, even more perplexing. The editorial stated earlier in the piece that "[t]he business of race classification is hardly scientific," but its solution smacks of the same genealogical absurdities denounced by scientists who testified for Phipps:

> If society must make a [racial] distinction, at least let it split the difference evenly: a person is white if 51 percent white, black if 51 percent black. And let us move quickly as possible toward the day when any distinction is no longer useful.[49]

How the state or anyone else could concoct a formula determining such a racial majority rule as this is hard to imagine. Furthermore, high school biology teaches us that generations are calculated in halves and fourths, making the 51 percent number illogical and irrelevant. The paper's solution suggests that one can be "more white" or "more black" in a comparative sense, when the reality of racial designation practices in the United States has always been to protect the hegemonic ideology of White purity. In the 1980s, there was hardly any support for the notion that someone who was "part white" should be considered only as White, but clearly it made sense that someone who was "part black" should be designated only as Black, no matter what combination of ancestors existed on both sides of the color line.

The dominant press did not approach the Phipps story in a way that significantly challenged racial categories; on the contrary, reports of her dilemma and resulting legal wrangles suggest that mixed-race people have no choices beyond passing for White or "settling" for being Black. Furthermore, key omissions of information and lack of attention to a wider range of mixed-race people limited the discussion of the meaning of race and the role of the state in determining racial categories. Finally, coverage of the case replicated a well-worn stereotype of mulattos: trapped in a biracial world, they are doomed to the fate of never truly fitting in with any group. In the next section, frames found in the Black press underscore the absences in the dominant press, but also reveal certain troubling similarities around the question of what choices people of mixed race can and should make concerning their identities.

Frames in Black-Authored Media

Three major frames shaped the majority of the Black press' coverage of the Phipps case: (1) the case concerned civil rights, not merely bureaucratic technicalities; (2) Phipps was part of a long history of controversy involving mixed-race individuals; (3) Phipps's desire to be classified as White was an affront to Black communities. Although these frames show that the Black press paid more attention to issues of justice, equality, and a broader context of racial history, the third frame functioned to curtail discussion of the place of multiracial people in the contemporary racial landscape.

Frame 1: Civil Rights, not Legal Technicalities

Much like dominant media writers, Black writers and commentators amplified the legal dimensions of the Phipps case but with a twist. Rather than treat the case as a legal anomaly, they contextualized it within a larger rubric of civil rights cases. *Jet* magazine's coverage of the case, which consisted of seven articles over a five-year period, began in 1982 and ended with the U.S. Supreme Court's decision in 1986 not to hear the case. *Jet* writers focused on how her case might bring greater justice to all Blacks. The magazine placed all of its articles on Phipps in a section devoted to civil rights cases and other racial legal matters. In the first four pieces, *Jet* zeroed in on the absurdity of the one thirty-second statute, the need to abolish it, and the racist notion that "Black blood" impurifies "White blood."[50] The magazine used quotations from anthropologists and a prominent Black scholar that the state's blood quota had no scientific merit, highlighting the double standard of the law. Said Dr. Albert Dent: "It's discriminatory because it only classifies Blacks. If someone had a thirty-second of White blood in them, would they be classified as White?"[51] The answer, of course, is no, not in a system where Black blood is considered simultaneously inferior and powerful. After repeating the statistic that many Whites have 5 percent African genes, the article ended with a quotation from Dent that endorsed Phipps's claim to Whiteness because he believed that Whites in Louisiana ignorant of their Black genes would not want to be subject to the one thirty-second rule.

Jet's implicit endorsement of Phipps's fight against the state of Louisiana was not broad, however. *Jet*'s coverage focused on and lauded the dismantling of an unfair, racist statute, not Phipps's desire to be White. So, the magazine applauded when the state overturned the one thirty-second law in 1983, but when Phipps's lawyer decided to pursue the task of eliminating racial labels on *all* birth certificates, the coverage changed.[52] By 1984, headlines and opening paragraphs no longer presented the state's laws or legal decisions but instead focused on Phipps's desire to be designated White.[53] Phipps's interest in eliminating the use of racial labels on any state documents conflicted with a key Black political interest—to ensure that the state recorded race in order to track and prosecute cases of racial discrimination. So began the implied critiques of Phipps's quest to change her state records. The sixth article in the series quoted the court's ruling at length, ending the article with the following statement: " '[Racial classification] provides statistics which are an essential tool for planning and monitoring the public health programs, affirmative action and other anti-discrimination measures,' the panel said."[54] The final article, as will be shown below, was particularly pointed in its critique of Phipps's goal to maintain and live a White identity.

Frame 2: Racist History as Context for Passing

In contrast to the dominant media's "Southern Anomaly" frame, Black writers framed the Phipps case within a history of passing, racial double standards, and a host of laws passed across the country, not just in Louisiana, that punished those who crossed the color line. In *Ebony* magazine, evidence of a nationwide obsession with passing, including laws against interracial marriage and other forms of social intercourse, was used to contextualize the Phipps case. The writer noted, "Whatever the outcome of the Phipps case, the problem of racial classification will continue, for the national definition of race is still vague."[55] *Ebony* also traced the problem of racial designation back to *Plessy v. Ferguson*, which reinforced the national standard of hypodescent, or the "one-drop rule." Under hypodescent, the dominant society assigns a racially mixed person the identity that corresponds to the racial group that has the lowest social status.[56] In contrast to dominant press accounts, *Ebony* announced that states other than Louisiana still had racial classification laws and guidelines.[57] For example, writers revealed that in Texas, the father's race determined that of the child; in West Virginia, the law was to follow the guidelines of the National Center for Health Statistics, whose code states that a child is recorded as "Black" if either parent is Black.[58] Black columnist Dorothy Gilliam told *Washington Post* readers that she "couldn't brush this [story] aside as a single eccentric's identity crisis," and that "this story is as old as the nation."[59] Furthermore, unlike the photos showcasing Phipps in the dominant press, the Black press contained a variety of visual representations. *Ebony* did not limit its photos to her case; rather, the magazine printed photos of other "passers" who have been caught up in the judicial system in previous decades. Thus, the reader was invited to compare Phipps's appearance to other controversial figures from the past rather than alone and outside of the historical context as in the dominant newspaper photos. In *Ebony*, she was presented as part of a lineage, so to speak, of liminal figures, but in the dominant press, she was put forth as a rarity to be examined alone.

It is notable that although the Black press did take pains to historicize the Phipps case, it also did not mention the other, successful challenges to the one thirty-second law that occurred in the 1970s. Perhaps this is because of discomfort with the plaintiffs' wish to be White rather than Black. The Black press has always been a champion of racial pride, and the act of passing or desiring to be another race is anathema to communication of pride. As described in the previous chapter, portraying passing as a positive act is rare in the Black press. Unlike the subjects of the "post-passing" narratives of the 1950s Black press, [60] the plaintiffs who sued the state of Louisiana to declare White identity in the 1970s (although they exposed a racist double standard for determining identity) did not communicate that Black identity is desirable or equal to White identity.

Frame 3: Passing as Challenge to Black Community Integrity

With regard to the dominant press frame of multiracial people trapped in a "shadow world," Black writers agreed in the sense that passers are problematic people who have identity choices to make. Both implicitly and explicitly, Black authors indicated that all people with any African heritage should choose a Black identity—and be proud of it. The issue of pride, both personal and group-centered pride, became important for Black writers. Susie Phipps was depicted as succumbing to self-hate caused by racism. Gilliam declared, "It's naïve to get caught up in this as an 'interesting' court case; it is having your head in the sand to be shocked. Susie Phipps is doing what many blacks are doing—running away from being black."[61] For Black commentators, questions of racial discrimination constituted the main focus; this case was seen as neither strictly nor primarily about procedures of law. Racial designation laws were described as tools used against Blacks to secure White privilege. For Gilliam, the question was not whether the state had an interest in recording Phipps's race, but that such mechanisms have been used as weapons to divide and psychologically damage Black people. Passing was portrayed as pathological and disrespectful to the Black community.

Like Gilliam, Smart-Grosvenor took Phipps to task for her—and her husband's—apparent racism.[62] The article was peppered with implicit and explicit references to Phipps's internalized racism, beginning with the title, "Obsessed With 'Racial Purity,'" which could have been applied to both the state of Louisiana and the plaintiff's state of mind. *Ebony*, like the *New York Times*, included testimony from her relatives that they considered the family colored, supporting the accusation that Phipps was trying to pass for White and run from her Blackness.[63] Smart-Grosvenor clearly believed that Phipps was knowingly passing and that her current personal quest for state-endorsed Whiteness was demeaning.[64] "Blacks look on passing for economic reasons—so you can get a better job—with a bitter-sweet eye, but passing for white *just to be white* is to most of us an anathema, no matter how little black blood you have."[65] In contrast to some of the Black-authored narratives of the early twentieth century that expressed a smug satisfaction that some blacks were getting over on whites by passing, this quote reveals that passing is not always pleasurable for people who are "in on" the pass. Indeed, save for the comments of one interviewee in *Jet*, we found no other Black voices supporting Phipps's goal of whiteness or acknowledging any pleasure over her ability to pass for so many decades prior to her court battles.

Jet's coverage, which was initially supportive of Phipps's quest to overturn the one thirty-second law, moved gradually toward a gentle implied critique of her personal motives. In the final *Jet* piece on Phipps, the opening sentence stated, "It looks as if Susie Guillory Phipps, 51, of Sulphur, La., might have to live with the official designation 'colored' rather than the label 'white' that she is seeking."[66] And, whereas in previous articles all mentions of her slave ancestress were accompanied by the mention of the White slave owner who was also Phipps's ancestor, this article only mentioned Margarita. Describing the Supreme Court's refusal to hear the case, *Jet* wrote that the Court "would not get involved with Mrs. Phipps's argument," a statement that seemed to reduce her case to a personal vendetta rather than a wide-ranging legal problem of national significance. The article implied that Phipps should give it up and "live with" the knowledge—private and public—of her Blackness.

Despite their focus on the moral and social questions surrounding the case, Black writers did not offer any potential solutions to the dilemmas presented by multiracial identity. Personal feelings of shame and group affinity were raised, and the influence of the state in these matters was spotlighted, but these reports left the reader with the same options as the accounts in the dominant press. Furthermore, Black writers were invested in the notion that one has "Black blood" and that it makes you Black, no matter how small the fraction. Similar to the dominant press, the Black press barely confronted the court's role in constructing Whiteness and granting White identity. Black writers recognized the arbitrary one thirty-second quota as unjust and unfair, but not as part of the architecture of *White* identity; in these news narratives, the one thirty-second law was, as in the dominant press, a generator of *Black* identity. As if in possession of some fantastically imagined gravitational density, one drop of Blackness dramatically pulled attention and emphasis away from the dominant end of the color hierarchy, leaving Whiteness to dissolve, unnoticed and unexamined. In sum, both dominant and Black texts contributed to the operation of Whiteness as a "strategic rhetoric" that renders invisible its nature as a rhetorical construction.[67]

Conclusions

Against the dominant media frames that portrayed Susie Phipps as trapped in a shadow world and her case as a local issue about legal technicalities, Black writers and media outlets foregrounded the civil rights dimensions of her case and emphasized histories of racism and community integrity as larger contexts for understanding the case and its primary litigant. Visible through these frames are multiple, sometimes competing constituents of Black and White identity: blood percentages, genealogy, self-identification, and state documentation, for example. Ultimately, judges in the state of Louisiana upheld the integrity of state laws and state records and thus thwarted Phipps's effort to be(come) White. Furthermore, no journalists or editorialists asked the question, "What is white?" This failure can be seen as a reinforcement of the invisibility of Whiteness that, as Aida Hurtado suggests, allows the assumption that Whiteness is "natural" and "unproblematic."[68] Likewise, Diana Fuss notes that "in American culture, 'race' has been far more an acknowledged component of black identity than white; for good or bad, whites have always seen 'race' as a minority attribute."[69] The press accounts of the Phipps case did not challenge the notion that race resides within "black blood" rather than in the regimes of White identity or privilege.

These frames and criteria of identity suggest several conclusions about race and media practices prior to the emergence of the multiracial movement in the United States. First, the comparison of dominant and Black press reactions to Phipps reveals that on the issue of passing there are major differences and a few notable similarities between dominant media and Black media. The varying interests of these groups can serve to narrow the scope and length of debates over identity, and, by extension, affect the length and quality of discourses concerning these events and issues in the public sphere. In the Phipps case, the localizing of the story and the lack of editorial response in the dominant press cut off many avenues of discussion. Similarly, despite an acknowledgment of the larger historical and national implications of the case, the Black press did not explore the potential identity crises the case could elicit across the nation; rather, they depicted Susie Phipps and others like her as victims of self-hatred. The "one-drop rule" system of racial classification, although it is revealed to support a double standard in the Black press, was never challenged in the dominant press and was implicitly endorsed by the Black writers in the name of solidarity.

As critical rhetoricians remind us, marginal peoples do not always (or necessarily frequently) produce oppositional or liberatory texts.[70] The politics of identity seem to demand that individuals be labeled or choose labels that reflect their solidarity with a particular group or set of groups. People who exist on the margins of traditionally defined identity groups, however, do not have easy choices or "natural constituencies" to reference in their quest for recognition. The tensions between group and individual identity are highlighted in this case and those in the following chapters, where larger, more established social groups aimed to classify or reclassify individuals who clearly did not seek identification with those groups.

The comparison of dominant and Black media reports about Susie Phipps also exposes the continuation of narrative themes from the nineteenth and early twentieth centuries. As summarized in the previous chapter, dominant media emphasized the painful and tragic dimensions of mixed-race individuals. Black media acknowledged a broader range of outcomes from passing in addition to the painful backlash enacted by Whites. Black writers lamented the damage to community pride and spirit resulting from passing for White, but they also related histories of race passing in which the passers accrued material gains by fooling Whites. These differences between dominant and Black accounts of passing continued, although for the Black press the pleasures of getting over were far less salient in this late-twentieth-century case. As the following chapters will also suggest, the Black community's cultural transformations and political gains since the civil rights movement make it highly unlikely that choosing or elevating one's white heritage over Black will be seen as a valid personal or political choice.

Dominant social groups and the state want to fix identities to police boundaries of privilege and to enforce legal standards, standards that often disadvantage marginalized groups. For marginal groups, fixing identity can illuminate institutional discrimination and oppression and make it easier to articulate civil rights agendas and establish a political presence. Blacks, for example, are invested in a politics of identity to rally allies and fight injustices, injustices that are perhaps easier to locate and define when the potential victims ascribe to a discrete, often state-recognized identity. Supporting a politics of identity may be harder if group members want to perform more fluid, ambiguous, unnamable personae.

Thus, when a person is accused of performing the "wrong" racial identity, it prompts commentary and action not only from the state and dominant groups who feel "duped," but also from marginalized groups who see a need to assert their identity and redefine the passer for their own agendas. In the aftermath of discovery, passers do not seem to fit in either community. They are coerced by the state and dominant society to admit to and perform a marginalized identity that may limit their lives: Susie Phipps was forced to be documented as Black and is now publicly known as a woman who may have "hidden" her "true" identity. Although Black writers in the past have attempted to appropriate the passer to critique White racism and pleasurably imagine passers subverting White authority, contemporary Black journalists ultimately classified Phipps as a self-hating Black woman, forever damaged by internalized racism.

Neither set of articles analyzed in this chapter employed any imaginative thinking to get around dichotomous racial thinking. Although in hindsight the employment of multiracial identity may seem obvious, in the early 1980s, there was no immediately recognizable set of people or organizations asserting an alternative to the either-or choices presented regarding Phipps. Perhaps the *New York Times* attempt at creating a "51 percent rule" comes closest, but the inconsistencies within the editorial and the illogical, unscientific use of blood percentages by the paper's editors made this stab at offering an alternative racial option naïve at best. There appears to be a need for a critical mass or threshold of visibility for those who perform identities that cannot be easily captured by our current norms and language. This is illustrated by the fact that Phipps was linked to multiracial identity in 1992, when the organized presence of multiracial advocacy groups and celebrities in the 1990s inspired a mainstream journalist to reframe Susie Phipps as an example of multiracial identity.[71]

The higher profile of interracial celebrities, children, and families provided a set of sources and texts for the reporter in the '90s that earlier writers did not have. However, even had Phipps been categorized as "multiracial" in the 1980s, the tone of the coverage might have remained the same for the following reason: Susie Phipps did not and does not want the choice to be "multiracial": she wants to be White and only White. The reporters covering her story did not grapple with that desire outside of the tropes of mulatto identity invented in an earlier era. Furthermore, White identity and the problematics of racial categorization are not completely resolved by the creation of new categories, even if they are officially recognized by the state. If personal choice, state-recognized evidence, and biological realities of birth are all parts of the racial identity equation, one has to wonder, what would Phipps have to do in order to achieve her choice of Whiteness? Or, to put it another way, what changes would have to be made in how we think about White identity to allow a woman with a single known slave ancestress to be allowed to claim White rather than Black identity? While the next chapters do not claim to answer this question, they will continue to explore it from different angles.

Chapter Three

"Not as Black as the Next Guy"

A Peculiar Case of White Identity in the News

What do they want us to do, hang a sign on our front door saying we're black?

—Marsha Malone

When racially controversial issues—such as welfare or immigration—are covered in mainstream news, racial minorities are usually framed as victims, complainers, or instigators. Whites, on the other hand, rarely are the focus of such reports, nor are they often explicitly named as "White." One exception to this pattern is news reports about affirmative action, where both Whites and minorities are explicitly named. While the term *affirmative action* encapsulates a multitude of different government and private sponsored programs that seek to remedy discrimination against racial minorities and women, public debate over these policies has been largely focused on the effects on Blacks and Whites. During the 1980s, several key court cases challenged affirmative action programs, and officials in the Reagan and Bush administrations alongside conservative scholars, pundits, and foundations flooded the public sphere with anti–affirmative action rhetoric. These voices portrayed affirmative action as reverse racism, "special rights," and unfair to Whites. From some of this discourse, one might believe that it was better to be Black in the 1980s than White in terms of college admissions and jobs. Social statistics strongly suggest that this was far from the case.[1] However, two "White" brothers in Boston took this notion literally, and in doing so created an exceptional story of affirmative action, racial privilege, and bureaucratic definitions of race.

This chapter examines press coverage of the blonde, blue-eyed Malone twins, two aspiring firefighters with white-looking skin who claimed White identity the first time they took and failed a civil service exam, and then claimed Black identity two years later, qualifying for jobs under new affirmative action guidelines. Their saga presented a challenge to news media accustomed to framing Whites as innocent victims of affirmative action politics, and also brought into question the criteria used by the state to determine minority racial identity. The novelty of the case presented an opportunity for the press to create new frames to cover the story, particularly in terms of describing Whiteness. Because the role of Whites in this case of affirmative action abuse was so visible, I argue, it presented the media with a case of Whites and Whiteness in the spotlight, counter to the invisibility of Whiteness in racial discourse that is the norm. The result was an awkward mix of frames that had to incorporate explicit references to White criminal actions. The Malones' story provides us with an opportunity to observe not how Whiteness is occluded, but what happens when White invisibility is not a convenient or feasible rhetorical strategy. However, despite the emergence of some alternative frames and inclusion of minority voices, coverage reinforced the dominant norm that race and affirmative action are Black/White issues, even though there were opportunities to make the case that the uncertainty surrounding racial identities and policies in the United States go well beyond that dichotomy.

Before turning to the Malones' case, I present a brief overview of the shift in affirmative action discourse that occurred in the 1980s, and provide a summary of communication studies scholars' analyses of media coverage of affirmative action controversies.

Affirmative Action in the 1980s

In the 1980s and beyond, political and media discourses were peppered with narratives of Whites who lost opportunities to not-so innocent minorities. From Janet Cooke to Jayson Blair, from *Bakke* to "Soul Man," from Edwin Meese to Shelby Steele, political, academic, and media elites informed audiences about Whites who *merited* positions taken by *unqualified* minorities (usually Blacks), and minorities (usually Blacks) who were allegedly stigmatized as unqualified due to the mere existence of affirmative action. This dominant narrative featured innocent Whites who were being wrongly punished for racist practices that existed only in the past or in paranoid minority and liberal minds. At the beginning of Reagan's second term in office, the administration accelerated its attack on affirmative action programs using this rhetoric of reverse discrimination. In 1985, the Justice Department, led by Edwin Meese, notified fifty-one cities across the country that it would be investigating them for "abuses" in police and fire department affirmative action systems that "discriminate against whites by granting 'preferential treatment' to blacks, women, and other minorities," and that minorities who weren't "actual victims of discrimination" were benefiting from "unfair hiring quotas."[2] William Bradford Reynolds, the assistant attorney general for civil rights at the time, said that many of the cities were discriminating "against those who were innocent victims," that is, White job seekers and employees.[3]

Describing Whites as "innocent victims" was quite common in sound bites from Justice Department officials and attorneys representing White employees against fire and police departments in the 1980s. Indeed, conservatives announced and celebrated their quest to reshape the public's vocabulary of affirmative action by promoting terminology such as "special privileges," "reverse discrimination," "quotas," and "preferential treatment." The Reagan administration characterized this shift in language as part and parcel of curtailing affirmative action and moving the United States toward a "color-blind," merit-based society. And the administration was particularly fond of having its Black employees announce the end of "quotas," as was the case with chairman of the U.S. Civil Rights Commission, Clarence M. Pendleton Jr.

> Chairman Clarence M. Pendleton, Jr. said . . . [they] had shifted public concern from a "preference society to an opportunity society. I told him we've pushed the argument to the point where quotas are a dead issue . . ." Pendleton said he also told the president that the commission hopes to continue to reshape the debate over civil rights by holding hearings on affirmative action in higher education and releasing a report in early spring . . .[4]

The beneficiary of this reframing of affirmative action discourse was the White employee, constructed as innocent victim rather than a member of the group that historically and presently dominates and controls opportunities in the job marketplace.

In class action suits against cities and universities, lawyers and plaintiffs have claimed to speak for Whites as a group, all potentially harmed by affirmative action. In both anti- and proaffirmative action discourses presented in mainstream media, White job seekers, college applicants, and others are portrayed as innocent victims. While the Right frames this as unconstitutional discrimination based on race, the Left has avoided or been reluctant to approach the subject of White people who are directly affected by affirmative action policies. As Nicholas Lehmann wrote,

> The [pro-affirmative action] establishment's reasoning, never openly stated, would have gone something like this: *Sure, affirmative*

action generates white victims of reverse discrimination, but there aren't very many of them and they don't suffer too greatly. They go to Colgate instead of Cornell. Big deal. The most clearly outstanding whites . . . don't suffer at all. In return . . . [i]t creates a feeling of doing something to correct our worst historic wrong.[5]

On both sides, Whites are assumed to be individuals who earn their rewards in society rather than beneficiaries of centuries of racial domination that facilitated accumulation of socioeconomic and political capital. Neither the Right nor the Left, as represented in the dominant media discourses, link Whites to institutional racism or reveal any benefits they gain from the continued existence and residuals of institutional racism. Social scientists and statisticians have generated much evidence that the economic marketplace is still structured by racial and gender inequalities; from housing loans to harassment, women of all colors and non-White men are still negatively affected by racism and sexism as they navigate the job, housing, and education markets.[6] As indicated in the earlier review of this literature, its evidence and counterarguments, clearly many academics and activists could provide newsgatherers with alternative frames for stories on the effects of affirmative action that would shed new light on how Whites, women of all colors, and racial minorities have fared since affirmative action policies were enacted.

Positioning Whites as victims of affirmative action rather than minorities as victims of institutional racism in the job market meant, however, that White racial identity had to be named in order to depict this innocence. In class-action lawsuits, Whites, like Blacks, were represented as a group rather than as individuals. News reports of White employees who were allegedly mistreated due to affirmative action policies often violated the convention of applying racial descriptors only to non-Whites. As such, news reports on affirmative action are among the few involving race and public policy where Whites are explicitly labeled by their race.

Whiteness in Mass Media

The great majority of work on race and media centers on dominant media representations of and Whites' reactions to people of color. The last decade, however, has seen the advent of "whiteness studies," a subgenre of critical race theory.[7] This body of theory has inspired media scholars to investigate how White identities and privileges are structured, renegotiated, and maintained by mass media. One key element of whiteness that communication scholars have investigated is how the rhetoric of whiteness is one of evasion and invisibility in order to obscure the continued privilege and power held by whites in society. Whiteness is an often-unnamed norm to which all other racial groups are compared, implicitly and explicitly. In the dominant discourse, only non-Whites have racial problems; Whites are normalized and seen as outside these concerns, innocent in matters of race, somehow raceless. As Raka Shome summarized in a review of whiteness studies:

> [T]his research rightly recognizes that whiteness . . . is maintained and produced not by overt rhetorics of whiteness, but rather, by its "everydayness," by the everyday, unquestioned racialized social relations that have acquired a seeming normativity and through that normativity make invisible the ways in which whites participate in, derive protection and benefits from, a system whose rules and organizational relations work to their advantatge.[8]

The media are part of this system that reproduces whiteness in this evasive manner. As Dwight Brooks and James Rada found in their study of the Clinton-Lewinsky scandal, whiteness was reinforced as normal and morally upstanding without mention of the term *White*.[9] Although Black support of Clinton was widely scrutinized and labeled as "Black support," journalists didn't represent label Whites' views as "White support" or "White criticism." This reflects a main tenet of Whiteness studies, that "by erasing the presence of whiteness, media texts reinforce it as the unacknowledged standard and norm against which Blacks (and other non-Whites) are measured."[10]

Brooks and Rada suggest that studies of Whiteness and media must go beyond documenting the invisible nature of White privilege and begin to examine various formations of Whiteness in mass media. This chapter follows their suggestion by presenting a case where Whiteness is made visible. As Shome notes, Whiteness cannot remain unchallenged and unseen at all times. Specifically, when Whiteness is challenged or contested by other racial groups or crises, Whiteness has to be spoken about somehow in order to maintain or reinforce its hegemony. Thus, "when whiteness begins to feel insecure about its power and its future, it begins to mark itself . . . as an identity in crisis and therefore having a particular location that, like minority locations, needs to be defended, salvaged, and protected."[11] This particularity presents a challenge for an identity that thrives on its ability to deny itself and its import in the racialized public sphere.

Two circumstances which necessitate explicit marking of Whiteness that have been explored by media scholars are the fear of passing or miscegenation, and when the national identity—hegemonically constructed as White—is challenged by the increased presence or visibility of and/or critique brought by non-Whites. Carlson and Hasian and Nakayama examined the legal and rhetorical dimensions of "Blackness" and "Whiteness."[12] In their analysis of courtroom argumentation and press coverage of passing cases, these authors reveal the fictional and provisional nature of racial classifications, and how actors, including and especially the state, have difficulty trying to resolidify racial boundaries once the passer has transgressed them. Similarly, the previous chapter's analysis of media discourses concerning Susie Phipps found that White and Black interests served to narrow the scope of debate about racial identity in their respective presses, and reinforced the notion that White and Black were polar opposites.

In the wake of powerful social movements and cultural critiques of White supremacy, media representations reflect a desire to represent White identity in a way that distances the majority of Whites and White-dominated government institutions from racism. Kelly Madison's analysis of 1990s films that represented civil rights movements in South Africa and the United States found that "antiracist" White male heroes decentered and silenced the organization, labor, and innovations of Black Americans and Africans who led the movements.[13] Casting White men as the enemies of extreme White supremacists served as a strategy to relegitimate White male power. Similarly, Shome demonstrates how 1990s films concerning crises in the American presidency offered "a rhetoric of the 'good whites versus the bad whites,' . . . This is a problematic rhetoric in that it seems to locate the problem of whiteness at an individual level: as long as some 'bad' whites can be fixed and brought to task, everything will be all right."[14] As Projansky and Ono emphasize, "The issue is not whiteness, but what whiteness is so often called on to do.[15]" In these cases, popular cinema has functioned to reinscribe Whiteness as pure, good, and symbolic of the national citizen body, able to incorporate particular desirable traits of the racialized "other" and rehabilitate itself to return to normalcy and power. In this hegemonic process, however, the question of what it means to be White is raised, and in these moments of revelation of Whiteness, we can learn more about its construction and gaps in its armor.

Framing Affirmative Action in the News

Whiteness is also depicted as an identity under siege in affirmative action discourse. Affirmative action can be described as a "racial project" initiated by the state in response to Black (as well as feminist) social movements.[16] This racial project changed the landscape of higher education and the job market by trying to remedy long-standing practices of discrimination against Blacks and women. Of course, this project also served to challenge the privileged status of Whites and men in education and employment opportunities. But the meaning of this racial project is shaped not only by policies, but also by discourses emanating from institutions such as universities, think tanks, political parties, and, of course, the mass media. In the last twenty years, the judiciary has made multiple decisions about the nature, scope, and implementation of affirmative action projects. Clawson, Strine, and Waltenburg note that the Court "largely leaves it to others to shape public opinion regarding [its decisions]. The media play an important role" in this process.[17]

The conservative framing of affirmative action in the 1980s described above did not, of course, go uncontested. But, as Gamson and Modigliani's investigation of affirmative action frames demonstrated, conservative opinions came to dominate affirmative action debates in the press.[18] The researchers found two main frames were used to depict affirmative action: (1) the "remedial action frame," which focuses on affirmative action as a necessity "to redress the continuing effects of a history of racial discrimination"[19]; and (2) the "no preferential treatment frame," which depicts affirmative action as giving minorities unfair advantages. The first frame was popular in the 1970s, but the second became dominant in the 1980s, helped no doubt by the ascendancy of conservative spokespersons. Likewise, Entman's analysis of major newsmagazines' coverage in the 1990s found that anti–affirmative action statements dominated pro–affirmative action statements three to one.[20] The "most common oppositional consideration [was] that affirmative action constitutes reverse discrimination."[21]

Following Gamson and Modigliani, Clawson and colleagues found that the majority of mainstream news articles written about a major Supreme Court decision limiting affirmative action in the early 1990s continued to be dominated by the "no preferential treatment" frame.[22] Their study, however, also analyzed Black newspapers, finding that Black periodicals were more likely to frame the decision as a "dramatic setback" for civil rights.[23] Their comparison is instructive and suggests that Black readers are exposed to a broader set of frames about affirmative action than Whites. This could account for some of the variance in Black and White opinions on affirmative action.

Dominant newsgathering routines privilege the opinions of government officials, think tanks, and academics; thus in the Reagan-Bush era, it was more likely that reporters on government beats would gather more conservative viewpoints. As documented by Ellen Messer-Davidow, many conservative scholars, Black and White, who work for or get funded by conservative think tanks, have an easy route to public intellectual status; organizations such as the Heritage Foundation and the National

Association of Scholars have created "articulated systems" to manufacture and disseminate the opinions and scholarship of conservatives.

> The articles, opinion pieces, letters, and news stories, as well as a range of actions, are the individual products. The conservative journals and books, the think-tank seminars, and the grass-roots lobbying efforts, together with the mainstream media, are the distribution system.[24]

Through these efficient and well-connected networks of information and opinion dissemination, conservatives have been able to simultaneously make the argument that liberals have taken over the media, while at the same time conservative pundits and scholars dominate mainstream media debates about affirmative action.

Gamson, as well as Entman and Rojecki, stress that the media reflect political elites' versions of the affirmative action debate and that public opinion data suggest a disjuncture between lay public and elite opinions about the issue.[25] Although these authors recognize that polls are not perfect reflections of public discourse, their review of three decades of poll data on affirmative action reveals that the lay public's measured opinion is not always consonant with the mainstream media's framing of the issue. However, this body of content analysis work demonstrates that conservative elites have been quite successful at influencing at least the mainstream media's framing of affirmative action to portray policies as reverse discrimination or unfair to Whites. Furthermore, work by Kinder and Sanders and Entman and Rojecki suggest that the reverse discrimination/preferential treatment frames can influence Whites to respond negatively to affirmative action in polls and when faced with political decisions.[26]

While previous studies have shed valuable light on news framing of affirmative action and its potential effects on public opinion and discourses, they have not explored the underlying assumptions about race that are made within these frames. That is, they do not explore the way in which affirmative action's advocates and opponents understand race as a category or element of our lived experiences. The non–preferential treatment and reverse discrimination frames imply that race can never be a justifiable category for use in public policy. Most anti–affirmative action rhetoric either implies or explicitly states that racism no longer exists or is not widespread enough to justify continuing affirmative action. Indeed, some opponents, such as Shelby Steele, insist that affirmative action itself perpetuates racism by highlighting racial categories and stigmatizing minorities further.[27] But the debates over affirmative action spotlight the employment of racial categories in at least two other ways: (1) the strategy of representing Whites as a social group that has been jeopardized by affirmative action; and (2) the power of the state to determine who is assigned minority status and eligibility for affirmative action remedies.

Today, some Whites, certain people who claim multiracial heritage and, most recently, supporters of Ward Connerly's Racial Privacy Initiative (RPI) campaign, have claimed that the state should never have the power to determine racial identities or even collect and maintain data about racial characteristics.[28] These two streams of argument were rarely linked prior to the debate over new multiracial options on the 2000 Census. But in 1988, the issue of the state's role in determining race collided with affirmative action when the Malone brothers were accused of faking their racial identity to benefit from affirmative action policies in the Boston Fire Department.

How the "White" Malone Brothers Became "Black"

According to Boston Fire Department (BFD) and court records, twin brothers Philip and Paul Malone[29] first applied for jobs as firemen in 1975, but were not hired because they failed their civil service exams. In 1976, the twins' mother allegedly revealed to them that their great-grandmother was a black woman, showing them a "sepia photograph of a light-skinned woman." In 1977, they reapplied to the BFD and took the civil service exam again. Both brothers listed themselves as "Black" when they reapplied, and both received scores below the minimum for White applicants but above the minimum for minority applicants. In 1978 they were hired as firefighters and began a ten-year career in the department.

In 1988, Fire Commissioner Leo Stapleton was sent a list of names for possible promotion to lieutenant and was surprised to see that Philip Malone was listed as a Black candidate. The Malones were well known in the department because they were the only twins, and the commissioner had believed from his interactions with them that they were White. The brothers were called in one at a time to the office. When asked about the discrepancy between the race listed on their employment papers and their visual appearance, Paul replied that his father was Black; Philip replied that "someone" in the family was Black but he wasn't sure who.[30] These discrepancies led to the brothers' dismissal and a citywide investigation that generated allegations of identity fraud at other fire stations, in the Boston police force, and the Boston Public Schools. Many of the people whose identity was questioned had claimed Hispanic ancestry and status.

Ultimately, a handful of firefighters and teachers were discovered to have falsely represented their race in order to benefit from affirmative action policies. The scandal unearthed racial tensions in the fire department, eliciting bitter comments from White firefighters, many of whom supported the Malones, and Black firefighters who commented on the White-boys' network atmosphere of the BFD. The Malones sued the fire department and the state in an attempt to get their jobs back, but in 1990 the Massachusetts State Supreme Judicial Court ruled that the brothers had intentionally committed fraud and were denied reinstatement. As their case and the cases of the other alleged nonminorities made their way through city investigations and the courts, the dominant media were there, trying to make sense of "white skinned" men who said they had "black ancestry," and "white skinned" English-speaking people who insisted they were Hispanic because they had "Spanish" ancestors. Between September 1988, when the brothers were suspended, and August 1990, when judges decided the last appeals in their and other firefighters' cases, thirty mainstream newspaper stories were written, and one nationally broadcast news show reported on the case.[31]

Three frames dominated the articles that told the story of the Malones:

- Frame 1: Corruption and inefficient bureaucracy in the Boston Fire Department (BFD) and State of Massachusetts allowed this to happen.

- Frame 2: There is a problem with how the state defines race.

- Frame 3: The Malones' actions harmed minorities.

In addition to the three main frames, there were inclusions and omissions in the stories that emphasized Black/White relations in affirmative action discourse. Reporters repeatedly described the physical characteristics of the Malones, awkwardly emphasizing hair, eye, and skin color in a way that reinforced stereotypical visions of White features. Although there were many more employees investigated for alleging Hispanic identity than black identity, the focus was mostly on Blacks and Whites, and there was no sustained discussion of the state's methods of determining Hispanic identity. In contrast, the state's method of determining Black identity and long-standing racial tensions within the BFD and other Boston communities were discussed at length in the news.

Although this case certainly had import for African Americans, Hispanic Americans, and other minority groups, unlike the Phipps case I did not find coverage in newspapers or magazines created by and/or for these groups.[32] This lack of coverage can be attributed to at least two factors. First, in the late 1980s, there were few Black-owned publications and no known Hispanic-oriented periodicals produced in the Boston area. Second, the city's premier paper, the *Boston Globe*, employed two African American editorial columnists, Viola Osgood and Derrick Z. Jackson, both of whom commented on the case at length in their writing. Their presence and the mainstream newspapers' quick reaction to the case may have led African American publishers to believe the story was being covered with the right kind of sensitivity. Indeed, I will argue in a later section of the chapter that these columnists, alongside Bella English, a White *Globe* writer who took an explicitly antiracist stance in her reports, provided readers with counterhegemonic arguments and histories that were very similar to those often provided in African American newspapers in the Phipps case. The interventions and alternative frames provided by these writers underscore the importance of diversity in newsrooms. Thus, in this chapter, I contrast the work of these three columnists with the frames provided by beat journalists, masthead editorials, and commentary from White columnists who did not take an explicitly antiracist approach to the Malone case.

Frame 1: Problems in the System Facilitated the Malones' Racial Fraud

The first frame dominated coverage of the Malone case and the citywide investigations. Eighteen articles used this frame, which was supported with three main arguments. These added up to portray an affirmative action system gone awry at the hands of corrupt individuals in a historically White-only department. The first argument was that the Malones and their superiors were part of a cover-up. This was expressed in two ways: first, that the Malones lied to take advantage of the system; and second, that senior BFD officials allowed it. The *Boston Globe* supported this premise succinctly in its lone editorial on the case: "The disclosure that Whites were hired by the Boston fire Department after claiming minority status is more an indictment of the officials charged with overseeing the hiring process than of a few allegedly dishonest persons."[33] Integral to this argument was the notion that, due to their visual appearance and lack of social contact with Blacks, it was impossible for White officials to be ignorant of the discrepancy between their race on paper and their "real" race. Quotes and commentary from investigators and Black firefighters contributed to this part of the frame, and it was one place where Black voices were incorporated into the reporting.

> City Councillor Bolling said: "I understand it was common knowledge in the department that the Malones weren't black. It was a joke."[34]

To some familiar with the case, it is inconceivable that Stapleton and the administrators of the State Department of personnel Administration, David Haley, or at least their subordinates, did not know that Philip and Paul Malone had reported they were black.[35]

The second argument was that regardless of whether their statement of racial identity was true, higher-ups were ultimately responsible for their personnel records, and the Malones were made scapegoats for the bureaucrats. The Malones, their attorneys, and White firefighters contributed to this line of reasoning. In an interview with a reporter, the wife of Philip Malone stated that "They're being used as scapegoats."[36] Similarly, a sympathetic White columnist wrote with sarcasm and exasperation, "Naturally, the response of today's bureaucracy is to fire both men and penalize their families rather than reach out and slap the people who allowed such foolishness in the first place."[37] Supporters of the Malone brothers within the BFD also blamed the "system" for the problem, not the men who changed their racial designation to Black from White.

> "Any failure of the system is not the Malones' or anybody else's fault," [White fireman Mike Mullane] said. "If the system failed to attract qualified minorities and identify them, it's not the fault of anyone on the force now. It's the fault of the system."[38]

One commentator on the *MacNeil/Lehrer Hour* went so far as to employ the Malones as an example of just how bad it is for White people under affirmative action. After asserting that "the white community or white power structure" does not exist, Paul Roberts, an economist, in an exchange with Benjamin Hooks of the NAACP, argued that affirmative action has made being black economically valuable:

> ROBERTS: It's absolutely of economic value to have these quotas because now you have white people claiming to be black to get them.

> HOOKS: It's patent nonsense to say that.

> ROBERTS: It's not. It's a matter of factual record. You now have white firemen in Boston claiming they're black . . .[39]

Roberts and other proponents of this argument positioned the Malones as innocent, double victims of the affirmative action system, closer to the norm for Whites in dominant affirmative action discourse. First, they were held to a higher standard for test scores than Blacks, next they were found guilty by a system that should have corrected the problem of determining racial identity earlier. However, the facts surrounding their declaration of Black status confounded this attempt to portray them as innocent, destabilizing the narrative of White innocence in the politics of affirmative action.

A final argument was that the BFD was under pressure to hire Blacks and could not find enough qualified candidates. Because of the court order and public outcry, they hired the Malones to satisfy, what was in their eyes, an unfairly imposed quota. Again, White firefighters and supporters of the Malones contributed to this view, which implied that there are never enough qualified minorities to fill spots in White-dominated workplaces.

> Many firefighters, including Mullane, contend that to meet the hiring quota, the Fire Department hired out-of-towners. "That hurt more than anything," said one. "They hired a lot of out-of-state kids. These weren't black kids from Roxbury. Over a white South Boston or Charlestown kid it was . . . someone from North Carolina."

> "We've had convicted felons on this job," said another. "There was a kid born in Africa, another born in South America who couldn't speak a word of English."[40]

These firefighters clearly articulated the resentment felt by many Whites that minorities are taking jobs that "belong" to Whites, or that Whites are more deserving of those jobs. Indeed, the diatribe against foreign and out-of-state Blacks combined multiple stereotypes of people of color while simultaneously constructing a legitimate, local White populace's claim to jobs in Boston.

However, in a handful of pieces—most notably two authored by Black columnists—these assumptions were challenged with the experiences of African American firefighters. By emphasizing the history of race relations in the BFD and the discrimination suffered by Black employees, these writers, as well as Black interviewees, explicitly called out White privilege in the BFD as responsible for the Malones' ability to pass as Black on paper. The way in which Black contributors supported the corruption frame did not shy from naming the architecture of White power in the BFD.

The first way writers and interviewees introduced this argument was to recall how the White-dominated BFD resisted hiring minorities for years. They then speculated that the department used the Malones as a way to get around hiring "real" minorities after the court decisions mandating affirmative action in the 1970s. Although the voices of Black firefighters and their advocates were not found in the majority of the stories, one *New York Times* piece presented this argument through multiple quotes from African Americans involved with the BFD.

> "The ones who chose to ignore [the Malones' racial status] are equally culpable." In the 1980s, [Toni Wolfman, attorney for Black firefighters] said, fire department officials were inclined to look the other way; they "clearly manipulated the system because they weren't interested in hiring minorities . . ."

> "There have been candidates who have been suspect since 1976," [Lieutenant Walter Porter II, a black fireman] said. "But in a semi-military organization in which there is a lot of nepotism, the person you complain to could be the guy's father or uncle."[41]

In Derrick Jackson's column, Black experiences with a history of BFD racism and nepotism in the hiring system were aired.

> The disgust of the black firefighters is that the case of the Malones revived old wounds. The wounds of qualifications. It has been only a few years since white firefighters stopped taunting blacks for being accepted with lower test scores than whites. . . . Black applicants, who had no fathers and uncles to hand down experience in hooks and ladders, competed against whites with empty decks.[42]

In the following excerpt from the same piece, Jackson related how Black firemen said the Malones' ability to get preferential treatment reminded them of Dan Quayle's rise to political prominence on less than stellar academic merits.

> The black firefighters likened their situation to that of Jesse Jackson and Dan Quayle. Jackson, black, was deemed unqualified to be president or vice president by the white men of his own party. . . . Dan Quayle, white, failed the normal requirements to get into law school. He sneaked in anyway, using a program intended primarily for applicants of color. . . . Meanwhile, affirmative action as it was intended is under assault.[43]

Black firefighters and their advocates emphasized that collusion among Whites allowed the Malones to slip through the system unchallenged, asserting the continued existence of White privileges and power in the BFD and other institutions despite affirmative action. As such, they implied what is often explicitly stated about Black beneficiaries of affirmative action: without a system of privilege in place, Whites such as the Malone brothers and Quayle would not have qualified for their positions.

> "I can't believe that people didn't look the other way," attorney Toni Wolfman said yesterday. "If a black person came walking into the fire department in the 1970s and it was in his interest to claim he was white, I have no doubt the Boston Fire Department would say, 'Wait a minute, you're not white.' When a white person said he is black, they look the other way."[44]

> How, [Councillor Bolling] asked, could twins with Irish names, Caucasian features and no black identification from any perspective get into the force and stay on without collusion?[45]

This approach provided an opportunity to emphasize that even if the system of identifying minorities was flawed, affirmative action itself was still valid. As Eleanor Holmes Norton stated to one reporter, "[T]he problem of affirmative action is not defining who is a minority . . . but having the statistics—such as how many black accountants are available—to run programs fairly."[46] And, as seen above, Black firefighters who related their stories of harassment and difficulty in gaining positions in the fire department made the case that affirmative action policies had not yet achieved their purpose.

The notion that Whites could still pull strings to benefit under affirmative action was stated explicitly only by Black commentators. This is notable for two reasons: one, that it downplayed the continued existence of White privilege in the job market; two, journalists failed to include other cases where Whites had claimed minority status to gain jobs under affirmative action statutes. Just three years earlier, the New York Police Department (NYPD) went through a major controversy over White officers claiming Hispanic identity. Even though the *New York Times* covered both the Malone case and the earlier NYPD case, neither *Times* nor *Globe* journalists noted the similarity, making the Malones and their colleagues seem like anomalies. Had reporters linked the cases, they would have added to the framing of White deviance, rather than innocence, in affirmative action. Through such a link the marketplace for civil servants such as police and firefighters would be exposed as a place where White collusion was still a major vehicle to success, rather than a pure meritocracy. Additionally, if journalists had compared the recent NYPD cases to the Boston scandal, this would have produced an even larger *group* of Whites acting together to defraud the system, suggesting that these kinds of responses to affirmative action are indicative of a group-level behavior. This would portray Whites as a racial group, not as individuals, defending their long-held monopoly on city service jobs.

Frame 2: The State's Definition of Race for Affirmative Action Purposes is Problematic

Although each story, to some extent, explicitly or implicitly asked, "How should the state define race for the purposes of affirmative action?" this question was the main focus of two in-depth articles, one in the *Boston Globe* and one in the *New York Times*. Reporters and commentators questioned the fairness and mutability of state criteria for racial designation, and wondered how the system could make exceptions for individuals in a racial "gray area" who "look white but are actually black." The existence of such racially ambiguous persons was not in question, though most interviewees did not believe that the Malones belonged in such a category. Rather, whether any "White-looking Blacks" deserved inclusion in the category "minority" in the context of affirmative action was at issue. In these articles, three main arguments structured the larger frame.

The most prevalent assertion was that the state's system for categorizing and determining minority status was problematic. This was expressed in two ways by interviewees and reporters. First, the state's criteria for minority status had changed in the decade since the Malones were hired. The Malones' supporters claimed that when the twins applied for their jobs, applicants only had to state in good faith their racial identity, and they had done so. Thus, the lawyers and some White firefighters reasoned, the Malones shouldn't be held to the standard that was used to judge them in 1988. This new standard, referred to as the "three-prong test," evaluated racial identity with three questions: (1) can the individual be visually identified as a racial minority; (2) is the individual recognized by and/or involved in a minority community; and (3) do documents, such as birth certificates, list the individual as a person of color? In their final appeal, the Malones' legal team declared that the twins had reported their race in good faith under the old system, and that the Boston Fire Department had exceeded "a reasonable statute of limitations" and was being allowed "to hound these men like Victor Hugo's Inspector Javert.' "[47] Marsha Malone, wife of Philip, insisted to a reporter that the men had "claimed their racial heritage in good faith."[48]

Second, many of those who did not believe the brothers acted in good faith were also wary of the state's three-prong test. While they insisted that the Malones were lying about their Black ancestry, these critics stated that there were other people with legitimate claims to minority status who might not satisfy all three criteria. Black commentators insisted on the existence of "real" minorities who "looked white:"

> "It's entirely possible to look white but be black," [Barbara] Arnwine said. . . . But, she added, "What's so troubling about the Malones is that they held themselves out to be white until right before taking an exam that they had previously failed."[49]

> Color is not always the best way to tell if a person is black—you have to look at the history. . . . Besides, I know lots of black males with similar Caucasian-influenced features.[50]

Thus, African American sources and writers elucidated the slippery link between visible racial identifiers and family history, challenging the dominant view that race is legible on the body and offering a more culturally based definition of Blackness. But, as many interviewees noted, the state had no guidelines for how to evaluate such cases of "Caucasian-influenced" Blacks. One issue was the use of genealogical evidence or claims. The Malones and other firefighters, with varying degrees of proof, claimed to have distant relatives who were Black or Hispanic. But, as Boston City Councillor Bruce Bolling protested in one article, "There have got to be some limits [on how far back one could go on the family tree]. . . . What is reasonable?"[51] Setting those limits, however, was distasteful to many. Margaret Dale, legal counsel for the state's Department of Personnel Administration, which was in charge of evaluating minority status cases, told a reporter that creating some specific ancestral criteria would evoke South Africa's racial caste system: "We're not in South Africa, and we don't have blood percentages, and we don't want to."[52] The assertion that government agencies in United States doesn't use blood percentages is false, but was never challenged in this article or any of the others.[53]

Community recognition as a means of identification was also deemed suspect. Arnwine claimed that many White-looking Black families who could have chosen to pass "held themselves out to be black and traditionally maintained that posture through the centuries no matter how 'white' they looked."[54] This comment implied that those who intentionally pass for white are not eligible for minority status in cases of affirmative action, but those "white-looking" Black people who publicly assert and perform Black identities should be eligible for affirmative action programs. However, the question of how to determine which community should be relevant in terms of public knowledge and/or cultural performance was also raised. The Malones' attorney claimed that the firehouse was the community that mattered, and that the Malones' fellow firefighters and supervisiors "knew" they had written "black" on their personnel records.[55]

Perhaps a more interesting and troubling answer to the question of which community and culture should be tested was brought up by a Black firefighter interviewed by Jackson for his column in the *Boston Globe*. He told a story of a light-skinned colleague "who claimed to be black" but did not want to eat soul food the other black firefighters cooked; rather, he "always cooked corned beef and cabbage."[56] The implication was that this firefighter, like the Malones, was not really Black. On the flip side of the Black firefighter's test for community membership, a White firefighter suggested to a White *Globe* columnist that people claiming Black status should have to compete in a basketball game because "Blacks are much more skillful with a ball than white guys. That's not a racial statement, that's just a fact of life."[57] Both firefighters invoked essentialist renderings of community, culture and race, and these are certainly both suspect albeit in different ways. While the second comment on basketball would make most people cringe, the notion that one can reasonably expect all Blacks to appreciate soul food doesn't seem as distasteful, although it is no less essentialist. It is essentialist not in terms of all Blacks having innate dispositions to eat soul food, but in terms of all Blacks sharing the same cultural experience of making and/or eating soul food. Under each firefighter's test, a phenotypical African American who had neither ball skills nor a taste for soul food would fail.

Finally, people questioned whether it was fair to make employees document their race. Interviewees argued that the state should assume that most people will be honest about their race and therefore should not subject people to unwarranted investigations of their background. Stanley Moore, head of the Vulcan Society, a Black firefighters organization, said that although some sort of criteria had to be established to guard against fraud, "I'm concerned about the manner in which it is done. You don't just bring in a herd of people and say, 'what color are you and what color are you.' "[58] But, of course, the Malones and the other civil service employees who were found to be exploiting the system show that merely saying one is a minority clearly isn't sufficient to prevent abuses.

Frame 3: The Malones' Deception is Part of a Still-Racist System

The third frame contextualized the harm done by the Malones and their protectors within a history of racism in Boston and beyond. While this frame structured only three articles, the eight pieces that contained Black voices touched on it briefly as well. One main contention expressed was that racism in the system had cost Blacks many jobs, and that there was no way to compensate for the loss of opportunity suffered. Supporters of Black firefighters asserted: "The Malones' actions denied two minority firefighters an opportunity to be hired."[59] One Black firefighter told Jackson, on condition of anonymity, that

> "[t]he Malones don't deserve a dime. Somewhere out there are two black men who should have 10 years experience, should be up for lieutenant and should have the same house the Malones have . . ."[60]

This firefighter eloquently testified to the effects of disaccumulation caused by generations of White privilege and institutionalized racism. Not only were were unknown numbers of Blacks denied well-paying, union jobs in the fire department, but also the denial of these jobs meant a lack of other opportunities for those would-be employees. They did not accumulate wealth and occupational status as rapidly as the Malones, or homes and income to pass down to the next generation.

The second argument that structured this frame was that racism still exists in the BFD and in society at large. This was illustrated most strongly by the three columnists who took an antiracist and historical approach to the case, one of which was an editorial satire written by White *Boston Globe* columnist Bella English[61] titled "Color Coordinated." In the article, she described a trip to Milton to investigate the Malones and find out how they had successfully passed in a community which

> had 25,317 white residents and 530 blacks. Milton, which last year paid $626,000 in a civil rights settlement to Bancroft Hall, a black man arrested at gunpoint while waiting in his car for his daughter outside of her friend's house in a white section [of town]. Milton, where several real estate firms were charged with discriminating against blacks seeking housing . . .[62]

Naming the racial segregation and examples of racist acts that occurred in the Malones' Boston suburb, English rejected the main premise of anti–affirmative action adherents, that we have achieved a color-blind society. Explicitly mentioning the role of realty firms and the police in her description of Milton, English rejects the racial realist premise that it is only individuals, not institutions, who are responsible for racism. Her Black colleague, Viola Osgood, also engaged in pointed satire of the Malones in her piece, "New brothers in the family."[63]

> I want the Malones to know there are kinfolk willing to embrace
> them. And after passing for all those years, you guys may have a
> hard time adjusting to being treated like the rest of the family.
> Here are a few pointers. Don't be pressured or forced to run
> away by any of your Milton neighbors who "never suspected."
> We need you in Milton; there aren't enough of us there as it is.
> Expect to be stopped on "suspicion" if you get lost and end up
> driving hopelessly up and down some suburban street. Count on
> being turned away from certain clubs, and being harassed.

Like English, Osgood draws upon the history of Blacks passing for White
to send up the "not as black as the next guy" Malone brothers, making
the point that given current racial conditions, the Malones really don't
want to be "outed' as Black. Similarly, by featuring the experiences and
comments of black firefighters, black columnist Derrick Jackson emphasized the systemic and continued racism faced by minorities in the Boston
Fire Department and elsewhere.

> Through the mid-1980s, black firefighters have charted how blacks
> have been systematically given more negative marks than whites
> for tardiness or mistakes on the job. . . . "Now my buddy at the
> Malone's firehouse is telling me that white firefighters are put-
> ting the squeeze on him to give up his holiday check to help out
> the Malones," a black lieutenant said. "My buddy says he is a
> little scared. he is not sure how the white firefighters will react
> if he says no. After a couple of Budweisers, they start calling
> basketball African handball."[64]

As seen in the previous chapter and Clawson et al., by focusing on Black
experiences with racial hierarchy and including Black perspectives, news
media can provide new ways to view contemporary racial controversies by
placing them in the context of continued inequalities in the wider society.[65] In addition, these articles often raised historical evidence that was
not used in the other articles about the Malones. For example, both
English and Osgood called on the history of passing to structure their
satirical critiques of the Malone case, and Jackson made a subtle reference
to *Plessy v. Ferguson* in this sentence: "[Black firefighters] laughed at the
idea that when some whites found jobs tough to get in the 1970s, they got
black. That sure beat 1896, when Albion Tourgee, in arguing before the
Supreme Court against separate but equal laws, said, 'probably most white
persons would prefer death to life in the United States as colored persons.' "[66] These historic references, coupled with evidence of current rac-

ist practices, positioned the Malones as part of a longer history of White dominance of institutions rather than a peculiar, one-time case.

Inclusions and Omissions

Two other elements of the Malone stories that deserve note are: (1) journalists' recounting of details about the Malones' physical features and their alleged great-grandmother's picture; and (2) the omission of similar details about the physical features of and/or "proof" used by firefighters who were under investigation for claiming Hispanic status. This included and omitted information implied different standards for and meaning of racialized groups' identities.

The emphasis on the Malones' and their alleged great-grandmother's bodies reinscribes biological definitions of race. In almost every story, the Malones were described as "white skinned," or having "light skin." Many journalists also included their hair color (blonde) and eye color (blue) to complete a picture of stereotypical White, European American features. While in one sense the decision to use adjectives rather than definitive racial labels gave the twins the benefit of "innocent until proven guilty" consideration, when paired with the repeated fact that they changed their racial identity between tests, the physical descriptions placed the Malones squarely within the matrix of recognized White (almost Aryan) physical attributes, undermining their claim to Black ancestry. Many stories ran pictures of the twins side by side with a reproduction of the photo of their alleged great-grandmother, using the description "a light-skinned woman in a sepia photograph." As in the use of pictures in the Susie Phipps case, the photographs invite the reader to scrutinize and judge the Malones and their ancestress based on their visual appearance, reinforcing the notion that race can be "read" on the body.

The silence around the issue of how to determine Hispanic identity was significant. The lack of physical descriptions or pictures of the employees accused of faking Hispanic identity implied that, unlike Black identity, Hispanic identity may not be "in the blood" or on the skin. The absence of discussions of the evidence required to assess alleged Hispanic/Whites' claims was particularly noticeable, considering that one of the firefighters under investigation, Edward Kenney Jr., was the son of BFD Deputy Chief Edward Kenney Sr. While Kenney Sr. identified himself as White, his son listed himself as Hispanic on his employment documents. The father offered one comment to the media, that he had counseled his son against claiming Hispanic identity. But his son did not speak to the media, and no pictures of him or his father were ever printed. This story, one might assume, would be just as newsworthy as the Malones, given the angle of nepotism. However, journalists did not delve into this case or those of the other people accused of misidentifying themselves as Hispanic.

Only two of the thirty stories mentioned the state's criteria for determining Hispanic identity: "someone born in South America, Central America, Cuba, Puerto Rico, or the Spanish speaking islands in that region . . ." and who demonstrates "some cultural identification with Hispanics."[67] Although this definition includes a standard of cultural identification similar to the criterion of "holding oneself out in the community" used to identify Blacks, none of the reporters who covered the Hispanic identity cases questioned the fact that the only evidence of Hispanic identity Kenney Jr. and his superiors presented was that "[h]e went back, I don't know how many generations. But they went back and they had it," it being genealogical evidence of a "Spanish" ancestor. Although he was initially dismissed from his job, Edward Kenney Jr. successfully sued for reinstatement, an accomplishment that was barely mentioned and without any discussion of how he proved that he hadn't misled the BFD. That no journalist or editor decided to investigate this tangle of contradictions is stunning. The father claimed White identity, the son's birth certificate listed him as White, and neither of the two spoke Spanish or were born in the nations or regions listed by the state's criteria. There wasn't even a report of a sepia photograph to back up the claim of genealogical evidence. It seems that the media's default position on affirmative action, that it is a Black/White issue, prevented an interrogation of the definition of Hispanic identity, and artificially limited the story.

As White (or Black) as They Want to Be: The Power of Whites in Affirmative Action

The Malone case sheds light on many questions concerning race and the media. First, this chapter affirms past research on affirmative action in the news, finding that the media still focus on African Americans and Whites. Like Clawson and colleagues, this analysis suggests that Black commentators may bring new frames and information to the debate on affirmative action. Although we cannot assume that all Black journalists and/or black-owned media sources will utilize different frames than White journalists or White-owned news media, on the issue of affirmative action, Black writers continued to emphasize civil rights issues and the racism faced by African Americans. Unlike the dominant anti–affirmative action frames found by researchers cited earlier, the Malones' story did not elicit a flood of negative views on affirmative action. Rather, scrutiny of the alleged White frauds did not lead to a call for ending affirmative action as scandals of Black affirmative action "cheats" (e.g., underqualified Blacks) have.

Indeed, many commentators voiced the opinion that affirmative action remained a legitimate and necessary policy. Thus, the replacement of "innocent White victims" of affirmative action with White perpetrators of race fraud prevented journalists from following the prevailing trend for affirmative action, that is, finding pro- and anti–affirmative action elites to provide sound bites. As they reported the case, journalists could not depend upon normal scripts, and the focus on racial identity extracted the case from the routine of elite-driven news framing.

This chapter highlights an instance where Whites are clearly visible and are *not* normal. Because the Malones and some of their White peers were found guilty of fraud, their stories disrupted the "innocent victim" narrative usually seen in stories of affirmative action. Indeed, the verdict of fraud, added to the repeated statement that their test scores were extremely low for White or Black applicants, further distanced the Malones from the "innocent White" prototype, because innocent White victims are assumed to be better qualified than Black job seekers. Due to the overarching corruption frame and certain omissions, the representation of White deviance was not as strong a theme as it could have been. By presenting the Malones and their colleagues as anomalies in the Boston system and not linking their cases to similar ones in New York and other locales, the Malones were portrayed as bad apples who were able to slip through an imperfect system. As with journalists who covered the Phipps case, the lack of connection worked to contain the problem locally. Had reporters connected the cases, a different framing possibility would have been that many Whites were using their privileged connections to other Whites to "beat the system" around the country, representing Whites as a group. This would have brought Whites closer to the depiction of Blacks as *group-oriented* in their reactions to race issues. This kind of focus may also have raised the question put forth by Robertson on *Mac Neil/Lehrer*—Is minority identity really worth more on the job market because of affirmative action? In-depth reporting on that question could have produced interesting statistics about the realities of race and employment in the late 1980s.

Like the code of silence that encourages policemen to not testify against their colleagues in cases of brutality, the White firefighters who shared in the joke of the Malones' racial identity were in collusion based in shared White identity. The resentment voiced by White firefighters such as Mike Mullane is institutionally reflected in: (1) hiring practices; (2) workplace hostilities against Black and Latino firefighters; and (3) the slow rate of promotions for minority firefighters. Really, the only aspect of the BFD hiring system that was questioned in depth was the mechanism for confirming racial identity. The nepotism and cronyism of the fire department was reduced to the case of a few bad apples; neither were the qualifications of those Whites who benefited from the racial ruse rigorously investigated, nor was their collective investment in White group identity examined, save in Viola Osgood's scathing column. Indeed, the White personnel who managed the Malones' hiring were never censured or investigated for their role in the situation; when journalists failed to critique and follow up on the reinstatement of alleged Hispanic fraud Edward Kenny Jr., they effectively conceded that Whites in control of the BFD could continue to provide opportunities for Whites to abuse the affirmative action system.

This case also provides an example of a crisis in White identity that does *not* function to manage legitimation crises in Whiteness, as found in some prior studies.[68] In every aspect of the case, Whites were suspect, from the Malones to their supervisors to some of their co-workers. Although the Malones' supporters tried to portray the twins as innocent victims, the larger framing of the controversy privileged a reading of the brothers as White frauds, and the Boston Fire Department as guilty of corruption. Shome and others have found that oftentimes in media narratives Whites incorporate particular aspects of Black or other minority identities in a way that benefits the social order while simultaneously reestablishing White normativity. The Malones and their co-offenders performed a much different form of incorporation. The firefighters claimed a racial identity in name only; the Malone brothers and their attorneys attempted to segment "ancestry" from all other markers of racial identity for one, personal purpose: achievement in the job market. As Philip Malone's wife complained to the *Boston Globe*, her husband wasn't "as black as the next guy," but the family shouldn't be expected "to hang a sign on our door saying 'we're black,' "[69] making it very clear that the Malones had no desire to "hold themselves out" in their community as Black. Their claim of "black ancestry" reflected no attempt at syncretism between cultures, let alone tolerance, acknowledgment or public acceptance of this "other" identity. Their decade-long success is itself a demonstration of White dominance of the Boston Fire Department rather than a rejection of particularly violent and ugly forms of White racism, as seen in Madison's analysis of popular films. Thus, the story of the Malones and their colleagues does not satisfy the desire to relegitimate White male identities or distance this identity from socially unacceptable displays of racism; rather, it produces more problems for the legitimacy of the White individuals involved as well as the institutions dominated by Whites.

Lastly, this analysis corroborates previous work in finding that the dominant press frames most racial issues, particularly affirmative action, as a Black versus White dilemma. This was a particularly disappointing aspect of the media's coverage of the Boston investigations since the majority of firefighters and city employees who were investigated for racial fraud had claimed Hispanic, not Black, identity. Although a few of the alleged Hispanic frauds did resign early on in the investigations, some of the accused firefighters and teachers retained both their positions *and* their Hispanic status, notably the son of a senior BFD official. The added intrigue of nepotism in this case, one could assume, would make it as least as newsworthy as the Malone scandal.

There are at least three possible reasons beyond the media's reliance on the Black/White divide that issues surrounding claims of Hispanic identity were not explored thoroughly. First, given the reliance on Black/White conflict in affirmative action reporting and reporting on other racial conflicts, reporters may not have had the same network of community and elite contacts in Hispanic communities as they did for Black and White communities. This is not an excuse but rather a critique of how dominant newsgathering practices may be affected by dependence on particular frames. Second, although a few articles contained information about how different state agencies defined Hispanic identity, the state's criteria for Hispanic identity emphasized *national origin* and *language* rather than skin color and community visibility. Although Hispanic/Latino(a)s are certainly racialized in the United States, reporters seemed to follow the state's lead and framed Hispanic identity more like a nationality or nonracialized ethnic culture.

Third, because the state's definition of Hispanic focused on nation and language, it is possible that the journalists themselves understood or accepted Hispanic identity as an "ethnic option"[70] rather than an essential racial identity as Blackness is often understood in dominant discourse. Thus, in these cases, they may have believed that a "reasonable" claim of Hispanic ancestry—just as many people claim a laundry list of distant ties to multiple European ethnic groups. This seemed to be enough for the press to allow these firefighters' assertions of Hispanic identity to stand, and also may have seemed less problematic than a White-looking person's claim of Black identity. Ethnographic studies of journalists who write on racial issues would be useful, to explore whether they have different frameworks for different ethnic and racial identities.

Although this case occurred more than twenty years ago, the assumptions about race that structured the stories about the Malones resonate with current public debates about the nature of race, affirmative action, and the role of the state in identifying minority groups and managing racial projects. The recent controversial changes of the racial categories used by the Census Bureau in 2000 along with Ward Connerly's new crusade to end the use of race in government records are both phenomena that the Malone case speaks to today. Specifically, the Malones' attempt to privatize their claim of "black ancestry" and separate themselves from any social or political consequences of racial identity/identification is instructive. The Malones' case suggests that, in a society structured on racial inequalities, race is never a private matter. Whether individuals or the state are utilizing the assumption that race is biological or cultural, the discourses around the Malones, like those in the Phipps case, reveal that there is an expectation of public visibility and or performance of race. People are expected to display, declare, and associate themselves with a racialized identity, not only on a form stashed in a file cabinet or a sepia photograph hidden in shame from the rest of the family. Thus, state and social actors compel racially ambiguous individuals to make declarations about their racial identity in some public manner.

Cases reported at the margins of racial identity, while rare, are useful dispatches for exploring how racialized news frames are constructed and can be disrupted. In particular, the Malones' case reveals that journalists and other public opinion shapers can use these cases as opportunities to alter their representations of controversial issues that have, up to that moment, followed particular patterns. Exceptional stories can serve more enlightening purposes than titillation in the public sphere, especially when they center on important public issues. Failure to deepen our discourses about race and identity in the public sphere would be, as Patricia Williams recently wrote, "but one face of the collective abandonment of the political problem of race; it substitutes a calculated and loveless escapism for civic commitment to the transformative notion of human equality."[71] In order to produce a more complex picture of race that allows for the ambivalences, frustrations, as well as the commonalities among and across racial groups to speak, individual journalists, elites, and other news shapers need to rework their prior frames and include diverse voices to open up previously limited discourses on race. The next chapter provides an illustration of the opposite result—an exceptional case of race and hiring that was framed squarely within the conservative consensus of the meaning of race in our society.

Chapter Four

Descended from Whom?

Defining Maria Hylton in the News

This chapter concerns the scrutiny brought to a job candidate's racial pedigree, making what might have been a routine faculty hiring process into a minor firestorm over the definition of Black identity and its applications in affirmative action. Law professor Maria Consuelo O'Brien Hylton's parents are a Black Cuban woman and a White Australian man. In 1994, Northwestern University Law School began considering her for a position, possibly in relation to a retention package for her husband, also Black and a law professor. During this process, groups representing Black and Latino law students as well as feminist groups protested her candidacy. Each group claimed that she would not represent or meet their needs because of her background and theoretical interests. In addition, the school's first tenured Black law professor, Joyce Hughes, told her fellow faculty members that she would not support the hire, and declared that Maria Hylton was not "Black in a United States context."

The Hylton case made its way into major newspapers' headlines and editorials and sparked conversations within and outside of academia. When the press reported on this case, as with the Malones, affirmative action was a major issue. But the discussions of how institutions should determine if a person is "authentically" black[1] went in a different direction. In particular, reporters and commentators gravitated toward the perceived irony of one group of Blacks denying a Black woman the privilege of representing herself as Black in a job search. This focus, I argue, fit in with two recurrent themes in the dominant media of the mid-1990s and beyond: (1) judging which (if any) black people "deserve" affirmative action; and (2) coverage of political and cultural conflicts within the Black public sphere. These preoccupations were part and parcel of the neoconservative assault on the use of race in public policies created to decrease racial inequality in higher education and the workplace. Indeed,

101

these strands of discourse included accusations against Black political leaders and activists, who were said to be using and abusing the "race card" to silence Black conservatives and to force unfair hiring practices. Through this focus on Blacks' alleged misuse of race, conservative commentators (and the journalists who solicited their commentary) reinforced the idea that people of color monopolize race matters, obfuscating the role of Whiteness in racial politics. This approach was consistent with the conservative consensus on race, that Blacks who assert that race and racism are still relevant factors in social life are doing a disservice to other Blacks and society. Media coverage of these issues was exemplified in the frenzies over the Clarence Thomas nomination, controversial Supreme Court decisions and public referenda on affirmative action, "Black-on-Black crime," and the "failure" of the Black middle class and Black celebrities (notably Michael Jordan and other athletes) to give back to and uplift the "Black underclass."[2]

Press coverage of Maria Hylton's case, unlike the Malone and Phipps situations, was not so much about the role of the state or other powerful white-dominated institutions in determining who is Black, but about cultural heterogeneity, dissent, and political confusion within Black communities in the 1990s. This alleged turmoil was contrasted to a mythic, homogeneous, unified Black public sphere of the 1950s and '60s. The case also represents an iteration of the strategic invisibility of Whiteness, wherein White observers of Black "pathology" distance themselves and Whiteness from current configurations of race and power, even as they discuss race explicitly. Additionally, press coverage of Hylton's experience with Northwestern failed to evaluate claims about race, color, identity, and ideology with a complexity that could have illuminated debate over how affirmative action and other policies to support racial diversity should work given the demographic trends that could alter our sense of who is Black or who is a "racial minority" in the United States today.

Discovering Diversity (and Pathology) within Black Communities

Herman Gray's *Watching Race* analyzes how conflicting images and messages about Blackness, race, and race relations came to television in the 1980s and 1990s, producing overlapping meanings and new challenges for imagining Black life.[3] Kristal Brent Zook also describes the surge of Black cultural production that occurred in the late 1980s and early 1990s. In books, film, and television, Black auteurs "wrestled with the unspoken pleasures (and horrors) of assimilation, the shock of integration, and the pain of cultural homelessness" in the post–civil rights era.[4] As she and other writers have observed, the emergence and increased visibility of the growing Black middle class, alongside a burgeoning global market for Black culture (exemplified by the success of hip hop) and continued evidence of racial inequalities and discrimination, spurred multiple media productions of Blackness. But this often complex creative reaction to Black life postsegregation was not reflected in documentary genres. Specifically, Gray explains how news and political messages clashed with this surge in popular black-themed sitcoms, like such as *The Cosby Show*. This exposed audiences to very different visions of the "realities" of Blackness in the post–civil rights era. In their focus group study of *Cosby*, Jhally and Lewis found that White viewers of the successful Huxtable family on TV articulated the view that "other" Blacks—those on welfare, those in low-status jobs—weren't trying hard enough to make it. According to the world of the sitcom, Blacks were making it on the level post–Jim Crow playing field; images of welfare moms in the news, then, were the result of individual failings, not social failings.

During the Reagan era, neoconservative pundits launched successful attacks on Blackness through the rhetoric of welfare queens, "black-on-black" crime, and the war on drugs. In his book on the emergence of "Black-on-Black" violence in the media and political landscape of the 1980s, David Wilson documents how misleading "crime-wave" reporting combined with well-placed and widely disseminated studies of crime and race from right-wing think tanks invented a neoconservative discourse of an epidemic, centered in the alleged failings of Black families and urban cultures.[5] Wilson argues that this discourse was used to support and push through more punitive sentencing laws by creating "a 1980s and 1990s black crime panic across America" that persuaded political representatives and the majority public that more law and order was needed to protect innocents from a generation of a new kind of hyper-dangerous, predatory young black male criminals.[6] Similarly, Martin Gilens's work illustrates the impact of "welfare queen" rhetoric and images on public opinion, finding that White Americans were swayed to believe social welfare programs should be drastically cut.[7] Thus, at the same time that 1980s and 1990s television sitcoms provided a space for black popular culture to be transmitted to ever-larger multiracial audiences, many in those same audiences were also exposed to frightening portrayals of Black urban communities falling apart due to violence, drugs, and overdependence on welfare, provided by politicians and members of the news media. The contradictions between the portrayals of Blackness in the press and the cultural imagery flooding the airwaves created a tension that has still not been resolved in how Blackness is configured in mass media.[8]

In addition to contradictions created by entertainment and news narratives, Zook notes that "[u]nlike the 1960s and before, who 'counted' as black was no longer clear by the 1980s. Nor was it clear who now suffered enough to be a 'legitimate' family member."[9] The issue of legitimacy and Black identity was not limited to artistic output or even Black-authored texts. As African Americans negotiated integration and its meaning, mainstream media outlets simultaneously pursued their own investigations of the question, What does being Black mean thirty years after the legal victories of the civil rights movement? In addition to the televisual output reviewed by Zook and Gray, at least two other phenomena shaped the answers to these questions in the dominant press: (1) the media successes of conservatives, whose members declared a color-blind society achieved or imminent in a wide variety of news media outlets; and (2) a string of racially charged public events, including the trial of White police officers for the beating of Rodney King, the Clarence Thomas/ Anita Hill hearings, the Million Man March, and of course, the O.J. Simpson trial.[10]

Major newsmagazines provide a convenient timeline of this interest in Blackness. In the 1990s, multiple feature-length cover stories on Blackness and race populated newsstands. In April 1995, *The New Yorker* published an issue titled "Black In America," which included essays from prominent scholars and artists such as Henry Louis Gates Jr., Ralph Ellison, and Anna Deveare Smith. From the provocative cover story "Race and Rage: Affirmative Action" in 1995 to the 1997 cover "Black Like Who?" *Newsweek* ran the gamut of the attention paid to the "new" diversity within Black communities. In these pieces, portraits of young and old, men and women, liberals and conservatives, were accompanied by statistics about Black achievement (or failures) in education, the job market, marriage, and childbearing. Between the pictures and the charts, commentators on the Left and Right pontificated about either the continued lack of opportunities for many Black Americans, or the failure of individual Blacks to make good on opportunities afforded by the civil rights movement. By 1997, writers at *Newsweek* felt confident declaring that

> [i]n the '90s, black families are divided as whites were in the '60s—and hip hop is their Vietnam. . . .[11] Three decades after the heyday of the civil rights movement, black America is facing a generation gap.[12]

The mainstream press contrasted a picture of Black cohesion in the 1960s with a fragmented contemporary Black public fighting itself. Oftentimes, the problems of the Black community were blamed on the "crisis in black leadership." Pundits, scholars, and others lamented a generation without a unifying central leader like Martin Luther King Jr. They criticized prominent figures such as Louis Farrakhan and Jesse Jackson for not living up to King's "color-blind" dream. Sources depicted new generation of Black activists and leaders as unable to agree on whether racism or personal and cultural failures are the root causes of continued inequalities across racial groups.[13]

In a few instances, this discourse of Black fragmentation included discussions of mixed race Blacks. The main problem presented was how Blacks perceive people of mixed race. The February 13, 1995, cover of *Newsweek* cover asked readers "What Color Is Black?" and showcased a matrix of African American faces of different hues. The feature inside informed readers that, despite poll findings that Blacks and Whites still disagreed on many questions concerning racial progress,

> the world is changing anyway. By two other measures in the same *Newsweek* poll—acceptance of interracial marriage and the willingness to reside in mixed-race neighborhoods—tolerance has never been higher. The nation's dialogue, meanwhile, is changing so rapidly that the familiar din of black-white antagonism seems increasingly out-of-date . . .

> America is beginning to revise its two-way definition of race. . . . What color is black? It is every conceivable shade and hue from tan to ebony—and suddenly a matter of ideology and identity as much as pigmentation.[14]

In these paragraphs, the author claims that our nation is rewriting race outside the Black/White binary, but the whole piece is focused on one side of the binary: the Black side. Indeed, even the color spectrum invoked, "from tan to ebony," misses the presence of many people of multiracial heritage who "look more white" than Black, such as Susie Phipps or artist-scholar Adrian Piper.[15] As the article continues, the writer introduces us to "biracial Americans," whom he distinguishes from the first multiracial Americans, who, we are told, appeared as early as Jamestown. However, we are told that members of this biracial generation "are the first to stake a claim to multiracial status, discomfiting in the process blacks and whites who are reluctant to reconsider racial categories."[16] Again, in contrast to the use of the term *multiracial*, the story is centered on Blacks, Whites, and those of Black and White multiracial descent. Of those interviewed for the piece, all who have some non-White heritage are also of African American descent.

Furthermore, as the piece wraps up, the author claims that "the demand for recognition by emerging multiethnic and multiracial groups . . . implicitly threatens the tradition of black solidarity. . . . Black intellectuals and political activists . . . are worried by the prospect of change."[17] Not a page after declaring that both Whites and Blacks are "discomfited" by the idea of multiracial identity, the author focuses only on *Black* resistance to the multiracial category. Effortlessly, the "discomfited" Whites of a sentence or two earlier drop out of the equation, leaving only Blacks as obstructionists of the new biracial people's dream of self-nomination. The reader is encouraged to forget the racial thinking of Whites, their experiences of racial discomfort, or any other relationship they may have to this new racial identity. To end the piece, the author suggests that to facilitate the "ultimate blending of black and white, [a]ll it requires is patience, faith—and a measure of good will,"[18] all traits hard to see in a Black public portrayed as stubbornly holding onto racial "entitlements" such as affirmative action, holding "grudges" about Jim Crow and slavery, and unwilling to be "color-blind" in the 1990s. This simple solution also ignores the role of institutions in how different racial groups interact. As I demonstrate in the next two chapters, this multiracial rhetoric is most often combined with personalized comments and photos of people of Black, White, or Black/White descent. Importantly, Blacks are used most often when journalists illustrate traditional racial groups' discomfort with bi- or multiracial identification. The case analyzed here conforms to this pattern of focusing on African Americans' discomfort with multiracial identity and (supposedly) civically unhealthy preoccupation with racial identity.

The Hylton Case

Maria Consuelo O'Brien Hylton was born in the United States to a Black Cuban mother and a White Australian father in 1960. She grew up in a middle-class area of New York, attended an elite college and law school. She joined black law organizations both as a student and as a professional. Her work focused on economic aspects of the law; some of her published articles argued against certain programs valued by feminists, such as paid child care leave. She married Keith Hylton, a Black lawyer with interests in economics. In 1994, she was a tenured faculty member of DePaul University Law School in Chicago and he was in a tenure-track job at Northwestern University Law School in nearby Evanston. He was one of only two Black law professors at that school. When Boston University approached the couple with an offer of tenured positions, Northwestern began to investigate bringing Maria Hylton in as a faculty member in order to retain her husband, described by the dean as "a valued member of the faculty."[19] Keith Hylton was considered, in the words of another colleague, "one of the leading black law professors in the United States."[20]

When the school began the process of vetting Maria Hylton's file, African American, female, and Latino American law students protested. The head of the Black students' law association said that Hylton should not be counted as a Black candidate and that her views on the law, combined with her racial background, would make her a poor mentor for Black students. Contrastingly, a member of the Latino law students' organization stated that Maria Hylton should not be viewed as a Latino candidate either, because she "seems to identify more as a Black."[21] A feminist group on campus accused the university of recruiting a person who was not "a star" just to satisfy a male spouse. In addition to the students' outcries, the only other Black faculty member at the law school, Joyce Hughes, opposed hiring Hylton. Hughes contacted Maria Hylton when she was being recruited and asked questions about her background; the Hyltons allege that she told them she could not support Maria's candidacy because she was too conservative, and implied that she was not "black enough" in Hughes's estimation.[22] At an October faculty meeting, Hughes allegedly argued that Maria Hylton should not be considered a "minority candidate."[23] Later, in December, at the end of the controversy, Hughes wrote a memo to her colleagues outlining her views on Maria O'Brien Hylton's ancestry and why it disqualified her from being considered as a minority candidate:

> It is misleading to label as Black any person whose skin color is dark. . . . [A] person whose parents are (white) Australian and (black) Cuban should not be considered a Black candidate. . . . [W]hile there are said to be 100 million people of African descent in Latin America and the Caribbean, they are not African American and are not Black in the U.S. context. . . . For most African Americans, descent is from 12 generations of enslaved Africans.[24]

Hughes also provided her colleagues with a list of elements to consider when hiring Black faculty:

1. Color does not determine who is African American or Black, to use a term polls say most African Americans prefer. (Note that I use a capital B.)

2. Faculty (of any race, any color, any ethnicity, any gender) who will validate African American students are necessary in institutions of higher education.

3. "Minority" faculty should not be concentrated in any particular [theoretical] orientation.[25]

Arguing against hiring another conservative economic law professor on its face seems legitimate, since intellectual diversity is a hallmark of universities. However, those who protested Hylton's hire did not only reject her approach to legal questions; they also mentioned her parentage and relationships to particular racial groups as disqualifying elements of her portfolio.

Framing Maria O'Brien Hylton

Eleven newspaper articles were written about the Hylton case. Two of these were letters to the editor written by Northwestern officials. Eight of the stories appeared in major publications such as the *Chicago Tribune*, *Boston Globe*, and the *New York Times*.[26] Of these eight, three were masthead editorials that appeared on the main editorials page, indicating that the editors of three major papers found the case important enough for their official comment. Only one story was found in an African American periodical (*Black Issues in Higher Education*), and none in English-language Latino or multiracial periodicals. Thus, I did not create a separate section for ethnic news, as in the Phipps chapter, due to the fact that this case did not garner attention from the Black press.

The overarching frame constructed by reporters and editorialists covering the Hylton case was that the concerns of the students of color and Dr. Hughes were unreasonable and had no legitimate place in higher education. The articles painted a picture of "identity politics" gone overboard; the excesses of "political correctness" had come home to roost in the universities that spawned it.[27] Two ironies were seen by the majority of commentators: first, that Black people would accuse another visibly Black person of not being "Black enough;" and second, that the same "liberals" who fought for freedom of ideological expression and inclusion for people of color in the academy were vigorously attempting to exclude "one of their own." However, this focus on the ironies of the "P.C. wars" eliminated deeper consideration of the politics of color and identity, and also drowned out the well-articulated concerns some students had about academic diversity and the mentoring needs of students of color in the law school. Furthermore, the articles overwhelmingly zeroed in on the politics of Blackness, even though Maria O'Brien Hylton is part Cuban and faced opposition from Latino students as well. As in coverage of the Malone case, the press continued to cling to a dichotomous, Black/White vision of racial politics. Three main arguments supported the dominant frame: (1) Hylton's Black opponents were racist and unreasonable; (2) conservative Black thinkers are unjustly subject to the tyranny of "politically correct" liberals who dominate academia; and (3) university administrators and faculty should not be swayed by minority identity politics, although some methods of creating or maintaining racial diversity on campuses are credible.

ARGUMENT 1: UNREASONABLE, RACIST PEOPLE OF COLOR AMBUSHED HYLTON

In both of the Chicago newspapers and in the *Boston Globe*, editorialists and sources lambasted students of color and Professor Joyce Hughes for what was construed as a peculiar kind of intraracial prejudice. Thus, racism was located in the minds and actions of a circumscribed group of Black and Latino law students and one faculty member. This discredited and displaced their critiques of racism in the academy, instead construing their critique of the Hylton hire as a personal vendetta. The title of the *Chicago Tribune's* masthead editorial about the case read: "Racism takes an odd turn at NU."[28] Similarly, other reporters chose to include Maria Hylton's own assessment of Professor Hughes's memo: "I think the memo is offensive. I think it's racist."[29] Every article included excerpts from or paraphrased Hughes's memo and its definition of what Black means, often with surrounding judgments about its use of race. Although the *Journal of Black Issues in Higher Education* did not explicitly call Hylton's opposition racist, its lone article on this case (the only one published in a Black periodical) summed up the problems with Hughes's memo as follows: "It now appears that Maria Hylton's 'white blood' excluded her from being appointed to the faculty of Northwestern University School of Law."[30]

All of the articles mentioned that Maria Hylton came from an interracial family, and seven of the eleven pieces mentioned Hylton's parents' races in detail. Not all of the articles explicitly mentioned her parentage as a source of the opposition's rancor. But when the facts of her ancestry were combined with the excerpts from the Hughes memo, all of the articles implied, as explicitly stated in one *New York Times* news piece, that

> [i]t was, in fact, Professor Hylton's racial and cultural identification (or lack of it) that fueled much of the tempest. The daughter of an African-Cuban mother and an Australian-Irish father, Professor Hylton says she does not define herself in racial terms.[31]

At this juncture, it makes sense to note that the accusation, "You're not Black (or Latino or Asian, etc.) enough," is cited by multiracial activists as a central feature of oppression faced by people of mixed race.[32] But I argue that the Hylton story, as reported in the dominant press, was not about multiracial identity; rather it was a story about the politics of Blackness and the problems of identity politics. Indeed, none of the journalists or commentators drew upon sources in the multiracial movement or linked Hylton's case to the already highly visible call for a multiracial identifier on the 2000 Census.[33] Only one reporter, Irene Sege of the *Boston Globe*, linked Hylton's case to "a world changed by intermarriage and Third World immigration,"[34] but the main thrust of her piece was to condemn Hylton's opponents for hypocrisy. As Sege wrote, "The very groups that push for faculty diversity . . . all opposed Maria Hylton." Furthermore, her biracial identity was overshadowed by the writers' dependence on themes concerning Blackness and the (over)use of Black identifiers to describe Maria Hylton. For example, four of the eleven articles used "Black" in their headlines to describe her:

- Black Prof. Fails Political Test[35]

- "Not All with Dark Skins Are Black": Definition of Who is "Black" Plagues Northwestern School of Law[36]

- Rule of Law: Not Black Enough for This Law School[37]

- Not Black Enough?[38]

Two other stories also used the term *black* in their headlines, one as a pun, and the other as a reference to Hylton's husband, but without other knowledge of the story, a reader could reasonably think the second use of the label referred to both husband and wife:

- Academic Blacklisting[39]

- Battle to Keep Black Law Professor Leaves Bruised Egos and Reputations[40]

As the next section illustrates, Hylton's Black identity was of utmost importance in the second argument: that conservative Black thinkers are unfairly under attack by the "P.C. police."

ARGUMENT 2: RACIAL McCARTHYISM AND P.C. IN THE ACADEMY

In the vein of the "culture wars" and the not-so-distant controversy over Supreme Court Justice Clarence Thomas, the press took Black students and faculty to task for what *Chicago Sun-Times* columnist Dennis Byrne depicted as a resurrection of McCarthyism.

If this were still the '50s, the script would read that [Hylton] . . . was too radical, too progressive, even too black and too female to be offered the job. But this is the '90s, and the reasons may be that she wasn't black, female, and progressive enough . . . this is, to put it bluntly, the same kind of McCarthyism and blacklisting that infected the '50s.[41]

Irene Sege wrote that the Hyltons had become "the campus flash point in a disturbing debate about just what it means to be black. . . . Some students at Northwestern University are quietly quoting [NYU Law Professor Derrick] Bell's admonition against those who 'look black and think white' to justify their opposition to Maria Hylton."[42] In the same piece and in others, reporters quoted Keith Hylton's conjecture that the students were angry with him for his conservative views. And in her column, Melanie Kirkpatrick of the *Wall Street Journal* summed the case up as follows:

The latest dispatch from the campus PC wars comes from Northwestern University School of Law in Chicago. In the line of fire were two brilliant young Black law professors whose apparent sin was not being "progressive" enough thinkers. . . . [M]ost universities prefer minorities who first take a political test that only liberals can pass.[43]

The editors of the *Boston Globe* proclaimed that the hiring controversy could have become "a constructive debate" over the intellectual diversity of a law school, but was instead "obscured by a smoke screen of racial malarkey. It is a pernicious notion that real blacks cannot be conservative."[44] Just as some reporters and politicians framed Clarence Thomas as a martyr to identity politics, Maria Hylton was portrayed as a free-thinking Black woman under fire from rigid-thinking Blacks and liberals.[45]

The venom in many of the columnists' assessments of how universities favor "liberal" minority candidates is certainly disturbing. However, their attack is also problematic and inflates the power of minorities and liberals in the academy to screen out conservative thinkers. Kirkpatrick's assertion that "most universities" choose liberal over conservative minorities is easily dismissed if one takes into account the successful careers of many Black conservative thinkers at top universities, such as Thomas Sowell or Glenn Loury.[46] Beyond the academy, Black conservatives enjoyed enormous success in both mainstream and neoconservative media outlets in the 1980s and 1990s; a study by FAIR found that Sowell, Loury, and Shelby Steele enjoyed much more media exposure than Cornel West, Manning Marable, and Adolph Reed.[47] And, given their position in and funding by conservative think tanks and institutes such as the Heritage Foundation and the American Enterprise Institute, Black conservative thinkers often enjoy wide distribution of their ideas in mass media.

Byrne's invocation of McCarthyism was spurious as well: neither minority law students nor other people of color in the academy have the kind of power wielded by Senator McCarthy and his allies during the Red Scare. Targets of the anticommunist witch hunt were usually blacklisted from their professions for life; reputations and lives were ruined. In contrast, Maria Hylton and her husband went on to take coveted jobs at another prestigious law school, Boston University. Equating McCarthyism with the "PC Wars" is at best hyperbole and serves as an example of how neoconservatives have become expert at appropriating the rhetoric of progressive causes to dismantle antiracist policies. By presenting hegemonic ideologies and identities as under attack, conservatives position themselves as innocent victims of untested, rash ideas emanating from social groups who have no regard for justice, just their own "special interests."

ARGUMENT 3: UNIVERSITIES SHOULD REJECT "POLITICAL CORRECTNESS" AND IDENTITY POLITICS

In response to the flurry of negative press, the leaders of the Northwestern Law School wrote letters to the editors of the *Chicago Tribune* and the *Wall Street Journal*. They protested that the portrayals of the school and the hiring controversy were unfair, particularly in saying the school was using race or beholden to denizens of political correctness.[48] In these letters, the dean insisted that the law school only considered Hylton's scholarship, not her race, when evaluating her case. I agree with legal scholar Leonard Baynes's assertion that the dean's claim was somewhat disingenuous.

> Dean Bennett acknowledged that Northwestern was an affirmative action employer but denied that . . . race had anything to do with the steps they would take to retain [Keith Hylton] . . . or hire his wife. . . . Maria O'Brien Hylton's race and gender may not have been the pivotal factor in Northwestern's decision, but given the discussions about race and gender concerning her candidacy, these had to be major factors in her being considered for the position in the first place.[49]

Considering Baynes's critique, it may have been more productive for the law school to iterate its position on how and when race is used in hiring as part of its defense. Instead, the denial of race's role in faculty hiring—

particularly in this case—reinforced the position articulated in the third theme that emerged in the press: higher education has been hijacked by the "special interests" on the Left, who have abandoned merit in favor of identity politics. Without a clear explanation of how academic excellence and minority faculty retention are not mutually exclusive goals, the school's defenders left unanswered the charges that the "P.C. police" have taken over the campus, and that the law school's administrators were in league with those who found Maria Hylton's racial credentials lacking.

As columnist Byrne put it, "The School's majordomos who make these appointments wouldn't go into detail, but it wouldn't be a wild guess to suppose she didn't get the job because of the opposition of some faculty members and some black, Latino, and female organizations."[50] These admonitions, alongside the list of her career highlights—six of the eleven articles noted her Ivy League education, prestigious clerkships, and already tenured position at DePaul—made the rejection of her case even more perplexing for these writers. The contrast of her academic excellence with the so-called racist antics of her critics made their argument—that she was done in by identity politics—seem logical.

This logic rests on the assumption that issues of racial identity and identification have no place in academia, whereas many other scholars would argue that the legacy of segregated education makes this issue central to questions of fairness at institutions of higher learning.[51] As the University of Michigan Law School successfully argued to the Supreme Court in *Grutter v. Bollinger*, racial and ethnic diversity in law schools is crucial to preparing legal professionals, who will interact with clients and colleagues of different identity groups. By extension, a diverse faculty enhances the goal of training a diverse student body, particularly in professional schools where mentoring and networking are crucial to future success. Comparing his time in law school—when he was the only Black student in his cohort—and the composition of law schools now, Judge Harry Edwards remarked on the importance of mentoring, and the continuing likelihood that Black students will need Black mentors to help guide their progress:

> Nowadays, perhaps as a result of having available some African-American role models, it is not uncommon for Black students to seek out only African-Americans for guidance. Likewise, it is not uncommon for many persons who are not African-American to assume that the sole responsibility for mentoring young African-Americans rests with senior members of their race.[52]

Edwards then cited educational research that has found that racial misperceptions hinder both White faculty's and Black students' ability to engage in cross-racial mentoring opportunities. His discussion raises the important point that, until there are more general improvements in race relations, the presence of faculty of color will be crucial for mentoring opportunities. Additionally, Edwards notes that at schools with diverse faculty, students can observe people of different ethnic and racial backgrounds engaging in "dialogue based on mutual respect," a powerful demonstration of their future need to interact with and assert themselves on an equal plane with other lawyers, clients, and the like.

Despite the rhetorical gestures toward the need for honest talk about diversity and hiring at the law school, when discussing these issues the press did not go beyond blaming the immediate members of the hiring committee for falling into a P.C. trap. The *Chicago Tribune* editorialized that the law school's hiring committee was most at fault for the tempest over Hylton's background.

> [B]y not distancing itself from Hughes' memo and the racism in the student groups' motives, the committee—and the institution it represents—invites the assumption that it supports such foolish, shabby behavior.[53]

Other articles reported secondhand statements that the Hyltons were informed by certain members of the hiring committee that they were ready to recommend a tenured position to Maria, but the pressure from the students and certain faculty killed the case.[54] Many writers shamed the school's administrators for hiding behind the confidentiality of hiring records and not admitting that her tenure case went out of control in part due to student protests. The bottom line for editorialists and commentators was that Northwestern's failure to quash the excesses of "political correctness" cost the law school two talented professors to Boston University, as related in these quotes:

> Northwestern Law School is the loser—and it has lost more than a valued professor.[55]

> Come September, BU's law school will be ahead with three black tenured faculty members, while Northwestern has one. Both have more work to do.[56]

These quotes imply that recruiting and retaining Black faculty are important goals. However, readers were never provided with any compelling reasons for the retention of Black faculty. And, although most of the articles did not contain explicit support for affirmative action measures to ensure the presence of faculty of color, a few put forth the argument that controversies like the Hylton case could have a "chilling effect" on future hiring decisions. In effect, these remarks blamed the historical victims of racial exclusion for perpetuating their own scarcity at institutions of higher learning. Indeed, writers went so far as to claim that this one case was symbolic of an epidemic in Black-on-Black academic racism that would lead to a decrease in Black hires.

> The question of who is black now plagues the implementation of policies of affirmative action. . . . This past fall, the debate over who is, and who is not, an African American reached new heights of sophistry at Northwestern University School of Law.[57]

> For the Hyltons, this story has a happy ending. . . . [A]s tenured professors they'll be immune from attacks from other Joyce Hugheses about whether they are black enough or hold progressive enough views. Others at Northwestern and elsewhere may not be so lucky.[58]

In the end, not only were Hylton's "P.C." opponents deemed guilty of using suspect racial reasoning to oppose her tenure, but commentators accused them of shooting themselves in the foot by damaging the chances of future Black candidates. Placing the blame for a paucity of Black faculty on people of color echoes other narratives that became popular in the '90s, such as the hypothesis that Black youth reject good study habits and grades as "acting White." According to many mainstream commentators, in the realm of education, Black people don't know when to stop thinking about race, which limits their ability to harvest of the fruits of opportunities such as school desegregation or affirmative action. No mention was made, however, of the successful lawsuits and government actions taken to reduce or eliminate affirmative action throughout the 1990s. Decisions such as *Hopwood v. University of Texas*, and California's ballot initiative to eliminate affirmative action at the state's colleges and universities were greater threats to diversity in higher education than this particular case. Instead, Blacks and their White liberal allies were singled out as the cause of the race problem in academia. So even though the critics were in the awkward position of defending campus diversity at the same time they were trashing the people who created diversity on the Northwestern campus—students and faculty of color—they managed to get their main message across: racial identity should be left out of debates over hiring.

Omissions in the Press Coverage of the Controversy

One major omission in coverage of the Hylton case was a function of the reporters' own one-drop rule–influenced frames. After spending many lines of text ridiculing and criticizing the Hughes memo for its troubling definition of Blackness, none of the commentators seriously considered Maria O'Brien Hylton's Cuban heritage. The Hispanic Law Students' estimation that she considered herself "more black than Hispanic" was allowed to stand without asking what criteria they had used to judge Hughes. What makes someone less Hispanic than Black if her mother is from Cuba? Her black skin, or her affiliation with Black organizations, apparently, disqualified her. It seems that both in the Hughes memo and the Latino students' claims, that Black and Latino are incongruent identities. In the Hughes memo, familial roots in the United States limits the definition of who is Black in the United States; for the Latinos (albeit the press presented little commentary on this matter), if one declares Black identity, it creates a distance from Latino-ness. Both of these racial definitions are suspect, but the Hispanic opponents of Hylton were not put under the microscope. Although the Hispanic law students were included in the laundry list of liberal groups opposed to hiring Maria Hylton, beyond that there was no discussion of what it means to be Hispanic or speculation that their identification of Hylton reflected intra-Hispanic tensions, racism, or colorism. As in the Malone case, the press missed an opportunity for debate about how society envisions Hispanic ethnicity. Blackness trumped national origins, reproducing a variation of the one-drop rule lambasted by so many commentators, and reinforcing the prevailing notion that Black is primarily a U.S.-based racial identity.

A second omission in the coverage was that of the concerns many students and faculty of color have about faculty hiring, retention, and student mentoring. While it is certainly clear that Hylton's main opponents did use questionable criteria for racial identity to argue against her job candidacy, this does not negate other legitimate issues lost in the reporting. For example, only one article presented direct quotes from a member of the Black Law Students Association, who articulated specific reasons why they felt Hylton's candidacy was troubling unrelated to her parentage.

> For the African American students, the issue was not just her racial identification, said Sean T. Carter, president of the 50-member Black Law Students Association. They wanted someone who would teach in specialties different than those of the rest of the faculty. . . . "[O]ur emphasis is still that we need diversity on the faculty. There's a lot more to this than black people support-

ing each other because our skins match. The obvious reason to support someone is qualification, someone who has something to offer in terms of intellectual diversity as well."[59]

Interestingly, the *Boston Globe* editorial excerpted earlier stated that a debate on the breadth of intellectual diversity would have been welcome, but that such a debate was hijacked by race talk. The *Globe's* lament over the lost opportunity to talk about diversity of ideas in academia has to be taken with a grain of salt. One has to wonder why the editors didn't suggest that the reporting or opinion staff pursue this angle of the story. After all, the fault lies not only with the Hughes memo or organizations of minority law students; the press inserted themselves into the debate, and focused almost exclusively on the definition of Blackness. The law students and other faculty, it seems, may have had much more to say about intellectual diversity, given the lone quote that appeared in the newspapers regarding their discomfort with Hylton's work.

Beyond the press's inability to draw its attention away from the train wreck of racial definition presented by Hughes's memo, however, is the overriding sensibility that one can, somehow, separate a person's racial or gender identity from their thoughts and ideas. But for many of Hylton's opponents and other scholars, the questions of intellectual freedom and diversity cannot be so easily separated from the question of racial identification and one's relationship to Black collectives. Pretending that all law professors are chosen on the basis of their work, nothing more, is based on the colorblind thesis. The idea that these professors can be evaluated without attention to their raced, gendered, classed, and sexed identities is part and parcel of the ideology of objectivity that supports the hegemony of White, middle-class, heteronormativity.

Overlapping with the concern for intellectual diversity, some students and faculty were concerned that an unofficial quota for faculty of color would be used against future hires that may have brought different perspectives on the law. At a law school where only a single Black person had achieved tenure, one has to ask, how likely was it that additional Black faculty would be hired? Would a "soft quota" slow down recruitment of other talented professors of color? Given her ideological orientation, would she entertain students' concerns about racism in the sphere of law? Would she teach any courses to fill holes in the curriculum? Of course, the law school vehemently states that it does not use quotas for faculty or students; however, in practice, many Black faculty members have observed, "there is often an informal upper limit on the number of faculty of color a school is willing to hire. The upper limit is not necessarily fixed, but the need or desire to hire an additional faculty member of color declines in proportion to the number of faculty of color that the law school employs."[60]

The law students' desire to have faculty who understand their views and will be supportive mentors is also an important issue. While some commentators found this expectation unfair or ridiculous, legal scholar Leonard Baynes and others point out that faculty of color "often have 'unoffical' additional burdens placed on them, such as mentoring students of color and junior faculty of color, serving as the representative voice of people of color on various committees, and interacting with the larger community of color."[61] I bring these issues to the fore not to justify either the use of racial definitions such as Hughes's memo presented or the conduct of Hylton's opponents; rather, I seek to emphasize that other legitimate avenues of debate were not included in news reports and editorial commentary on the case.

In contrast to her conservative supporters in the opinion pages, the Black, female, and Latino law student critics of Maria Hylton's work considered her ideology and biography together. Their concern that she, like her husband, was a conservative legal thinker goes beyond just the assessment of her work to what she symbolizes as the Black, female author of legal scholarship that argues against policies and programs developed to assist women and African Americans. The power of the symbol of an African American and/or female conservative is well understood in the wake of Clarence Thomas, Ward Connerly, and Condoleezza Rice. The Black conservative can be used as the example that breaks (or proves) the rules about race. The identity politics driving this logic assumes that since a Black person advocates anti–affirmative action views, their opinions are more valuable because they show approval of a member of a subordinate group; they "prove" that women/blacks/Others can make it using the rules of dominant culture. As Angela Dillard argues in her work on "multicultural conservatives," these media stars argue that they speak as Americans, as individuals, "but it is as African Americans, Latinos, and Asian Americans that they have been courted and promoted by the Right. In merely exchanging one form of identity politics for another (another with its own orthodoxy and correct political line), the painful contradiction is almost palpable."[62] Their presence and success are used to argue that racial policy is out of date and unnecessary. They are showcased by conservative groups as independent thinkers who have consulted hard evidence, not personal interest or group loyalties, to see through race to colorblindness.

Through well-funded think tanks and easy access to media practitioners conservatives have been able to simultaneously make the argument that liberals have taken over the media and academia, while at the same time their own stable of pundits and scholars dominate mainstream media debates over education and culture.[63] As these spokespersons decry the lowering of standards in the multicultural curriculum, many of their scholars' reports are rarely subjected to peer review or other rigorous evaluation prior to publication because their foundations and think tanks do not require them to undergo such review; rather, the credentials offered by these institutes and foundations are substituted for those obtained in the academic system. Thus, the attack on diversity and "P.C." in the name of high academic standards is led by those who do not have to subject themselves to academic scrutiny, but who have unprecedented access to mass media networks ready to disseminate their ideas to the general public.[64]

Breaking Down The Race Card?
Mixing up Identity Politics, Right and Left

The press latched onto Maria O'Brien Hylton's story and populated it with readily available and recognizable figures: the maligned Black conservative, rabid "P.C." activists, and wishy-washy White liberals afraid to take a stand against minorities. Granted, the content of the Hughes memo and a climate suffused with images and narratives of Black infighting and confusion made this framing more likely. But this story became newsworthy, as did the Phipps and Malone cases, in part and importantly because of a breakdown in racial identification schemes. Indeed, if Maria Hylton had been from an all-White family, I doubt the resistance to her hire would have garnered as much attention from major newspapers. Perhaps if she were "Black in a U.S. context," to use Hughes's memo as a guide, there would have been some commentary similar to that filed during the Thomas hearings or the defenses of Ward Connerly during the Proposition 209 debates in California. But Hylton's biracial identity and the existence of the Hughes memo and its formula for Blackness gave the story legs, allowing (mostly) White commentators to accuse Blacks of using a perverted racial logic. African Americans fighting over who is Black enough was a perfect vehicle for arguing that identity politics have gone too far, and that Blacks are irrational about race, even to the point of damaging "their own." This rhetorical strategy allows White and neoconservative debaters to shift attention away from institutional racism and continued racial inequalities and focus instead on the alleged pathologies of Black culture or hypocrisies of Black civil rights activists.[65]

Beyond the continued attack on civil rights groups' insistence that race still matters in society, the press did not take up the issues mentioned in Sege's article: what does Black—or any other racial identity, for that matter—mean in a society changed by growing interracial marriage rates and shifting immigration patterns? Other than the brief mention in Sege's column, no one made a link between the controversy over Hylton and the ever-changing terrain of Blackness in America. People of African descent from all over the globe reside in the United States, transplanting very different ideas of racial, national, and ethnic identity with them. For someone of Afro-Cuban descent, this could involve a much different configuration of race, color, class, and nationality than someone who is descended from generations of African Americans. If the press had chosen to talk about the nexus of race and ethnicity suggested by *Afro-Cuban* (and, for that matter, *White Australian*), then they would have had to address the Hispanic students' determination that Hughes was Black, not Latino. Exploring how color, class, and nationality are articulated in Latin American nations would have expanded the conversation about what "Black" means—or will mean—in a U.S. context that is transforming constantly and may have shed more nuanced light on both the African American and Hispanic American law students' issues with Hylton's candidacy.

I am not suggesting here that Hylton's supporters or opponents should have endeavored to create some sort of scale of racial hierarchy or belonging based on skin color or national origin. Such a system would be akin to that evident in countries like Brazil, where a de facto system of color recognition mediates social status with whiter-looking people at the top and Blacks at the bottom. But even those who think they are light-skinned can find their relative skin privilege taken away at any moment.[66] For example, Michael Hanchard relates the story of Ana Flávia Peçanha de Azeredo, the light-skinned daughter of a prominent Brazilian politician, in his essay "Black Cinderella."[67] As she attempted to visit a friend, two Whit(er) Brazilians assaulted Ana Flávia for using the residents' elevator in their apartment building because they believed she was an insolent, Black servant refusing to use the service elevator.[68] Though she is certainly more privileged compared to the darkest Afro-Brazilian, Ana Flávia was still identified as darker, and therefore, lower, than the "Whites" who assaulted her. Belying the state's official narrative of a multiracially aware and tolerant nation,

> The seemingly arbitrary manner in which Ana Flávia the mulatta could become Ana Flávia the negra affirms the greater importance of the interpretive, as opposed to the phenotypical, criterion of racial difference. . . . Once identified as the enemy, the actual ideological or racial position of the signified had secondary importance.[69]

My link between Ana Flávia and Maria Hylton may seem odd since Brazil and the United States have very different racial systems. However,

I bring in the example for exactly that reason: in Brazil, the state's recognition (even celebration) of a mestizo population has not eliminated racist acts or thinking, even as it simultaneously allows for more subtle, malleable social relations along the racial spectrum. Hylton, like Ana Flávia, comes from a mixed race family, part of which has roots in Cuba—another Latin American country where skin color gradations matter. I propose that we consider both women's cases in tandem to open up the question of multiracial identity in a global, diasporic context rather than the limiting "U.S. context" invoked by Professor Hughes in her infamous memo. Columnist Sege only gave lip service to this complexity of race, class, and globalism when she mentioned the effects of interracial marriage and increasing immigration from the Southern Hemisphere. Her suggestion begs for a more thorough investigation to help us understand the Hylton case in terms of race, class, nationality, and gender. Journalists who covered Hylton's case never questioned what it means to be Black *and* Latina, as Hylton arguably is, in a "U.S. context."

While the press attacked the Hughes memo and the law students' protests, they did not distance themselves from the same reductive racial logic and only debated whether Hughes was "Black enough" and whether that question was valid. They never unpacked the implicit assumption in the debate, that one's skin color was (or was not) sufficient evidence of Blackness. Another option would have been to challenge Hughes's premise that the "U.S. context" was the most relevant one to judge a person's racial identity; indeed, I would argue that a broader, diasporic sense of Blackness would be more useful for describing Hylton and evaluating what her contribution might be to the university and to law students. Moreover, journalists should have been asking whether Hughes's vision of the "U.S. context" was still valid given the ongoing changes to the composition of Black communities in the United States. Finally, by projecting blame for racism and colorism onto Black law students and faculty, journalists revived a recurrent theme of White racial discourse. Centering discussions of racism on infighting between people of color displaces the role of Whites in creating and maintaining racial hierarchy. Locating the "race problem" within a Black public sphere or alleged liberal enclaves, such as universities, opponents of race-based policies can safely pronounce themselves colorblind and above racism while chastising Blacks for hypocrisy.

Related to this discussion of the question of what "Black" looks like as the demography of the U.S. changes, is how public policymakers should react to the new racial landscape. The Hylton case and the Malone case raise questions that are specific to multiracial identity. First, should people of multiracial descent be considered minorities for purposes of affirmative action? Beyond that single policy, should civil rights law protect multiracial individuals in the same manner as monoracial minorities? If so, then should a person such as Hylton be able to file lawsuits against whites who find them too dark as well as Blacks and Latinos who find them lacking in color or community relations? Although one could argue that Maria Hylton might have been able to file an antidiscrimination lawsuit against Northwestern, she did not. However, would she have had a leg to stand on if she had gone to court? In the past when suits have been filed alleging discrimination based on skin color differences, judges have dismissed them, failing to find any place in the law where intraracial discrimination or colorism can be punished.[70] Now that the government has decided to count people who list more than one race, it is possible to collect data and evaluate patterns of discrimination, although it may take a generation or two to build a significant set of data to find those patterns if they exist. Furthermore, work already done on multiracial populations reveals that many people of mixed heritage do receive some benefits from lighter skin color, but not all.[71]

Who's a Descendant?

At the 2004 reunion of Harvard University's Black alumni, a panel of scholars, including Lani Guinier and Henry Louis Gates Jr., discussed the finding that a great number of current Black students at Harvard came from either immigrant families or multiracial families. Similarly, researchers at Princeton reported that at twenty-eight elite universities surveyed, 41 percent of African American students identified themselves as part of immigrant families or as multiracial.[72] Some observers are alarmed at these numbers, and have argued that universities are ignoring the population of U.S.-born Blacks and have abandoned what they say is the real goal of affirmative action: to convey opportunities to those directly descended from slaves in the United States. In their reasoning, these are the Blacks who most deserve and need the remedies for racism and oppression affirmative action and higher education are supposed to help deliver. Indeed, at Harvard, some nonimmigrant, monoracial Black students have taken to calling themselves "the descendants" in order to differentiate themselves from Black immigrants and multiracial Blacks on campus and to call attention to the issue.[73] One problem with this formulation is that the students' definition of descendants from slavery seems to ignore the fact that many immigrants from the West Indies and other parts of the African diaspora *are* descended from former slaves. While one might argue that the specific experiences of slaves in the United States differ and deserve priority, like the Hughes memo, the tendency to center definitions of Blackness and community around U.S. experiences is troubling and, perhaps, counterproductive in the face of new forms of racism. Indeed, police abuse of Abner Louima and killing of Amadou Diallo suggest strongly that immigrant status is no protection from racial reasoning or profiling.

At present, no one has put forth a plan to identify "descendants" to allocate affirmative action benefits or determine eligibility for such programs.[74] To some, the entire issue may seem frivolous, particularly at a time when all affirmative action programs are under siege. Furthermore, as the Phipps and Malone cases illustrate, determining who is a "real" descendant is a tricky task. Drawing distinctions using the most common tools to identify ancestry—genealogy, genetics, and government documents—would be a difficult, time-consuming enterprise for any institutions and certainly frustrating and, perhaps, insulting for individuals and families working to gather such credentials. However, determining who is "really" Black, by interrogating ancestry, political opinions, comparing experiences of discrimination and reactions to racism, or assessing "what kind of Black" a candidate for a coveted position is, has not been such a rare occurrence in recent years. Indeed, such vetting may become more prevalent as the multiracial population increases and immigration patterns fluctuate. If the views of those who believe descendants deserve and need more aid did prevail, then there would have to be some system of differentiation. What criteria, documents, or other proof would be necessary?

As the Malone case demonstrates, self-report might not be the best method of determining who is a descendant; Susie Phipps's case also cautions that state records may not be trustworthy either, particularly those created prior to the 1970s. It also seems clear that the "three-prong" test used by Massachusetts could penalize people who are lighter skinned than the norm, but those armed with good genealogical evidence might be able to claim descendant status. But the Harvard discussion suggests that this same test could also be used to argue against the eligibility of someone whom most people would recognize visibly as black. The community element of the test is perhaps the most slippery part of it, and is used often in extralegal discussions of who is Black.

But this line of thought, I would argue, takes energy away from the question posed by sociologists, political scientists, psychologists, and other researchers: Why is racial stratification still so prevalent in our society? In order to deal with this question, we must turn away from the individual as the main site of racial identity and remember to look at group-level data and effects. To answer the question, "Why is the Black/White divide so deeply ingrained in our culture?" we need to go beyond personal identifications and look to social, structural, and historical phenomena. From this perspective, we have to ask ourselves whether or not the idea of a "bottom line" racial identity is necessary to ensure the enforcement of antidiscrimination law. No evidence was brought to bear against Maria Hylton that she *hadn't* shared experiences of discrimination. Indeed, accounts of her family and work life emphasized her involvement with Black organizations and personal experiences with racism. So whoever gets to define "bottom line Blackness"—whether it be the state, vocal members of marginalized groups, or the controversial person herself—we can see that it doesn't matter what "percentage" of "Black blood" a person has or what amount of community affinity they have. How an institution, powerful individuals, or groups decide what racial category you belong in is just as much a function of the descriptor's goals as it is a function of the person's skin color, ancestry, or other characteristics.

In recognizing that race, to a large extent, is in the eye of the beholder and his or her rules, though, I am not making an argument for color blindness. Rather, my goal is to recognize the double-edged sword of racial identity in the public sphere. We must be "color-aware," as Ronald Turner writes, in order to make amends and improve the racial climate of our society. But we may never create a set of a hard and fast rules that eliminates the discrepancy between the bureaucratic necessity of compartmentalizing race into a system and the lived realities of racial complexity. So perhaps we have to follow Elizabeth Alexander and recognize that a "bottom line blackness" operates for people of some/any African descent when interacting with others. That is, people who are identified as Black (or Black enough) by the dominant racial group are subject to exclusion and violence.[75] Though lighter-skinned or multiracial people may garner some benefits from colorism, Alexander's argument and Hanchard's example of Ana Flávia suggest that we should recognize that all people with some modicum of African ancestry have a greater likelihood than people with none to experience various forms of racism. What response they have, and how they think of themselves in relation to members of their own and other groups is largely up to them. But the possibility of it happening, as Ana Flávia's case shows, once the knowledge is public (or assumed) that someone has "a bit of the other" in them, everything can change.[76] This is what scared Susie Phipps into hiding the "truth" of her birth certificate from her husband for nearly a year, and convinced her siblings to abandon her lawsuit as it made its way to the Supreme Court. It is the public perception and employment of racial knowledge that triggers discrimination. Whether from dominant or minority groups, outsiders' evaluations of skin tone, language, or country of origin create identifications that spur particular actions. Whether state or social recognition of multiracial individuals as separate from "other" Blacks will challenge those identifications or prompt questioning of dominant racial paradigms at a broad level remains to be seen.

Chapter Five

Counting Race, Counting Controversy

Multiracial Identity and the 2000 Census in Asian American, Black American, and Dominant Periodicals

If you have ever used a pressing comb, CHECK BLACK

If you are a white woman and only date Black men, CHECK BLACK

If your skin has ever been ashy and you know what that term means, CHECK BLACK . . .

—Anonymous e-mail circulated on a Black listserv,
March 26, 2000

The first three cases analyzed in this book focused on media reactions to *individuals* who were accused of or perceived to be manipulating the color line and/or institutional uses of race in policy. The cases of Susie Phipps, the Malone brothers, and Maria Hylton, while on their face exceptional and quirky, were contextualized in terms of broader social issues affecting more readily identified citizens of color. This chapter and the next, on the other hand, focus on the decision of government officials to change the 2000 Census' system of recording the race and ethnicity of all citizens. Thus, the coverage of the Census racial controversy begins on a broader sociopolitical plane, but as with the previous case studies, the personal motives, needs, and rights of multiracial individuals were at issue as different parties debated the potential effects of any alteration to the way the U.S. government counts race.

The decennial Census has been the object of racial controversy in the last three decades, due in large part to the suspected undercounting of minority groups.[1] In the years leading up to the 2000 Census, a new

Table 5.1. Changes to Race and Ethnicity Categories on the U.S. Census, 1790–2000

YEAR	Categories included	Categories eliminated
1790	Free White male/female, Non-taxed Indian, Slaves (3/5 of a person)	
1870	White, Black, mulatto, quadroon, octroon, Indian	Non-taxed Indian, slaves, free White
1890	White, Black, mulatto, quadroon, octroon, Indian, Japanese, Chinese	
1900	Black, White, Japanese, Chinese, Indian	Mulatto, quadroon, octroon
1910	Black, White, Japanese, Chinese, Indian, mulatto	
1930	White, Black, Japanese, Chinese, Indian, Hindu, Korean, Mexican	Mulatto
1940	White, Black, Japanese, Chinese, Indian, Hindu, Korean	Mexican
1950	White, Black, Japanese, Chinese, American Indian	Hindu, Korean
1960	White, Black, Japanese, Chinese, American Indian, Hawaiian, part-Hawaiian, Aleut, Eskimo	
1980	White, Black or African American, American Indian and Alaska Native, Asian, Native Hawaiian and Other Pacific Islander.	
2000	"check-all that apply" system implemented	

dimension was added to this ongoing concern: the prospect of counting multiracial people separately from conventional monoracial groups. In the mid-1990s, the Office of Management and Budget (OMB) announced that it would consider changing how it collects race and ethnicity data on the 2000 Census. First and most controversially, the OMB considered the demands of peoples of biracial and multiracial heritage to describe themselves as more than one race or just multiracial. Second, the OMB proposed changing the list of racial groups offered as choices for respondents, such as separating Native Hawaiian from Asians and Pacific Islanders. At first glance, one might argue these potential changes were controversial due to the potential statistical complications they presented for social scientists and government agencies. For example, many people asked, How could comparisons of racial and ethnic groups across time be consistent or valid if the categories changed drastically? Beyond the numbers, the altered system—for the first time since the "mulatto" category was eliminated in the first decades of the twentieth century—would acknowledge interracial mixing. Additionally, the multiplication of the potential number of racial groups and subgroups counted by the Census Bureau raised questions of racial and ethnic minorities' power (actual or symbolic) as expressed in terms of population, potential voting blocs, and consumer groups. Thus, proposed changes to the racial categories on Census 2000 caused considerable alarm for many civil rights groups. Their concerns and the increased visibility of multiracial individuals and groups committed to a multiracial category on Census 2000 prompted discussions in the press about the way our government and society define race, and wider discussions about the meaning of race and ethnicity at the dawn of the twenty-first century.

During and after public hearings and input from various constituencies, including the creation of an advisory board composed of members of different racial and ethnic groups, academic disciplines, and civil rights organizations, the OMB tested different versions of the racial questionnaire, with and without a "stand-alone" multiracial category. In 1997, the OMB decided to implement the following changes to provide a multiracial option:

- Rather than add a single "multiracial" option, people would be allowed to check as many racial or ethnic categories as they wished.

- Those who chose White plus one other race would be counted as their non-White race for purposes of civil rights compliance.

- When particular multiracial combinations reach 2 percent of the population, this combination must be officially listed and reported in demographic data.

The "check-all-that-apply" option was heralded as a victory by many civil rights groups, who believed that this compromise would minimize any population losses. Even still, many publicly advocated that multiracial individuals choose a single racial identifier to maintain population counts and promote racial solidarity. For some multiracial activists, the lack of a stand-alone identifier was seen as a loss; others felt the check-all system was an important first step toward a new conversation about race and a way to prevent ill will between multiracial-identified and monoracial individuals.

Paul Peterson argues that "whether or not to classify by race is a political, not a moral or ethical, question. Put more exactly, the politically correct answer in a pluralist democracy is also likely to be ethically correct."[2] Although politics is certainly central to the issue of how the government names and recognizes racial groups, the discourses surrounding the 2000 Census controversy demonstrate how, as Craig Calhoun writes, the politics of racial identity exist at the intersection of the personal and the political.[3] The decision made by the Office of Management and Budget (OMB) to be *politically* correct in this situation, however, did not satisfy all parties and, for some, was deemed less than ethical. The demands of multiracial organizations, families, and individuals who lobbied enthusiastically for the ability to count themselves as more than one race were pitted against the grave concerns of established racial groups that fought for centuries to overcome oppression and share power in the government, the marketplace, and the public sphere.

This dramatic fight over racial naming practices drew the attention of the press and many public commentators who sought to make sense of the battle over how the government classifies individuals and groups by race. As in the cases of Phipps and the Malones, where journalists created frames that went beyond the nuts and bolts of state-sponsored guidelines for determining race, the debate over the (re)introduction[4] of a multiracial category extended beyond any single racialized issue. The reports on the Census racial controversy included concerns about multiple areas of civil rights policy, political partisanship, group identity, and cultural memory. The result is that news coverage of this contested issue included many of the themes that surfaced in the reports on Phipps and the Malone brothers as well as a handful that were not part of their stories. The most significant additions were due to three factors: (1) the highly visible campaign of particular multiracial organizations to change the 2000 Census, which introduced alternative ways of naming multiracial identity; (2) the perceived danger of a multiracial category to the implementation of various civil–rights era policies; and (3) the fact that a demonstrably large number of people of many racial backgrounds, not just Black and White, would have the opportunity to officially and uniformly make a different choice of racial identity versus the seemingly unique or uncommon choices made by the subjects of the previous chapters.

News about Race and the 2000 Census

The news media are major conduits and shapers of public opinion, and thus news reporting on the Census controversy impacts public discussions about the new system and its potential effects on our society. This chapter presents a comparative analysis of African American, Asian American, and dominant periodicals' coverage of the controversy over the multiracial category.[5] The previous chapters demonstrated that even when journalists and commentators were confronted with multiracial people, they drew upon dominant racial frames and largely ignored the growing population and organized presence of multiracial activists. In the Census story, the goals and preferred identity markers of these previously absent groups were unavoidable; however, who multiracial people are and what their identity means in society is not dictated solely by their goals and desires. Although multiracial organizations and individuals have tried to foster alternative ways of seeing multiracial identity, stories about the Census controversy reflected and were influenced by the organizational practices of journalists, the history and tenor of race relations in the United States, and the assumed audience (White, Black, or Asian American) of each type of news media analyzed below. These factors set the stage for particular renderings of multiracial people, their allies and opponents. As in the previous chapters, the multiracial movement and multiracial individuals are portrayed in relation to a broad set of contemporary racial contexts and projects as well as significant elements from the racial past.

The major frames for multiracial people in the early twentieth century were the "tragic mulatto," the deceptive passer, and the marginal man. Certainly, these stark stereotypes did not dominate recent coverage of the Census controversy; however, the narratives of the past do create the platform for the present. In this chapter and the next, I demonstrate how various news media are responding to the new conceptualization of "multiracial Americans" and how far from the (not so) old visions of "marginal men" and "degenerate hybrids" they have come. Through quantitative and qualitative content analysis techniques, I explore how other racial issues and groups are articulated with multiracial identity. The revision of a racial discourse does not automatically result in progressive change; rather, there can be unexpected effects even when "positive" stereotypes or renderings of racial groups are created in the media. For example, many scholars argue that the "model minority" stereotype of Asian Americans serves to erase anti-Asian racism and important intragroup differences among Asian Americans. Thus, even if the news media are contributing to a new, "positive" way of seeing multiracial people, that novelty may not lead to improvements in other arenas of racial politics or racial discourses.

A major criticism of the mainstream press has been that it still portrays America in Black and White when demographic changes have created a racially diverse population.[6] One could argue that the OMB's experimentation with racial classification provided an opportunity for journalists to provide a portrait of a more nuanced, multifaceted racial landscape than in the past by mere virtue of the new racial statistics provided by the government. Given that some of the proposed changes were advocated by "new" racial/ethnic groups, such as members of various Pacific Islander and Middle Eastern groups, and given that all racial groups would be just as affected by a multiracial category—if not more so—than Blacks, it would be logical for coverage of the 2000 Census to depart from the traditional binary approach to race. This could have inspired mainstream journalists to construct new racial frames and challenge older frames. Therefore, one guiding question for this study was, "Did journalists utilize traditional black versus white frames regarding race or create new ones to explain the Census controversy and categories to readers?"

A second related question that guided this study was, "How do journalists contextualize the Census changes for readers?" When we look across regions and international borders, it is clear that the United States has peculiar systems for determining the race and ethnicity of its populace. For example, the demographics and history of race relations in the Southwest vary dramatically from those of the Northeast. Likewise, many nations in the Americas that experienced slavery and European conquest have vastly different practices for determining racial identities. Brazil, for example, projects itself as a "multiracial democracy" with a multihued citizenry that is arrayed on a matrix of different color labels. Yet serious social and economic disparities exist between lighter-skinned and darker-skinned Brazilians.[7] Many people in the United States may be unaware of these differences or assume that the U.S. racial system—or the system particular to their region of the United States—is universal. These assumptions would be challenged with the release of new Census data. Official recognition and counting of multiracial people and the addition of more specific Asian or Latino categories in the Census could expand local notions of race. By unearthing and comparing racial histories across regions and nations, journalists could provide readers with an opportunity for greater understanding of the issues and would inform the debate about the new categories and their potential effects on perceptions of race. Although the changes to the census categories were complex and promised to have ramifications for multiple racial groups, the mainstream press offered up stories that were mainly Black and White. Similarly, African American journalists focused on Black/White relations, but with a specific focus on history and discrimination. Asian American periodicals, however, dispatched to readers a different vision of the new multiracial category and the politics it engendered around Census 2000.[8]

Asian American Reports: Cultural and Historical Approaches to Being a "Model Minority"

Asian American journalists and commentators reported on activists' and scholars' predictions of policy outcomes and cultural effects the racial categories of Census 2000 might have on their communities (and assumed audience members). Given that the Black and Asian American presses are created for and/or by particular racial/ethnic audiences, it makes sense that they both tried to provide more culturally specific information and thus we should expect to see many differences between these publications and the dominant press. However, there were some discrepancies in coverage that at first glance did not make sense. Specifically, Asian American writers were more likely to talk about marriage, miscegenation, and the landmark case *Loving v. Virginia* than African Americans.

On the one hand, this is not surprising, since Asian Americans marry members of other racial groups (usually Whites) at a higher rate than Black Americans. On the other hand, the Lovings were a Black/White interracial couple and there are many more popular contemporary narratives in U.S. culture regarding Black/White romance and marriage. It would be reasonable to expect that in the midst of a rash of popular films and television shows depicting Black/White interracial relationships such as *Zebrahead, Jungle Fever, Jefferson in Paris, ER,* and documentaries like *An American Love Story,* Black newspapers would have plenty of reason to cite and discuss interracial marriage statistics and the like to engage their audience. This relative silence will be explored later in the chapter.

Another unique aspect of the Asian American coverage of Census 2000 was that Asian writers were more likely to discuss a broad history of race and ethnicity categories on the census. Asian American articles included information not only about the history of Asian categories on the census, but White and African American categories as well. One

Table 5.2. Racial Issues Prevalent in Articles, Pre-Census 2000

Themes	Asian American Press N=33	Black Press N=64	Dominant Press N=32
Antimiscegenation law	36% (12)	3% (2)	18% (6)
Creation/evolution of Asian categories	33% (11)	6.2% (4)	3% (1)
Creation/evolution of white racial category	15% (5)	1.5% (1)	3% (1)

writer noted that "[w]ith the exception of Native Americans, this nation was founded on distinctions between free white people and enslaved black ones."[9] Although Asian American writers acknowledged that the Black/White paradigm dominates discussions of race in the United States, they did not reify it. Rather, by reinserting the experiences of multiple racialized groups into the history of the Census categories, Asian American journalists challenged the dominant articulation of the history of race in our society.

> For the first time, Americans of mixed racial ancestry will not be forced to choose one heritage over another.... But even more important than this new expression of self-identity will be the nation's new group identity. No longer black or white, Americans will for the first time be more accurately counted for what we have become: a unique people made up largely of successive waves of immigrants from around the world . . .[10]

> The original race categories used by the government were "Negro," "Oriental," "American Indian," and "Spanish American." But it was not until the 1970s that race categorization was standardized to make it more consistent.[11]

> Asian Americans were first tabulated in federal census data as "Chinese" in 1860. A "Japanese" category emerged a decade later and Filipinos and others of Asian ancestry had no option but "other" until the Asian or Pacific Islander category was established—in 1970. Moreover, categories have changed many times over and often carried arbitrary meanings. For instance, Asian Indians were counted as "Hindus" in censuses from 1920 to 1940; then as "white" from 1950 to 1970 . . .[12]

One possible reason for this emphasis on the malleability and historicity of census categories is the fact that in living memory Asian categories have changed dramatically in the last fifty years, while official categories for Black and White people have been relatively stable over that same time period. Furthermore, the Asian category is one that can be clearly demonstrated to be an amalgamation of many ethnic and national groups. Unlike "Black" and "White," terms most obviously linked to skin pigmentation, it is perhaps easier to see how "Asian" is a heterogeneous category because of strong associations of earlier labels with immigration patterns, religions, and countries of origin. Journalists for Asian American publications emphasized and puzzled over the political utility of the blanket term *Asian* and for the groups represented by the term.

> After all, the Asian American movement itself today is a coalition formed around a census category and the belief of other Americans that all Asians look alike. As Asian Americans become more organized, we must acknowledge our differences. This society is diverse, but there are further levels of diversity multiplying within diversity itself.[13]

Note that the last quote refers to an Asian American "movement" and "coalition," not an "identity" or "Asianness." This difference is crucial because it expresses a very different way of thinking about what a racial or ethnic category means. That is, as a collection of peoples who are very different from each other but have overlapping concerns and some common experiences—including the experience of Whites using racial stereotypes to prevent their ancestors from immigrating, owning land, or attaining full citizenship. Wu's description of the Asian American movement resonates more with antiessentialist theorists' conceptions of racial and ethnic identity than the essentialist language used often in everyday talk and dominant news media discourse.

In addition to an examination of the use of "Asian" to describe a variety of peoples, Asian American writers the brought to light two concerns that matched those of Black writers. First, would multiracial Asians still count as "Asian"; and relatedly, would the proposal to count multiracial Asians, Hawaiians, and other Pacific Islanders separately harm Asian American political interests? While these questions weren't as central to or prevalent in Asian American articles as in Black stories (see Table 5.2), it was a significant issue for the following reasons, found in Asian American periodicals:

> If people who formerly identified themselves as Asian/Pacific Islander now choose instead to mark "multiracial," programs geared toward Asian Americans will lose valuable numbers, resulting in less money for the API agenda.[14]

> Asian American advocates are concerned about the "check all that apply" plan, and with good reason. They worry that if the many Asian Americans of mixed race are classified as multiracial, it will decrease our numbers and therefore our visibility, clout, and eligibility for programs.[15]

For Asian Americans, the proposed Census changes were salient on multiple fronts of identity politics, and engaging the history of the government's creation of ethnic and racial categories was crucial to understanding the contemporary issues. One could argue that Asian American concerns should have been more prominent in dominant newspapers, since they have the highest rates of interracial marriage. Furthermore, the government's pretest of the multiracial category predicted that that Asian Americans would be most affected numerically by any changes to the 1990 OMB guidelines. Including Asian voices would have brought more legitimacy to the claims of multicultural awareness many dominant news organizations profess, and would have humanized the statistics provided to readers.

Another major feature of Asian American accounts was the inclusion of discussions and critiques of how Asian Americans are seen by— or not seen by—Whites. Neither dominant nor African American periodicals commented on the invisibility of Asian Americans in U.S. racial discourse; in fact, they rarely mentioned Asian Americans at all. This pattern of omission illustrates Asian American writers' contention that Asians are often left out of the national portrait. In contrast to dominant media coverage that largely excluded Asian Americans from discussions of racial discrimination and public policy measures dependent on racial statistics, Asian American periodicals highlighted how Asian and Pacific Islander (API) organizations were deeply involved with the debate over the meaning of the new Census system.

> "We oppose the check more than one [rule]," said Karen Narasaki, executive director of the National Asian Pacifica American Legal Consortium, who added that the rule is likely to affect the Asian Pacific American community because of higher rates of marriage outside the group.[16]

Furthermore, many writers lamented how the dominant portrayal of Asians as "model minorities" is a double-edged sword, obscuring important differences among Asian ethnic and class groups, and marginalizing Asian Americans' concerns about discrimination and hate crimes. Writers took care to explicitly name and describe particular Asian subgroups to illustrate the wide range of Asian American experiences, many of which do not conform to the model minority stereotypes and assumptions. One author noted that although "Asian Americans, as a group, reaped benefits in 1998 . . . such gains were not shared by all. . . . Anti-Asian hate crimes are down nationwide—but up in Northern California. And our efforts to be represented in the 2000 Census are imperiled."[17] Voicing concerns about racist acts is not part of the model minority profile; model minorities are supposed to believe racism doesn't happen, let alone complain about racial tensions.

Other articles stressed economic and social diversity within the Asian American community.

Tamayo Lott says the Census provides an ever-changing portrait of America. . . ." We're a more diverse population. We're getting older. We don't just have the nuclear family. We have single-person households that are elderly people living by themselves." There are also households of people not related to one another "as well as female-headed households, which is rising in the Filipino community more so than other Asian groups."[18]

The census subgroups for Asians are Indians, Chinese, Japanese, Filipino, Vietnamese Cambodian. . . . There are Asian New Yorkers that are well to do, but many live in poverty. Some are among the city's best educated, and yet a startling number are illiterate. . . . The report reveals that while Asian American families and a majority of Indians are least likely to be on public assistance, less than half of those families who appear eligible actually receive public assistance. . . . Unfortunately, though many Asian Americans are suffering, for too long they have been depicted and perceived as a "model minority" group, and partly for this reason, their serious needs have gone largely unnoticed and ignored.[19]

Airing these important intra-Asian differences, journalists rejected the homogenizing impulse of the model minority stereotype, and refused to participate in the erasure of economically subordinate Asian ethnic groups.

A few Asian American writers also criticized how particular bi- or multiracial Asian Americans have been fetishized by the media and, similar to black commentators, speculated that the danger of a color hierarchy lurked behind this exoticization of multiracial Asians. Teresa Kay Williams titled her article for *Yolk* "Racial Seduction: America's Gaze on Hapa Men." She stated that

[w]hat is fascinating is how the visible representation of Hapa public figures as "sex symbols" illuminates how race, ethnicity, color, gender and sexuality interact with one another. For the "spectators," to whom the socially constructed attractiveness of Hapa men is marketed and presented, these images of male beauty evoke meanings about Asian masculinity and attractiveness.[20]

Williams went on to evaluate how different male Hapa celebrities—Keanu Reeves, Dean Cain, and Tiger Woods—have been portrayed in dominant media and which of them are distanced (either by their own doing or via marketing strategies) from the Asian part of their heritages. In contrast, one writer in the dominant media gushed about how a Hapa man such

as Tiger Woods is the perfect multicultural advertising tool: Woods can
be marketed to Asians, Blacks, and Whites.

> In the popular marketplace the timing [of Woods's declaration
> that he is Cablinasian] could not have been better. . . . Companies
> like Nike, Calvin Klein, and Benetton are working ethnicity as an
> idiom of commerce; it adds value to a pair of sneakers or a cotton
> T shirt. . . . At a time when young people are buying corporate
> conceptions of "alternative," ethnic ambiguity confers both indi-
> viduality and a sense of shared values. Tiger Woods, says [Rob-
> ert] Triefus [spokesman for Calvin Klein], "represents the most
> exciting facet of this matrix."[21]

I will return to the theme of celebrating multiracial identity as "market-
able" in the next two chapters. Suffice to say here that the dominant
reporter's uncritical view of Tiger Woods's global popularity is partly a
function of the desire of consumers to buy into diversity for personal
satisfaction rather than embracing multiracial identity as a vehicle for
interracial understanding and justice. Asian reporters did not comment as
much on colorism or reactions within Asian communities to people of
mixed race. A handful of articles noted stereotypes held about mixed-race
Asians. For example, in an article for *Yolk*, Su Moon reviews a new journal, *No Passing Zone*, and makes comparisons between White racism and
Asian American responses to mixed race Asians.

> The heritage of American racism is dishonorable and insane. It
> is one being equaled by the racism within Asian American com-
> munities. The insensitivity and rejection of mixed-race Asians,
> with exceptional fits of "claim us if we're famous syndrome" are
> exposed. H. Rika Houston identifies a hierarchy which ranks
> monoracial Asian Americans, Eurasians, and Afroasians in mean-
> ingless descending order.[22]

In an *AsianWeek* article covering Hapa groups on college campuses, many
students interviewed by journalist Stacy Lavilla voiced frustration with
Asian Americans' stereotypes about Hapas and unfair expectations:

> "We were collectively offended by what [another Asian Ameri-
> can] was saying, because the bottom line was that interracial
> marriages were bad . . . they were sweeping generalizations, that
> interracial marriages were between all Asian women and white

men," recalled Greg Mayada, a founding member of [Hapa Issues Forum]. "A bunch of us got to thinking, and we concluded that that line of thinking was ignorance," Mayeda said. "There was no voice for children of mixed-race marriages to counter assumptions that were being made."[23]

This angle was not as prevalent in the Asian American press as discussions of tensions between biracial and monoracial-identified people exhibited in the Black press. Reporters were mostly ambivalent or supportive about the choices made by multiracial Asians. Indeed, commentary about the nature or psychology of mixed-race people most often came from those of multiracial descent. The diverse set of concerns included in Asian American articles on Census 2000 revealed histories and a set of issues and concerns untouched by the dominant press and the African American press.

Dominant News Reports: Statistics and African American Experiences

Two main characteristics of dominant publications emerged in comparison to Asian- and African American–owned periodicals. First, dominant publications focused on traditional political issues—such as electoral power—more than their Asian and African American counterparts.[24] Second, dominant press accounts most often used Blacks, Whites, and people of Black and White multiracial families to illustrate the effects of the Census controversy on individuals and how people think about their own racial background.

Policies, Interracial Conflict, and Power

Mainstream papers were more likely to include statements concerning the issue of congressional redistricting and the possible dilution of minority groups' voting power. Although some analysts, such as Skerry, are not convinced that census data are crucial to the policies singled out most often by reporters, the idea that there might be a strong correlation between racial policies and census statistics was introduced in many stories.[25] This theme emphasizes racial conflict, which resonates with prior research that finds journalists frame racial issues in terms of conflict and strife more often than in terms of cooperation or comity.[26]

More than one-third of dominant articles mentioned that changes to the racial data would have an impact on voting, school districting, and other bread-and-butter policies, as reflected in the following quotes.

Table 5.3. Political Themes Prevalent in Articles, Pre-Census 2000

Themes	Asian American Press N=33	Black Press N=64	Dominant Press N=32
Electoral and other traditional political issues	15% (5)	28% (18)	37.5% (12)
Republicans will use new category against minorities	3% (1)	12% (8)	37.5% (12)
Quotes from Census, OMB officials	33% (11)	23% (15)	62.5% (20)

> Racial data from the census are used in drawing boundaries for schools and congressional, water, and legislative districts.[27]

> The decisions people make [about the Census], while personal, will echo through public policy. The Justice Department uses racial data from the census to analyze voting patterns and evaluate redistricting proposals under the Voting Rights Act.[28]

> Any change in the racial classification system would have a major impact on traditional civil rights organizations such as the NAACP. . . . Such groups have been major backers of policies that rely on population counts utilizing the current racial categories. These include school desegregation programs and legislative redistricting practices under the Voting Rights Act.[29]

The dominant articles were also more likely to discuss whether the Republican Party would gain an advantage if a multiracial category was implemented on the 2000 Census. This speculation was prompted by Newt Gingrich's vocal support of the stand-alone multiracial category. The party politics angle fit in with the first emphasis, the possible effects on congressional districts and overall voting power.

Multicultural Numbers, Black and White Portraits

The mainstream papers were more likely to use government sources for information and also provided more charts, graphs, and general demographic statistics than Asian American and Black American papers. Despite their presentation of numerical data about *all* racial groups and the possible demographic shifts the new race and ethnicity guidelines could produce, the multifaceted numbers did not lead them to present a multiracial or ethnic portrait of the people who would be most affected by the change. The OMB's pretests of different race and ethnicity question-naires predicted that Asian and Native Americans would experience the most change if a multiracial option were to be included.[30] But these sta-tistics did not translate into coverage of opinions in Asian or Native American communities. Rather, when journalists presented the personal stories to illustrate statistics and the potential social and cultural effects of the new census race/ethnicity plans, they featured people of African American descent. Often, this meant including negative opinions from African Americans, both mono- and multiracially identified.

> Ms. [Candy] Mills [editor of the magazines *Black Child* and *Inter-race*] is impatient with those who contend that a multiracial cat-egory is necessary. . . . "Many of these multiracial activists, both black and white, want to minimize their child's African heritage."[31]

> For Detroit teacher Donald Parker, whose mother is white and father is black, there were no options. Parker's parents married in Detroit during the Eisenhower administration, when only a hand-ful of states allowed interracial marriages. "I consider myself black because you didn't have a choice. That's what you've always been told," Parker said.[32]

These quotes are typical of the articles that included interviews with nongovernment sources. In addition, dominant papers and magazines almost exclusively printed op-ed pieces and essays written by leaders of Black organizations, Black or White academics involved in Afro/American Studies, or multiracial persons of Black and White heritage.[33] In addition, when pictures or illustrations were used, photos of Black/White couples, and biracial children of African and European American descent domi-nated those used to present people in the articles.[34] Thus, when journal-ists, essayists, and editors "personalized" the multiracial category, they suggested that (1) the majority of multiracial people are Black/White, and (2) Blacks are the group most concerned about or threatened by the use of multiracial categories.

When the press discussed specific government policies that could be affected by a multiracial option on Census 2000, Black organizations such as the NAACP were mentioned more often than Asian American, His-panic American, or Native American advocacy groups—and the latter rarely appeared. In many of these articles, quotes and examples empha-sized the experiences and concerns of people of African American ances-try even when reporters cited studies and statistics that Asian American and Native American population counts would be altered most by the inclusion of a multiracial option. For example, in a *Washington Post* article about the announcement of the OMB's decision to use the check-all-that-apply format, only the NAACP's reaction to the policy was included.[35] Similarly, another story about the decision opened with sentences, "Check the black box and be black for a day. That's what Patricia Williams, executive director of the San Diego Black Chamber of Commerce, is urging people of mixed ancestry to do when their Census 2000 forms arrive."[36] One *New York Times* article noted that, like Black groups who called on African Americans to only check the Black box to identify themselves on the 2000 Census, "The Asian American Legal Defense and Education Fund has made a similar request" that multiracial Asian Americans check Asian only on the 2000 Census.[37] However, the quotes used later in the piece were almost exclusively from African Americans. Furthermore, reasons for resistance to the multiracial option were described as follows:

> Dozens of federal programs—to assist minority businesses, to ensure that banks award mortgages to *Black* neighborhoods, to protect minority communities from environmental hazards—depend on racial data from the census.[38]

Black Americans were the only minority group linked to a specific racial policy; Asians and Native Americans were not singled out in this manner in any of the dominant articles analyzed. The presentation of "multicultural," yet impersonal, statistics followed by specific mentions of Black organizations and articulations of African American personalities and concerns obscured the lived experiences of other racialized ethnic groups. The overrepresentation of Black opinions and profiles of Black/White interracial people suggested that it was mostly African Americans who were wary and had the most to lose from a multiracial category on the Census. In addition, linking the effects of the change to policies associated with African Americans reinforced the misconception that only Blacks benefit from race-based public policy. As in the Malone and Hylton cases, the dominant press collapsed a potentially multiracial story into a biracial narrative. Similar to mainstream coverage of the Hylton case, the overrepresentation of Black opinions made it seem as if Black people were trying to deny bi- and multiracial people their individual rights. In dominant news stories, African Americans were framed as people pushing identity politics and taking a hypocritical position on racial self-determination.

African American Responses: Memories of Colorism, Fears of Losing Political Power

It is notable that, despite a smaller number of publications in circulation and fewer resources, the Black press published twice as many stories about the proposed Census 2000 changes than the dominant press. This comparison indicates the how important editors and writers believed this issue was for Black readers. This is understandable when one considers the concerns African Americans have about undercounts on the Census, as well as strong memories of government abuse of racial categories in public policy. The United States certainly does not have a good history of deploying racial categories for the benefit of people of color. For these reasons and more, it is not surprising that the overwhelming majority of articles appearing in Black newspapers and magazines framed the idea of a multiracial category and multiracial identity as a bad idea. Four arguments supported the negative frame:

- A multiracial category will dilute Black political power by decreasing the official count of the Black population.

- Multiracial people are seeking superior racial status via the multiracial category.

- White conservative politicians backed the idea of a multiracial category as part of their attack on civil rights legislation and programs such as affirmative action.

- Acknowledging multiracial people separate from Blacks will engender skin color hierarchies such as those found in apartheid South Africa, the Old South, or Brazil.

Reduction of Black Numbers Means a Weakening of Black Power

The first argument, that a change in Census categories would decrease Black population counts and political power, appeared in nearly every article in the African American periodicals (see Table 5.3). Many commentators predicted dire consequences if a change to the Census racial system resulted in a decrease in Black population statistics, as these quotes illustrate:

How many of us who classified ourselves as "Black" in 1990, will now switch to being "multiracial" in the year 2000? Who knows? If only 25 percent of this nation's Black population changes its

racial status, the Black population should drop by 6,750,000. That
is a significant decrease when allocating voter districts, and distributing health, welfare, and education allotment.[39]

If significant numbers of blacks begin checking the multiracial
box, it could trigger changes in census [*sic*] based formulas used
to distribute aid.[40]

The *Baltimore Afro-American* dramatized the fear that a multiracial category would dismantle Black power in the headline: "Census—the multiracial threat."[41] Even after the OMB issued the guidelines that a person
who checked a Black along with White would be categorized as Black, the
Los Angeles Sentinel's Larry Aubry still viewed the option to check more
than one race as a threat. "The growing diversity of California and the
nation's population could prove costly to African Americans, who will lose
funds and other resources because of dwindling numbers. It is especially
important that black Americans not inadvertently dilute their own strength
by multiracial/ethnic categories on Census 2000."[42]

Multiracial Identity Will Be a Vehicle to Whiter Status

Like the articles analyzed in the chapter on Susie Phipps, Black writers
were suspicious of the motives of multiracial people to pursue a different
category. At the top of their list was the concern that options to call
oneself "more than just Black" would reinforce or revive colorism. Many
commentators predicted that lighter-skinned Blacks would jump at the
opportunity to make racial choices that would make them feel superior to
other Blacks. Indeed, the Black press contained more negative opinions
about the motives of multiracial people than both dominant and Asian-
American articles.

While the dominant press also contained some of these criticisms,
they were expressed by interviewees or guest columnists. In the Black
press, masthead editorials, regular columnists, as well as interviewees in
general reporting stated their belief that individuals in the multiracial
movement were trying to foster colorism and gain status as a result. They
drew upon the history of passing and patterns of internalized racism to
explain their predictions.

This [new category] could be a setback and because of that, a lot
of people are reluctant to embrace it. It makes sense because if
someone marks multiracial on an application, that can set up a
system of discrimination against Blacks because multiracial means

Table 5.4. Colorism Issues Prevalent in Articles, Pre-Census 2000

Themes	Asian American Press N=33	Black Press N=64	Dominant Press N=32
Multiracial people want White status	6% (2)	42% (27)	25% (8)
Multiracial category will increase intraracial tensions	0% (0)	31% (20)	9% (3)
Creation of multiracial category will institute colorism	0% (0)	20% (13)	9% (3)

at least you have something else in you and, in many people's eye, that's better than Black.[43]

"I can see a whole host of light-skinned Black Americans running for the door the minute they have another choice."[44]

These opinions, as discussed in earlier chapters, are not founded on mere speculation. There are historical and contemporary examples of communities and families of light-skinned Blacks who enjoyed access to economic and social privileges denied darker Blacks, and some explicitly practiced discrimination against darker Blacks. There is a wealth of anecdotal evidence as well as emerging sociological studies that document how people of color with lighter skin are favored in the public sphere by Whites and some other people of color.[45] For example, lighter-skinned Black women are more likely to gain work as actresses or models, or be seen as more appealing candidates for dating and marriage because they are viewed as closer to dominant beauty standards.[46] This mix of experiences and history has created a formidable stereotype that lighter-skinned blacks look down on those who are darker, and that darker-skinned people desire lighter skin for themselves or their offspring (aka "the color complex"). For multiracial-identified Blacks, lighter skin and the expressed desire to be recognized as both Black and White can convince other Blacks that their identity choice is a function of internalized racism.

Multiracial People are Playing into the Hands of Conservatives

The third argument voiced in the Black press focused on fears that Republicans were duplicitously using the multiracial movement to advance a larger anti–civil rights political agenda (see Table 5.3). Unlike mentions of this in the dominant press, Black commentators were more likely to voice the belief that Blacks were being sold out for politics by Republicans and Democrats.

> Politics, rather than accurately reflecting the nation's history of racial mixing, dictated the OMB decision to allow people to check more than one race, according to Wilson. "It was a political decision," he said, "a compromise between [President Bill] Clinton and the Republicans in the Congress who were hoping to confuse things so that it will mask the slipping back of affirmative action programs."[47]

Likewise, the *Ebony* article, "Am I Black, White, or In between?" featured the following sentence under the main headline: "Is there a plot to create a 'colored' buffer race in America?"[48] And in the *Philadelphia Tribune*, a writer stated:

> The issue here is not whether groups advocating for families of mixed race have good intentions and real concerns about how they are identified. The concern here is whether these groups are unknowingly playing into the hands of those who are seeking a divide and conquer strategy against an African American population whose political power is already under attack in the courts.[49]

In the Black press, commentators portrayed multiracial people as politically naïve at best, and aiding and abetting the Republicans' attack on civil rights legislation at worst.

A Multiracial Category Will Foster a Color-Based Caste System

The Black press was nearly unique in comparing the proposed multiracial category to racial categories in other countries, such as South Africa (see Table 5.4). As one editorial declared: "We do not need another category of folks such as 'coloreds' (multiracials) in South Africa which shoved Blacks down another notch on the equity pole."[50] Commentators predicted that the light-dark hierarchy that existed more visibly in this country in prior eras in Southern states would reemerge if the government officially counted multiracial people.

> Mixed race or multiple racial check-offs will reinstate practices that were part of the pre–civil rights era in the Old South. Con-

cessions to "coloreds" were often made to the exclusion of their darker brothers. This system was designed to create dissension between Black "Blacks" and Blacks of mixed race. To this very day some African Americans talk about "good hair" and light skin as badges of honor.[51]

Notably, many Black publications featured quotes from famous multiracial Blacks who oppose the idea of a distinct multiracial identity and endorse the use of Black only to describe themselves.

Some biracial brothers and sisters might do well to heed advice from Lenny Kravitz. "You don't have to deny the white side of you if you're mixed," he says. "Accept the blessing of having the advantage of two cultures, but understand that you are Black. In this world, if you have one spot of Black blood, you are Black. So get over it."[52]

Asked about comments by [Tiger] Woods, the young golfing sensation who won the Masters Tournament, that he prefers not to be called black because he comes from a variety of racial backgrounds, Powell said: "In this country, which I love to the depth of my heart and soul, if you look like me you are still considered Black." Powell said that although he has white and Indian blood, "I'm a black American, African American, whatever rolls off your tongue most easily."[53]

These endorsements of a singular Black identity by popular figures worked to legitimize the opinion that multiracial Blacks should not pursue alternative modes of identification. Indeed, it mirrored the official and unofficial campaigns by many organizations for people of color to get people to check only one racial category. They also implied that other celebrities—particularly Tiger Woods—who do not identify solely as Black are doing a disservice to Black communities. By extension, other less-famous individuals of multiracial descent were also doing harm to Black collectives.

One Census, Three Approaches to Multiracial Identity

The comparison of these three sets of texts reveals limitations within and significant similarities and differences across different racial groups' print media discourses about racial policy and racial history in the United States. This comparison was not meant to produce a "winning" narrative strategy, but rather to highlight how the cultural assumptions and political goals of journalists, elites, politicians, and other sources of opinions and information used by media shaped the articles. The juxtaposition of the three types of periodicals provides a lens through which to see how far coverage deviated from usual norms of racial reporting, particularly for mainstream news.

Even in the face of an issue one could describe as the ultimate multiracial topic, creating new racial categories to fit a quickly changing demographic picture, dominant periodicals focused on the Black/White angle, emphasizing African American experiences of interracial marriage and organized opposition to a multiracial category. Asian, Native, and Latino-Americans were virtually absent from discussions of the 2000 Census, despite the fact that the Census Bureau's own statistical projections predicted that these populations would be most affected by the proposed changes to the ethnic and racial categories. Thus, the mere presence and significant numbers of a "new" population, multiracial people, and/or concrete policy changes that involve non-Black peoples is not necessarily enough to break the framing of race in dominant reporting.

Indeed, dominant reporting of the controversy reinscribed the links between "race," "minority," and Blackness. The almost exclusive focus on reactions from people of African American descent allowed dominant journalists to avoid confronting or even considering the question, "What does multiracial identity mean for Whites?" As recent Census data shows, 93 percent of those who did check more than one race on the 2000 Census checked "White" as one of their choices. Thus, another way media makers could have framed the issue was that not only would the category "Black" be affected, but White as well. As Shah and Thornton noted in their comparison of Latino, Black, and mainstream reports on racial issues, by ignoring Whites "and the impact of White privilege, the general circulation press . . . participates in the process of racial formation by linking culture and structure in specific ways [and] avoids discussion of certain structural issues such as power holding and how that effects local distribution of resources." This process erases the role of White-controlled institutions in the marginalization of ethnic minorities.[54] By emphasizing Black resistance to the multiracial identifier, the dominant press not only avoided discussion of Whiteness, but also displaced their own institutional power onto Blacks, who were portrayed as the barrier between multiracial people and their right to self-naming and inclusion in the American social body. None of the Black organizations or individuals held the power to exclude multiracial people from We the People; nor had they in the past been accomplices in drafting the antimiscegenation laws that legitimized exclusion of mixed-race people. But Black Americans were cast as the main opponents of multiracial people.

Writers and interviewees in African American periodicals also focused on Black/White interracial relations, but they did so in the context of a longer history. Concerns with the external pressures of white supremacy, internal color hierarchies, and the destructive effects of both on Black communities were central to these articles. This focus is understandable given ongoing backlash against civil rights legislation; the neoconservatives' embrace of the multiracial category was certainly cause for suspicion and alarm. It is clear, though, that the critique of the racial categories of Census 20000 extended well beyond Newt Gingrich's motivations. Harsh opinions about the goals of multiracial individuals and advocacy groups, who were portrayed as wanting to be White, or as naïve about the way racial politics really work in the United States, were included in many articles. Although this aspect is understandable given the painful history of colorism and passing, it is troubling that the work of multiracial advocates who reject these hierarchies was not included in the majority of articles.

The Asian American discourses around racial and ethnic labels of the 2000 Census presented the clearest challenge to dominant approaches to group identity. These articles explored the political necessities of labeling groups, and discussed the difficulties of achieving solidarity across cultural, class, and national lines. Indeed, the Asian American periodicals appeared to be the most "multiracial" in their considerations of Census 2000. Although they shared with the African American press fears of what the new labels could mean in terms of reducing/diluting Asian American numbers and political power, particularly in the context of how Asian Americans are marginalized in politics, these fears were matched with discussions of what the label *Asian* meant. The origins and validity of the term were deconstructed: writers portrayed the label *Asian* as a government-produced term that encompassed a range of ethnic, national, linguistic, class, and generation groups. This intragroup diversity was not celebrated uncritically; rather, commentators noted how the label *Asian* functioned differently for different Asian subgroups, rewarding some for their successes and erasing others who had not shared in the economic and social privileges allegedly enjoyed by "model minorities." Thus, the political utility of the label *Asian American* was debated and no sense of essential "Asianness"—outside of the complaint that White Americans assume Asians are all alike—was explicit or implicit in the articles. The model of group identity presented by Asian American writers resembled a patchwork quilt of coalitions—some links stronger than others, some groups more privileged than others. Although there was no consensus across the pieces as to how Asian Americans could use the heterogeneous model of identity to their clear advantage, the discussion of malleable, intersecting identities was refreshing and took the discourse in a direction more akin to what some critical race theorists see as a major contribution of multiracial identity to our understanding of race: divesting ourselves of the myth of static racial categories and participating in deeply historicized and contextualized discussions of the meaning of race.

Unfortunately, a multifaceted, multicolored approach to the racial identities on Census Bureau forms did not make it into the dominant press, the press that reaches the majority of Americans, particularly those Americans who normally associate only Blacks, not Asians or Latinos, with racial policy. The absence of Asian American and other non-Black minority voices in the dominant press allowed the Black/White paradigm to remain unchallenged, and subtly reinforced one aspect of the model minority stereotype: Asians and Hispanics don't make a fuss about racial issues like Blacks. The reality of the Census' implementation of the multiracial option necessitates further discussions and arguments about the multiple, liminal, shifting nature of racial and ethnic identities. The visibility of multiracial-identified people, with or without clear government policies for recognition, signals the need to develop different approaches to race in different contexts and to include a variety of groups' voices and experiences of race and ethnicity in the United States. The entrenched Black/White framing of racial issues in dominant discourses is hard to shake. In the following chapter, we will see how the Black/White paradigm continued to be salient, albeit among a host of other concerns and with a different and stronger neoconservative spin akin to that deployed in the Maria Hylton case. Yet again, several commentators blamed Black and other civil rights organizations for clinging to an outmoded definition of race in the United States that was dissonant with the documented emergence of "Generation M" in the 2000 Census numbers and statistical projections. Whereas in the coverage that preceded the implementation of the census the focus was on what problems a multiracial category might cause, the "hard data" gave confidence to those who were ready to declare race a long-gone problem.

Chapter Six

After the Census

The articles analyzed in this chapter were written after the 2000 Census, and the majority were published after the Census Bureau began to release the new race and ethnicity data to the public. Thus, one major difference between the articles analyzed here and in the prior chapter is that journalists, political actors, and commentators had "hard numbers" rather than speculation or predictions at their disposal to inform their discussion of multiracial identity. Beyond the numbers, the news discourses produced in the wake of the data release emerged in a different political context. The new Bush administration and Republican-dominated Congress, along with conservative pundits and other right-leaning newsmakers, gave little if any indication that they would support affirmative action or other race-conscious policy matters.[1] Indeed, the Bush White House signaled that dealing with racial inequality was not a priority with the appointment of noted conservative John Ashcroft to the post of Attorney General. Soon after, the administration filed a Supreme Court brief *against* the University of Michigan's affirmative action policies in the case *Grutter v. Bollinger*. In words and deeds, the new president revealed that he was in step with neoconservatives who espouse "colorblindness."

The second element that changed the setting for the post-Census media coverage was the attack on the United States on September 11, 2001. After September 11, discussions of immigration and multiculturalism were affected in ways unanticipated in the pre-Census years, when nationalism and terrorism were the backdrops for reports on the nation's diversity and identity. After the attacks, the questions of who is and what constitutes an American citizen were heightened in news discourses. Thus, the picture of the nation's diversity provided by the Census Bureau was a crucial snapshot of who we are, and deciding what the multiracial population meant in that context was subtly, but importantly, different than in the previous years of news coverage. How our society deals with or absorbs people of a broad range of ethnic, racial, and religious backgrounds has been an ongoing, central question for the American republic. In the wake of September 11, however, this issue came to the forefront, and the presence of multiracial Americans, I argue, became a convenient, "literal" metaphor of a successful, "natural" melting pot. For a nation desiring unity, peace, and an end to intergroup tensions, the multiracial individual became a convenient, reassuring example of people "overcoming" difference.

As other scholars of news and popular culture have demonstrated, at times of national anxiety, racially Othered groups are often put under heavy scrutiny and scapegoated. This occurred with Japanese Americans during World War II, and again in the 1980s, when hysteria over Japanese economic and industrial competition brought in a new wave and update of mid-century stereotypes of rapacious, ruthless Japanese invaders.[2] Similarly, legal and illegal immigrants, as well as Spanish-speaking Latino citizens, have been demonized periodically in public campaigns for punitive policies (such as California's Prop 209 and attempts to create English-Only amendments) and in media representations.[3] In these cases the racial Other is framed as a cancer on U.S. society, a threat to national unity and strength. In contrast, mainstream media coverage of multiracial people today, I argue, presents a case of the racial Other being framed as a *solution* to alleged social ills: individual racist opinions and race-based policies. In the Reconstruction period and in the decades thereafter, miscegenation and mixed-race peoples were pariahs and symbols of impurity, but today they are reimagined as a natural byproduct of improving race relations by a dominant culture uneasy with the task of conceptualizing race and racism beyond interpersonal interactions.

Responses to Census 2000 Data in the Asian American Press

Overall, the Asian American press framed the emerging multiracial data as an opportunity to reflect on Asian American politics in general. Although many of the themes presented in the prior chapter continued in the Asian American press, there were some changes in emphasis. Two major themes emerged in Asian American reports on the 2000 Census data: (1) concerns about political ramifications of multiracial Asian counts; and (2) Hapa experiences with Whites and Whiteness. In addition, I will address the presence of two articles that mentioned the use of multiracial people in marketing, mainly in order to segue to the discussion of dominant periodicals' views on the multiracial image.

The Numbers and the Political Possibilities

Perhaps the largest shift numerically occurred in the number of stories that mentioned the political ramifications of the census data for Asian

Americans. In the 1996-2000 articles, only 15 percent contained discussion of the link between Asian American politics and the count of multiracial Asians, while 58 percent of the post-2000 articles did. For example, *A Magazine* titled one of its pieces "Number crunch: Wondering how to make sense of Census 2000 and how it will affect you? Here's a rundown."[4] The headline suggests that the numbers are certain to affect readers. Within the article, a large paragraph was devoted to the meaning of the multiracial data, implicitly separating multiracial Asians from other Asian Americans. However, not every piece presented multiracial Asians as a distinct group apart from other Asians. Writer T. O'Sullivan, for example, classified multiracial people with all people of color in his report for the *Asian American Reporter*.[5] He included multiracial people in his representation of the census totals for Oregon minorities, showing them as part of the trend that will have non-Whites outnumbering Whites in the future. O'Sullivan also predicted that, given the success of ballot proposals such as Connerly's Prop 209 in California and other backlash politics against Blacks and Latinos, people of color are not going to gain equity speedily just because they become the numerical majority.

> There are many who see this numerical shift as a threat, or they see a need to start developing affirmative action strategies of their own towards whites. This kind of fear suggests that somehow people of color have a conspiracy in place against the dominant culture. . . .
>
> The change is coming. In fact, it is already here in many ways. What the mainstream needs to do in order not to get left behind is to embrace the different emerging groups and make it a point to learn about us. After all, we have to continually learn about the mainstream.[6]

Asian American writers approached multiracial-identified people as allies against the socially and politically dominant White racial group. And, in the latter half of the above quote, the writer put the onus on the mainstream (Whites) to move from their sense of the center to the periphery, to "embrace the different emerging groups" rather than demanding assimilation from the "majority-minority" population.

In an editorial titled "Most Indian State," the writers expressed concern about undercounts in Asian American communities alongside worries about how the Republicans will use the multiracial numbers.[7] "[The] minority population totals is a complicated issue that has yet to be untangled. The census numbers confirm the high proportion of interracial marriages in the Indian community." In this editorial, the main context for the multiracial Asian population was wariness about how data will be used, potentially against racialized communities such as Indians. A feature on Hapa Issues Forum (HIF), however, quoted extensively from the HIF executive director, Sheila Chung. She framed the multiracial numbers in this way: "These data not only provide more accurate information on race, but help us challenge our invisibility in the APA [Asian Pacific Islander] community."[8] For multiracial Asians, then, the census data served as legitimation of their place as an important subgroup within the Asian American community, not apart from it. In contrast, African American reports that expressed desire for solidarity with biracial Blacks rarely included their testimony. In the remainder of the report, it was clear that HIF members felt that solidarity with Asian Americans was of utmost importance. For example, when discussing the Racial Privacy Initiative with HIF conference participants, the writer elicited this information:

> Labeled by some at the [HIF]conference as the "Racial Ignorance Initiative," it is slated to be on the March 2004 ballot. "We see race, it is not hidden," said Curtis Takada Rooks [who is half-Japanese]. . . . "This initiative will take away your choice, my choice, our choice."[9]

This vocal resistance to the conservative "colorblind" agenda is virtually nonexistent in mainstream news media interviews with people of mixed race. It is crucial to see resistance by Hapas to the conservative agenda, especially given how, under Newt Gingrich's leadership, Republicans latched onto the multiracial movement in the mid-1990s; some observers still link multiracial people with neoconservatives. However, the organizations in the movement are quite diverse, and as the HIF interviewees demonstrate, many people of multiracial descent do not endorse the ideology or policy proposals of neoconservatives such as Ward Connerly and Gingrich. Information from local and regional multiracial groups—as well as groups affiliated with people of Asian descent, who are rarely covered in other news outlets—is important to broadening the public's awareness of multiracial organizations, identities, and political agendas.

Spotlighting Hapa Experiences in Asian and White American Spheres

More than half of the stories published in Asian American periodicals contained personal interviews with multiracial Asian Americans. As in the mainstream press, many of these articles began with personal experiences, and then transitioned into discussion of data trends and politics.

For example, an article began with the story of a Korean-Czech woman, and then provided the following data analysis: "The 2000 Census

Table 6.1. Multiracial Sources Directly Quoted in Articles

	pre-Census 2000	post-Census 2000
Asian American	30% (N=33)	58% (N=12)
Black American	30% (N=67)	25% (N=38)
Dominant	50% (N=32)	40% (N=110)

revealed that among the 12.5 million APAs, around 2.1 million are hapa. This data places hapas at 16.8 percent of the APA population, the second largest APA subgroup behind Chinese Americans, who make up 19.5 percent of the APA population."[10] Other stories included concerns that despite the numbers, many Asians do not accept Hapas. Janet Ng's piece for *AsianWeek* focused on the problems multiracial Asians have fitting in, focusing on the experiences interviewees had as children.[11] Experts she interviewed emphasized that "[t]here is tremendous pressure to conform to one race versus being multirace in our society. Whites, blacks, or Asian American communities still do not accept and do not feel comfortable with the mixing of the races."[12] Another interviewee, Matt Kelley, founder of a nonprofit organization for multiracial people, said that the Hapa kids he has counseled say that "it's just automatic that they are rejected by the API community."[13] Kelley also mentioned that in Seattle, the largest-growing group entering the juvenile justice system is multiracial kids, suggesting a need for more targeted interventions to prevent ostracism, and that the "rainbow child" image of advertising and dominant news media does not accurately reflect the experiences of many multiracial children, who are targets of bullying, are abandoned, and are not all middle-class.

Two articles dealt with tensions in Asian American communities over the high rates of out-marriage. They noted that some people are dismayed by the increasing number of interracial marriages involving Asians, fearful that out-marriage will lead to dilution of cultural knowledge. However, both pieces suggested that ostracizing interracial couples or multiracial people was invalid as a political or social strategy. An editorial in *Little India* urged Indian Americans to look at the facts before shunning interracial marriages, stating, "Indians and Asians as a group have among the highest proportion of interracial marriages in the United States, higher than other racial groups."[14] And while they admitted that some are still shocked by the numbers the Census Bureau provided, the editors concluded that "it is time to celebrate and embrace all of these multiple expressions of the Indian American identity." Furthermore, the editors linked the intermarriage issue to a larger, historical Indian diaspora in "Malaysia, Singapore, South Africa, Mauritius, Trinidad, Guyana, Senegal, Fiji, and Surinam, where Indians migrated almost a century earlier and forged a multiplicity of new blended identities." While one could argue that the depiction of Indian migrations might be romanticized, the paper acknowledged that the mixing represented in the census data was merely the latest iteration of cross-cultural interaction, reframing Indian identity as a multicultural, shifting entity rather than a monolithic, unchanging essence.

Likewise, the article "The Face of Race" discussed the variables that will affect the future ethnic composition of the United States, in particular Asian American communities, including interracial marriage.

> Hypothetically, if 40 to 50 percent of Asian Americans are marrying non-Asians and all of their multiracial children identify as Asian Americans, there could be a marked increase in the share of Asians in the U.S. The existence and recognition of multiracial people also challenges our assumptions about racial categories as being fixed and separate from one another. This not only has implications for whom we think of as "Asian American" but also who is considered to be an average "American."[15]

The author then speculated that the new "American"—if intermarriage continues at a high rate—will look like "the new Betty Crocker—a computer-generated amalgamation of 4,000 women of different racial and ethnic backgrounds—rather than the classic blonde-haired, blue-eyed 'All-American' beauty." Like the *Little India* editorial, this conjecture might be a bit romantic in terms of the blending of races. It also resonates with the hopes expressed for "Eve," the computer generated fantasy of miscegenation and the future of race by *Time* magazine, which Caroline Streeter argues is an exemplar of "safe hybridity"; multiracial people who are attractive and exotic without being threatening to dominant culture.[16] Although Kao's mention of the amalgamated beauty comes after a critical look at beauty ideals, the use of the new Betty Crocker is unsatisfying from a critical standpoint because it still seems to reduce the problem of racial hierarchy to one of race mixing or a facile acknowledgment that we are "all Americans" who happen to have different, multicolored skins. This resonates with (although the author is clearly not aligned with the same political motives) the post–September 11 attempts to flatten racial difference in favor of national identity, exemplified in the AdCouncil's television spots featuring a parade of Americans of different skin hues declaring to the camera, "I am an American," as if making national identity primary to one's self-definition can nullify the workings of racial definitions.[17]

But the personal experiences and opinions related by multiracial Asians in Asian American periodicals did not merely provide interesting individual details; many also asserted political views and critiques of racial hierarchy in the United States. Many of the articles in the Asian American press consisted solely of interviews with Hapas, providing a longer record of conversation and topics addressed during the interviews. Five of the seven articles that included direct quotes from multiracial Asian Americans contained sections that focused on the interviewees' opinions on Whiteness and racial privileges enjoyed by those who are White and/ or part-White. These sorts of conversations were almost completely absent from mainstream news texts. In these fragments of discussion, many multiracial Asians expressed strong opinions about the ignorance and prejudices they face from Whites, as well as their own desires to reject the privileges of lighter skin.

In "The Pursuit of Hapa-ness,"[18] a whole section of this roundtable interview with multiracial Asians was titled "Race isn't a biology, it's a politics." The section header came from an interviewee who said she wants "to distance herself from whiteness politically" because even as she acknowledges that her lighter skin has given her some privileges, she doesn't want to be associated with "those white people" who are racist. Another woman followed up by saying that she doesn't "really relate to white at all. . . . My main frustration with white people I've come across is that there's no urgency [for them] to think about racial issues. They can go through every day and not think about it. . . . Privilege is not having to struggle with race issues."[19] Later, another participant related being "ashamed of" an instance where he let someone on the phone assume he was Dutch. Another participant remembered how she thought she was White when she was younger.

> I mean, I knew my father was Chinese but I didn't think anyone could tell. The famous story of me realizing was when I was in fourth grade . . . and a bully from my class starts going "Ching chong, ching chong." I turned around to see who he was talking about and didn't realize it was me. That's how oblivious I was, because my parents were very much of the mind that we had to be American, and American to us was white.[20]

Continuing the mistaken identity theme, the article "HapAmerican" begins with Hapa participants listing the ignorant questions they have been asked by Whites: " 'Have you seen *Snow Falling on Cedars*? Are you

Japanese?'[21] Christine Hamilton recalls . . . 'Another lady said, "You look like Lisa Ling," ' she says . . . 'I mean, I look nothing like Lisa Ling.' "[22] Likewise, interviewee Michael Riego told *A Magazine* "Because of my last name, Riego, a lot of people I talk to over the phone think I'm Italian or Spanish. But when they finally meet me, they'll say something like, 'Oh, I thought you were Italian,' which is really a different version of, 'Wow, you have such great English.' It's disheartening."[23] Thus, in answer to the question posed in another article, whether Asian Americans will be "model minorities," assimilated, or will Whites continue to view them "as an unassimilable minority," the stories related by Hapa-identified individuals here suggest that Whites often assume Asian-looking people are foreigners, or all look alike, even if they have some White heritage.[24]

Beyond personal experiences with Whites, writers and interviewees related opinions about Whiteness itself. Kao, for example, contrasted the dominant White beauty ideal with the prospect of an amalgamated part-Asian woman becoming the standard in "The Face of Race."[25] Maria Blanco of MALDEF told a reporter for *AsianWeek* that the so-called Racial Privacy Initiative "gives ways for whites to hold onto the past and ignore the new California."[26] Similarly, in an *Asian Reporter* piece subtitled "Where did all the white people go," the author took on the issue of White political and economic dominance.[27] After assessing of the recent spate of anti–affirmative action campaigns on the West Coast, the writer noted that

> the global white population is less than 12%. Worldwide, a small number of whites control the majority of wealth. . . . Here in the United States, no one really addresses that issue of the small group of mostly white men who control everything, so we don't have a name. We were good enough, however, to name it for other countries: apartheid.[28]

With that crushing indictment, O'Sullivan named racism as entrenched in the American system and its institutions in contrast to the racial realists, who locate racism in the hearts and minds of individuals. Later in the article, he stated, "Ethnic people are just as different as white people are, which is to say that the Poles and the British are joined only by the color of their skin, but everything else is unique to their respective cultures." The author named White privilege, attacked essentialist racial stereotypes that lump people of color together but differentiate among White ethnics, and grounded his arguments about the changing racial makeup of the U.S. in questions of social and political power, not a toothless multiculturalism.

Selling Hapa Identity

While only two stories mentioned the use of multiracial people in advertising, here I make note of the tensions between two stories that appeared in the July 31, 2001, edition of *A Magazine* and those in the mainstream press. Both were features on high-profile Hapa men. The first, "He's got the look" features Michel Riego, a fashion industry executive who is part Filipino. When asked by the interviewer how his Filipino heritage impacted his work, he replied:

> "I've cast half-African American/half-Caucasian models and Asian Americans, Latin Americans, African Americans, more of what's representative of the true landscape of the population out there. . . . Even in the Midwest, it's becoming pretty diverse. You're getting intermarriages, so you're coming up with biracial children and teens, so I cast them in these campaigns. . . . In the new Jordache Originals campaign, I cast a South American girl who was meant to be this cultural melting pot embodied in one person. She's not blond and blue-eyed, and that was different from what the company has always done."[29]

In Riego's eyes, his work at the company was helping to change the brand image from one of Whiteness to one of diversity, or as he put it "representative of the true . . . population out there" in the United States. A few pages later, however, activist Matt Kelley viewed the use of multiracial models with more skepticism.

In his interview, Kelley said, "Unfortunately, I think that hapas are being used in TV and Madison Avenue primarily to provide more 'palatable' images of Asian Americans to a mainstream audience that still equates Asian Americans as Asian first, and Americans second."[30] But right after that cautionary statement, Kelley said he believed that "hapas have been fortunate to have pioneering hapa role models like Maria Root, Ann Curry and Tiger Woods. That makes me optimistic for the future."[31] Unlike Riego, Kelley made a distinction between how a "mainstream" (read: monoracial and/or White) audience perceives Asian American and Hapa identities and how Hapa or multiracial people view Hapas. This distinction, I would argue, is important, given that audiences bring their own particular ideologies and reading strategies to media texts, possibly producing very different meanings from those intended by the text's creator(s). Thus, as Carolyn Streeter argues, the exoticization of multiracial women may still continue to produce neo-mulatta stereotypes that, instead of being symbols of the ills of miscegenation, are used to invite erotic interest and mask continued racial inequalities.[32]

African American Press Responses to Census 2000 Racial Data

One theme of the previous chapter was that the Black press expressed the most skepticism about the government's plan to change racial classification on the 2000 Census. Indeed, some of the writers and commentators were plainly hostile to both the unfolding political and bureaucratic processes and to those multiracial individuals pressing for the change. However, in the wake of the initial data on how many Blacks chose more than one racial category to report their identity, there was a more diverse set of thoughts on the meaning of the *actual* racial data generated by the 2000 Census than during the period of speculation and struggle prior to the change in the racial categorization scheme. Three main themes emerged in the post-2000 articles. First, there were more discussions of possibilities of coalition and inclusion with multiracial people and other people of color. Second, there were broader discussions of how the concept of Blackness is changing overall, and what that means in terms of the future of civil rights battles and traditional approaches to organizing Black publics. Third, the issue of whether or not Hispanics outnumber Blacks— and whether people can be simultaneously Hispanics and Black—surfaced with the numbers and reaction to the political hype around the possible Hispanic "usurpation" of Black political clout.[33]

Looking to the Future: Considering the Heterogeneity of Blackness

One key difference between the pre- and post-2000 articles is that the articles published in the wake of the Census were much more future-oriented than those written in the 1990s. Two key indicators of this were: (1) a decrease in references to other racial systems of the past, such as those instituted in the antebellum South or apartheid South Africa; and (2) a decrease in negative opinions about multiracial people's motives for choosing more than one racial category to describe themselves.

Instead of looking back to very painful, real, and important memories of colorism and discrimination to understand the new census data, or lambasting multiracial-identified Blacks, African American commentators were focused on the present and future ramifications of the data and the people represented by the numbers. However, orienting around contemporary issues did not mean that concerns were erased; rather, the most

Table 6.2. Themes in the Black Press before and after Census 2000

	1996–May 2000 (N=67)	June 2000–2004 (N=38)
Census change will create institutionalized color hierarchy	20% (13)	7.9% (3)
Multiracial people want to be "whiter" than Blacks	42% (29)	13% (5)

prevalent issue raised in the Black press continued to be, How will this new group affect Black political power and economic status in the United States? Journalists and commentators were still concerned that Black political power could be diluted by multiracial identification, as illustrated in the following quotes.

> Civil rights activists and government officials said the increasing number of Americans who identify themselves as multiracial will change how poverty is tracked, civil rights is enforced and how racial balance is achieved in schools . . .[34]

This first quote, in contrast to most reports in the dominant press, reminds the reader that racial data is used for political as well as descriptive purposes. The next quote reiterates themes found in the previous chapter, that the multiracial count and/or its use by conservatives will damage African American political projects.

> [An African American] Friendship [Pennsylvania] resident also expressed concern that the U.S. Census may have undercounted the number of African-Americans because of a new racial category designated as "bi-racial."[35]

> The political right has co-opted the multiracial movement with the intent of gutting civil rights enforcement.[36]

The concerns about the Census' impact on Black political power, however, were not accompanied as often by questions about multiracial individuals' desire to be White or gain status, as seen in the chart above. This is somewhat surprising, given that more people of African descent chose more than one race than the Census Bureau initially predicted, and the prevalence of the accusation, found in the previous chapter, that some biracial Blacks wanted to "jump ship" or "be White." However, I argue that condemning the choice of bi- or multiracial Blacks is not politically prudent in the Bush era. As the next pages illustrate, concerns about the overall power of non-Whites and the continued erosion of race-based policies that benefit people of color were at the forefront, and multiracial people were reimagined as allies rather than race traitors. However, in contrast to Asian American reports, this new view did not translate into seeking more direct information from biracial Blacks. In addition, the retreat from attacks on the motives and character of multiracial people may be partly tactical; once it was clear that the number of people willing to identify as both Black and another race was larger than predicted, political actors may have seen a benefit to courting rather than shaming that cohort into partnership with African Americans. This is also evident in the response to the data on Hispanics.

It seems that concerns over predicted "competition" with Latinos and the very real threat of continued conservative encroachments on civil rights policies inspired a more open discursive strategy for discussing the place of multiracial-identified Blacks in African American politics and community life. Indeed, only four stories published in the Black press after 2000 suggested that multiracial Blacks should choose one race over multiracial options, where in the pre-Census articles many more explicitly articulated that position. Only two stories articulated the idea that multiracial people were victims of racial self-loathing, a prominent theme in the earlier group of articles, as well as in reports on Susie Phipps in the 1980s (see chapter 2). In contrast, one optimistic writer enthusiastically embraced the idea that intermarriage will continue to increase and generate a large population of mixed-race families who will bridge racial divides naturally:

> Jesse Jackson's Rainbow Coalition may eventually succeed beyond its wildest dreams . . . genes may be able to do it simply by forcing an issue in a way that bigots will be unable to resist. . . . Fortunately, genetics dictates a future in which most of this discrimination will come to an end.[37]

Notice that although this "melting pot" prediction mimics discourses in the dominant press described below, the writer also includes mention of present-day bigotry that must be forcefully confronted. However, the level of racial optimism in this piece was not matched in most other articles, which often included the problem of continued racism in acknowledgments of biracial identity. As one writer noted, "Being multiracial can mean being able to . . . celebrate the traditions of more than one culture while growing up. But it can also mean listening to people make racist jokes in front of you because they think you are White, and never being sure where you fit in."[38]

In addition to being less negative about a separate multiracial identity, writers included discussions of how the categories "African American" and/or "Black" may be changing in the present and future given the results of the census. Rather than looking to past models of multiracial identity in Black communities—where skin color gradations and terms such as "mulatto" and "quadroon" mapped onto class divisions—Black commentators coupled multiracial identity with phenomena such as Caribbean immigration and age cohorts to discuss an ongoing shift in how Black identity is conceptualized.[39] With the census numbers showing that more Blacks than predicted chose more than one race, Blackness, they argued, needs to be rethought, in political and sociocultural terms, to acknowledge not only the multiracial challenge but also generational differences, immigration, and class issues. Editorialists and commentators quoted in news articles acknowledged that multiracial-identified people were not going to lose their desire to choose more than one race, regardless of the merits of monoracially-identified Blacks' political and social concerns. These articles looked forward strategically and philosophically to ask the question, What results will emerge from the ongoing redefinition of "Black" in U.S. society as "Generation M(ultiracial)" grows up and continues to intermarry, and as immigration flows, particularly from Latin and Caribbean nations, change the population that "looks Black"? *Jet Magazine* titled an initial piece on the census data: "How Census results could redefine America's definition of black."[40] After presenting data on who said they were Black and some other race, the magazine noted: "Blacks 17 and younger were nearly four times as likely as Blacks 50 and older to identify themselves as belonging to more than one race."[41] Another writer claimed that the 2000 Census was a landmark in racial categorization:

> Historically, the decennial Census has produced a simple paint-by-number picture of America. . . . But the 2000 Census reveals a far more complex and subtle portrait—an America where nearly 7 million people identify themselves as multiracial.[42]

In contrast to the pre-2000 reports, these writers presented multiracial identification as an opportunity to see the complexity of race in contemporary American Black communities, not just as a threat to those communities. For example, a report in the *Indianapolis Recorder* declared that "Multiracial category on census raises questions" about who identifies as Black and what it will mean in the future.[43] This piece included, interestingly, quotes from multiracial activist and editor Charles Byrd, who predicted that the "multiracial category is the beginning of the end of race in America . . ."[44] Given Byrd's alliance with Ward Connerly, it was curious to find this statement without any qualification about the speaker. Its presence, though, does attest to a greater flexibility in the Black press to include a greater variety of opinions about multiracial identity than in the pre-Census period. Similarly, the *Tri-State Defender* published an editorial with the title: "What does being African American mean and who said so?"[45] Beginning with a discussion of Tiger Woods's choice to identify himself as multiracial rather than African American, the editorial gave him the benefit of the doubt that he chose this path because to say he's Black "would be inaccurate. If that is his reasoning, I whole-heartedly agree." This concession then led to a discussion of the one-drop rule and a challenge to readers to rethink racial identity.

> [H]ow long are we as people of color in America going to allow others to define for us who we are? To take that a step further, what about the tens of thousands of men and women and chil-dren of color who are of multiple ethnic origins? Those who would classify all "non-pure whites" as African American would likely submit the stereotypical image of rape or coercion by White men of Black women as a mitigation of the "mixed" ethnicity of the offspring.[46]

The editors concluded that such an assumption is faulty in today's so-ciety, particularly given the increase in consensual relationships and marriages across the Black/White divide.[47] However, there were still a handful of articles containing negative comments about interracial dat-ing and marriage. One article in this set was titled, "Why brothers date 'others.' " The journalist included lengthy and disparaging quotes from Black women who felt Black men choose White and Asian partners because they have absorbed and endorse racist and sexist stereotypes about Black women.[48]

Other writers expressed a sense of inevitability or resignation that multiracial identity is here to stay. These authors advocated the position that Black communities and organizations needed to pay attention to the numbers of multiracial-identified Blacks in a changing racial landscape. As one jounalist concluded, although "[t]he [U.S. Census] numbers may be an imperfect measure of how biracial the U.S. has become . . . the fact that Uncle Sam is plugging them into a calculator shows it is high time to take notice."[49] His quote suggests that, whether Blacks like it or not, the power of the numbers supercedes any qualms about the validity of biracial or multiracial identity choices or data. The author suggests use of this data by the government demands a practical, tactical response from Blacks.

A few commentators who agreed that "the multiracial category check off was inevitable, due to the increase in interracial marriage and children,"[50] reminded readers that the change in racial perceptions would be gradual and differ from generation to generation.

> While the struggle between what race a person thinks he or she is and what race society, particularly older generations, chooses to label them will undoubtedly continue, the Census results have gone far in redefining America's definition of Black.[51]

Despite this sense of inevitability, though, many commentators still argued that those who claim more than one race detract from more pertinent racial issues. For example, Dr. Manning Marable argued in an op-ed piece for the *Westside Gazette* that biracial people may not have the same level of need for civil rights protection as those originally envisioned in 1960s legislation to remedy discrimination against Blacks in the United States. He stated that race has changed since the civil rights legislation of the 1960s: then, "minority" usually meant only "Black/Negro" whereas today's multiculturalism has broadened the definition of minority, meaning that policies intended to redress Black/White inequality are now being used to benefit peoples who may not share the same legacy of racial hardship. Although in one sense, the "broadening" of the term "minority" continues to reflect a White/other division that supports institutional racism and hierarchy, Marable asserted that in practice this expansion of the category is working to benefit people who can often share in aspects of White privilege.

> Increasingly, individuals who by traditional U.S. standards would be considered "white" demanded financial support on fragmentary and even fictive connections with American Indians, Hispanic, Caribbean, and African American heritages. . . . Some "biracial" individuals have attempted to make a case for themselves as a special, discriminated class worthy of relief.[52]

Likewise, Dr. Robert Smith of San Francisco State University, interviewed by the *Indianapolis Recorder*, suggested that the multiracial numbers could be artificially inflated by Blacks and Latinos whose other ancestries are farther "down the line" than their parents' or even grandparents' generation. He also speculated that since only 2 percent of Latinos chose Black as their race, "[i]n the end, the Black/White thing will continue to be the central dilemma when we talk about race. . . . These other ethnic groups will become white before Blacks will."[53] Such quotes serve to remind readers that Blacks have historically been positioned at the bottom of the racial ladder, and that other groups may benefit from participating in a lightest-to-darkest color hierarchy. However, in the next section it is clear that the Black press sees this potential as a call to accelerate the formation of interracial coalitions against racial domination.

Bracing for Divide and Conquer Tactics

Related to Dr. Smith's remarks, African American periodicals were more likely than both Asian American and dominant publications to comment on the possibility that the census data would help Hispanics "overtake" African Americans in political, economic, and social opportunities.[54] The primary focus of articles that included information about both the multiracial count and the Hispanic count was the possibility that the Hispanic data would be manipulated in ways to reduce African American political and economic power.

Of the articles that brought up the issue of whether Hispanic Americans outnumber African Americans, most expressed the belief that the groups should work together to resist divisive strategies of Whites. One reporter relayed the opinions of a Black congressman to emphasize this desire for coalition: "With the U.S. Census showing Hispanics are becoming the nation's largest minority in America, Rep. Jesse L. Jackson Jr. (D-2nd) Thursday called for a 'natural' political bonding of Latinos and Blacks to fight for human rights."[55]

A handful of articles also included statements and statistics concerning how a large percentage of Hispanics used the racial category "White" when filling out the census forms. These statistics were used in two ways: (1) to imply or state explicitly that Hispanics use the White category to distance themselves from Blacks; (2) to contextualize Latinos' use of "White" in terms of culture and/or nationality. One source told a re-

Table 6.3. Comparison of Hispanic Population and Politics Theme, Post-Census 2000

Theme	Black (N=38)	Asian American (N=12)	Dominant (N=110)
Census results for Hispanic population may harm African Americans	18% (7)	0% (0)	4.5% (5)

porter " 'Forty-eight percent of Latinos identified themselves as white, and that is the dilemma,' said Smith. 'If a person has a chance to choose, white or Latino, they will choose to be white . . .' "[56] A columnist for the *Washington Informer* explained the large number of white-identifying Hispanics with the following paragraph on Latin American "interpretations" of race and class:

> For example, it is likely that many Hispanic immigrants have over-identified as "white" having a Latin American interpretation of what it means to be "white" rather than an American conception. In Latin America, it is said that upper class status whitens. . . . I once heard famous black (very black) soccer star Pele say that "when he was black" he had a different attitude about life. He meant, of course, when he was poor.[57]

His xenophobic assumption of immigrant status aside, the writer's point about the varied approaches to race in North and Latin American societies is well placed in a debate where Whiteness may be in the process of becoming "not all white," to use jon powell's phrase. If some groups, by virtue of interracial marriage and/or skin tone, are granted greater access to the social, political, and economic privileges enjoyed by Whites, then Whiteness is adjusting to the new racial landscape in a way that retains certain color barriers and reframes others. This, one could argue, is reflected in higher rates of intermarriage between Asians and Whites than Blacks and Whites. However, powell's statement refers to a radical notion of Whiteness as an "impure" category just as "Black" is an "impure" racial category. In this regard, although "model minorities" are given access to some greater benefits, Whiteness is still seen today as "pure," to a large extent. As the dominant news media framing of multiracial identity in previous chapters reflects, multiracial people are seen as being *of color*, not *White*. Whiteness is still in the eyes of the beholder and based on the *absence* of color, in society as well as the state, reminding us of the crucial role of cultural context to our understandings of race. So while Hispanic American "ethnics" must also choose a "race," European American ethnics do not choose either on Census or other forms—their ethnicity is assumed to be White always.

A few writers who consulted Latino scholars provided some more contextualization and nuanced reasons why many Latinos chose White on the census. In the *New York Beacon*, for example, an article focused on the place of wealth and class in determining Whiteness in Latin American nations. Additionally, one scholar noted that fear of racism may encourage Latinos to call themselves White in the United States.

And in the United States, some Latinos who also have African heritage may describe themselves "white" because they fear the discrimination that comes with being identified as black. . . . [But] "[i]n Latin America, the 'one-drop rule' doesn't work at all," said Silvia Pedraza, a University of Michigan sociologist.[58]

The writer also noted that there were differences in racial identification of Latinos by region: Hispanic Americans in Texas were more likely to identify as White, while Puerto Ricans in New York were more likely to use Black to identify their race. He also quoted a demographer who claimed that the Census Bureau had reclassified more of the Hispanics who chose "some other race" as White than as Black.[59] This article was exceptional in that it both included the information that Hispanics were the group most likely to choose "some other race" over White or Black than all other groups, and noted that the White/Hispanic combination could be inflated by Census Bureau intervention. Thus, one could argue that the choice for many Hispanics was perhaps not between Black or White, but rather a choice to refuse both labels, which are deemed by many to be insufficient to describe their identities. That more African American writers did not know about or utilize this tidbit of information could make it harder for readers to see the complexity of the issues surrounding how the Census Bureau identifies Hispanics and how Hispanics may be identifying themselves.

Dominant News Media Responses to Census 2000 Data

In the years prior to Census 2000, dominant news sources were focused mainly on predictions of problems the new system would cause for monoracially defined people of color. There was a focus on Black resistance to a multiracial identifier, and many personal stories and opinions of people of Black and White descent. As the actual data began to be released to the public, however, writers had hard numbers and statistics to use as a foundation for reports, editorials, and essays on the meaning of multiracial identity. The number of articles containing the terms *multiracial* and *census* tripled in dominant publications. In contrast, the number of stories with the topic decreased in both African American and Asian American publications. This suggests that multiracial identity became significantly more newsworthy to dominant news organizations once the data were released.

If the mainstream press (re) discovered multiracial identity in the mid-1990s, it shaped its discovery much differently than in the past. I have argued in the previous chapters that, when covering controversial individuals of multiracial descent, the press rarely covered them as *mul-*

Table 6.4. Layout Characteristics of Stories, Post-Census 2000

	African American (N=38)	Dominant (N=110)	Asian American (N=12)
Front page stories	10.5% (4)	40.9% (45)	0% (0)
Photos of multiracial people included	7.8% (3)	32.7% (36)	16.6% (2)

tiracial, but rather as part of or in relation to a specific *monoracial* group. These narratives worked in a traditional, binary logic of distinct races and did not recognize the growing population of multiracial people in the United States. However, with the census controversy, a vocal set of multiracial advocates, and actual data documenting the size of the new racial group, the press latched onto multiracial people as a "new" racial identity, a new generation of people with unique, natural characteristics, the most important of which is their role as a "bridge" between cultures. I argue that in the mainstream press, "multiracial" has become a new "model minority" identity, in two senses. First, multiracial individuals are seen as model in their (assumed) attitudes about racial difference. Second, they and their families are presented as models for the future of race relations, modeling a world where color and culture are no longer barriers. This model minority status is different from that imposed on Asian Americans. Asian Americans are not seen as vehicles for healing racial tensions; rather, they are valued as "models" for not participating in behaviors or holding attitudes about race associated most often with African Americans. As such, model minorities become intermediary groups, buffers between Whites and other people of color. Multiracial people may also be positioned in this way, but in addition, their "model" status is based in part on the hope they will eliminate racial conflict in their demographic wake.

According to the dominant press, the main problem with the multiracial category was the mechanics of dealing with a new kind of racial data. As in the previous set of articles, mainstream media used more charts and numbers to illustrate the Census and multiracial identity. In addition, they included more opinions about how the new data presented problems in terms of historical continuity. For example, they quoted from statisticians who feared that the new set of categories would make it harder to compare present and past decades of data on minorities since those who counted themselves as "Black" in 1990 may have chosen Asian and Black in 2000. But this disruption was minimal compared to the predictions of positive social outcomes to be generated by the multiracial generation.

Marketable Multiracial Identity

Although the marketability of multiracial identity was not the most dominant theme of either Asian American or mainstream publications, the contrast between how each presented the issue of the newfound popularity of multiracial celebrities and models is telling. Dominant media references to multiracial chic were rarely critical of the trend. Rather, the presence and fashion of multiracial people was explained with the same sort of optimism used to explain the census statistics on race mixing in America. Tiger Woods, for example, was often used to personify the brave new world of multiracial identity, particularly among the younger generation.

> Young, gifted and multiracial, Woods is the perfect role model for the millennium. White and black, Asian and Latino, Woods draws fans from across the rainbow coalition.[60]

Beyond lauding Woods in particular, though, the dominant press echoed marketing publications in their enthusiasm for multiracial identity as a perfect fit for the "postethnic" marketplace.[61] Although at first glance the chart makes it seem that Asian American newspapers and magazines were as interested as dominant periodicals, note that only two articles contained the idea in the Asian American press, and recall that one was highly critical of Madison Avenue's willingness to exploit Hapas. In the mainstream news, though, the use of multiracial models to successfully lure Generation Xers or Yers was applauded. In the *Style* section of the *New York Times*, for example, marketing executives declared "the demand is weakening" for blond-haired, blue-eyed models because,

> "Today what's ethnically neutral, diverse or ambiguous has tremendous appeal," said Ron Berger, the chief executive of Euro RSCG MVBMS Partners in New York. . . . "Both in the main-

Table 6.5. Celebrity and Marketing Themes in Post-Census 2000 Articles

	Dominant (N=110)	Black (N=38)	Asian American (N=12)
Tiger Woods used to illustrate multiracial issue	23.6% (26)	10.5% (4)	16.7% (2)
Multiracial people are good for marketing	12.7% (14)	2.6% (1)	16.7% (2)

stream and at the high end of the marketplace, what is perceived as good, desirable, successful is often a face whose heritage is hard to pin down."

Ambiguity is chic, especially among the under-25 members of Generation Y, the most racially diverse population in the nation's history.... "We're seeing more of a desire for the exotic, left-of-center beauty that transcends race or class," Amy Barnett, [*Teen People's*] managing editor, said.... Nearly seven million Americans identified themselves as members of more than one race in the 2000 census.[62]

This "ambiguity," however, is not part of the "fluidity" of race lauded by scholars of passing, for example. This ambiguity is about exoticism and intrigue, providing opportunities for consumers to fantasize and speculate about the Other with no expectations of critical consideration of power and racial categories. This particular article did include two quotes from multiracial individuals who did not appreciate the attention they got from curious onlookers, but the bulk of the article was devoted to how lucky multiracial actors and models are today now that the market wants diversity and ambiguity to evoke exoticism.

Likewise, in a review of Leon Wynter's *American Skin*, a book critic brushed aside concerns that racial inequality still exists despite the wave of integration in marketing and entertainment described by Wynter in the book. Instead, the critic looked forward to a future where the consumers of multiracial chic would usher in a day when only the human race matters:

What's important to Wynter is the fact that multiracial marketing does sell—it indicates that Americans see their own experience as ethnically diverse and like to see that diversity reflected in advertising and entertainment....

Wynter renames Generations X and Y... the first generations "certified as ready for nonwhite role models by corporate mass media." They are the generations who believe American is not merely a synonym for white. And if Wynter's book has anything to say about it, they are the generations who will create an America in which there's only one race (human) one culture (American) and only one kind of skin—not white, black, yellow or red, but American.[63]

This incredible optimism, that interracial coupling alone will create a generation of racially tolerant kids, was not a feature of Asian and African

American news stories. Here we see a strong suggestion that *national* identity can supersede (and is more relevant and valid than) racial or ethnic identity. Erasing the nation's racial past with the biology of race mixing continues as a trend in other dominant accounts, as I will explain below.

Other feature writers were also optimistic about Generation X's and Generation Y's ability to shed the racial past and immerse in multiculturalism.

> Among today's post-ethnic youth, cultural diversity is casually presumed as a normal aspect of daily life, and in the highly fluid youth marketplace, cultural identities are exchanged and shed as simply and efficiently as if they were eBay transactions.[64]

The above quote is taken from an article that included a three-quarter page graphic with a "quiz" on what "new" mixed-race label "fit" two columns of multiracial mug shots. For example, Tiger Woods was a match for " 'Cablinasian' = Caucasian, Black Indian & Asian," while "Negripino" was a match for a mug shot with the label "African American and Filipino." One accompanying caption goaded the reader, "You know Latino, Chicano, Hispanic and Anglo, Amerasian, African American and Native American. But do you realize . . . how far behind the times you are? Get with it!"[65] The graphics and text suggested that Generation Y, in contrast to the Baby Boomers, were "with it" and could identify and label humans of mixed race because of their immersion in this postethnic marketplace. In the same piece, a father proudly described his daughter to the authors as follows: "[She] listens to hip hop, belongs to the Asian engineering society and has a crush on a black guy," encapsulating the multicultural, hip, and tolerant vision of Generation Y articulated in other aspects of mainstream reporting on the Census.

The rash of interracial couplings in Hollywood movies also garnered attention in the mainstream news in a way not seen in Black and Asian American publications. A headline in the *San Diego Union Tribune's* "Lifestyle" section stated, "It's all about the box office if interracial couples are cast."[66] The writer interviewed Dr. Sharon Lee, a sociologist, for insights such as these:

> Lee . . . says the newly introduced option of checking off more than one race in the 2000 Census has put a spotlight on diversity. "The population as a whole is getting more diverse . . . more people are living in places where they are meeting people who are not going to be exactly like themselves," she says. Some trace a connection between the increase in multiracial couples and the

hip-hop era, as people listen to different types of music and interact with various ethnic groups.[67]

Other experts from marketing and academia insisted that the market was responding to a trend driven in part by a younger generation with multiracial tastes.

The *Times-Picayune* declared in a headline: "Teen movies embracing interracial couples."[68] Contrasting opinions from critics portrayed the interracial teen romance as either a tool of movie marketers who want to attract younger viewers who have "grown up on MTV and have exposure to so many different ethnic groups, it's no big deal anymore," or that these movies' portrayal of mixed-race couples "as a normal romance shows positive development" in terms of Hollywood and society's acceptance of interracial relationships. A critic for the *Boston Globe* also viewed the surge of interracial romance flicks as a sign of triumphant multiculturalism among youth.

> Making the transition easier is a new generation of actors . . . that people don't particularly view as black or Latino. Helping the transformation is the highly courted teen and 'tween audience that equally embraces white Justin Timberlake, a biracial Vin Diesel, or an African American Nelly.[69]

Thus, multiracial individuals and romantic couples satisfy the tastes of the new generation of multicultural youth, and in some cases, their parents.

This uncritical assessment of these celebrities' racial identities and performances is troubling and ahistorical. Vin Diesel, for example, was "outed" as biracial after coming on the scene as a new White-looking action hero; Justin Timberlake's solo career, one might argue, is based on a misappropriation of African American culture that allows him to be cool and down with Blackness but at the same time have none of the negative baggage of Black sexuality and style weigh his stardom down, as the Super Bowl debacle so obviously illustrated.[70] "African American Nelly," for example, probably would not have been exempt from harsh criticism had he exposed the breast of, say, Britney Spears on CBS. The 'tween audience is not just embracing a multicolored array of entertainers, they may be buying into some troubling reiterations of skin privilege.

Beyond the world of consumption, dominant articles were much more positive than Black articles. While Asian-American writers also included more opinions that the Census Bureau's use of multiracial classifications was a positive development, their quotes and assessments were directed mostly at Hapas' potential to challenge racism; the mainstream press' predictions that counting multiracial people would have a positive impact on society, as explained below, were focused on how the new identity group would eliminate race itself, not necessarily racism.

New Power Generation:
Will Multiracial Children Change the World?

Despite a perception that this country's number one failing is race relations, more and more Americans are striking up romances with people outside of their racial groups.... The proliferation in interracial marriages could lead to a future where race has outlived its usefulness and has been stripped of its power. When we can't talk abut each other's differences, we just might have to begin talking about similarities.

—*Seattle Times*, February 14, 2002

A large portion of the articles, as in the pre-2000 writings, used individuals and personal narratives of racial identity to help introduce and explain the results of the 2000 Census' assessment of race in the United States. However, in the post-2000 set of articles, there was not as heavy a focus on people of Black/White descent, although the majority still came from part–African American backgrounds. What is notable and different from the pre-2000 coverage is the nearly exclusive focus on multiracial youth.[71] Multiracial teens, children, and infants were mentioned constantly in mainstream accounts of the nation's changing awareness of and approaches to multiracial identity. The emphasis on age and demographic projections resulted in a frame of near-biological determinism in the dominant press; journalists implied and some commentators explicitly stated that the new generation of multiracial people could, just by virtue of their existence, solve America's racial problems. Three main themes shaped this frame concerning multiracial youth: (1) multiracial youth are disproportionately younger than other racial groups, and will outlive and, eventually, outnumber those with monoracial identities; (2) multiracial youth are growing up at a time when it is easier to be biracial and have an inherent multicultural perspective; (3) increasing interracial marriage and births will force people, through family ties, to accept people of other races.

From upstate New York to the West Coast, writers detailed the coming of the multiracial generation. A report in the *Seattle Times* declared in a headline that this generation is "Multiracial and tearing down old hierarchy."[72] This piece was unique in that it referenced racial hierarchy explicitly and repeatedly in its interviews through interview quotes from Matt Kelley, an activist also interviewed by Asian American publications. It also contained the author's own opinions and experiences as a multiracial person. However, the great majority of articles in the mainstream press did not speak critically about racial hierarchy; rather, they implicitly and explicitly assumed a correlation between increased intermarriage and decreasing racism—or, the decreasing significance of race. Many of these articles pegged their hopes and assumptions on the youngest members of Generation Y. The extreme youth of multiracial individuals was seen as an enormous benefit for society. The children and teens interviewed and analyzed by journalists were described in tandem with multiple statistics including birth rates, intermarriage rates, and polls on racial attitudes. The numbers and profiles of multiracial teens and kids were then used to back up predictions of racial harmony to come.

In its breakdown of racial data for Iowa, the *Omaha World-Herald* created a subheader, "Multiple Races," which contained the information that "[a] majority of the 31,778 Iowans who said they belonged to more than one racial category were children younger than 18. . . . Children younger than 18 account for just 25 percent of the state's total population, but they were 53 percent of the multiracial group."[73] While this summary article did not speculate as to the impact of this youthful generation, it is notable that the age discrepancy was highlighted for a group that was small compared to the rest of Iowa's population. In contrast to the "just the facts" approach of the *Herald*, a headline in the *Denver Post* boasted, "Kids top racial chart: Multiple choices on census forms reflect diversity."[74] The writer claimed that since young people were more likely to describe themselves using more than one race, "it stands to reason that classrooms will be increasingly multiracial—as a result of a steady rise in interracial marriages."[75] A writer for the *Christian Science Monitor* declared that multiracial youth are "blurring distinctions among black and white, Asian and native [sic] American—which may one day help erase racism in the United States." This hope was backed up with the following demographic data and projection: "[T]he largest cohort of multiracials are 4 years old or younger. Demographers predict more growth because the number of interracial marriages is on the upswing."[76]

On the flip side, the *Pittsburgh Post-Gazette* printed a piece that focused on two elderly gentlemen, one Black and one White, and quoted their recent awareness of how "miscegenation" had become acceptable to them at the end of their lifetimes, due in part to their own kids' marital choices. Mr. Keene, an African American, said that when his son married a White woman, "I accepted it. I didn't have any problem with it. Probably years ago I would have, but I didn't [when my grandkids were born] and I don't now. They are lovely children and I wouldn't give anything for them."[77] His White counterpart was more ambivalent, saying, "Personally, I think that there are enough problems in a marriage without introducing any further problems. However, if the couple moves away from both sets of parents, then I think it's easier to accept."[78] The article suggests that these men are in the last generation to have misgivings about interracial marriage, and in the future, such opinions will be extinct. However, there is still a gap between endorsing interracial marriage in theory and endorsing such a union in one's family, particularly among Whites. Additionally, generational opinion change is not a lockstep, linear process; certainly there will be pockets of Gen Y that do not condone and/or will not take part in interracial dating or marriage. Finally, we must remember the caution of Brown and colleagues, that historically there has been a discrepancy between racial attitudes and actions. Thus, swings in opinions are not always matched by significant behavioral and social change.

As in the Asian American press, dominant writers often used personal stories of multiracial individuals as a way to frame the data. In a piece for the *Buffalo News*, Jay Rey profiled fifteen-year-old Lisa Lopez, a teen of Hispanic and African American descent, to segue to the declaration that she is part of

> a growing youthful movement symbolizing how racial identity has blurred. The nation is just starting to get a taste of this now that, for the first time, the Census Bureau is keeping data on multiracial Americans. . . . The multiracial population is largely a youthful generation. Locally, 74 percent are age 34 and under; 54 percent are under 20, like Lisa Lopez . . .[79]

Similarly, an article about the high number of interracial families in the armed forces was titled "Acceptance amid the diversity," and contained numerous quotes from family members who asserted how much easier it was for their children given the critical mass of multiracial children at Andrews Air Force Base.[80] Like other features on multiracial people, it contained several large pictures of Black/White couples and their children to accompany the statistics and testimony of the families. The article, which was centered on the first page of the Metro section of the *Washington Post*, frames a large photo of an African American army officer kissing his White wife, who is embracing their biracial daughters. Likewise, the second page of the article showcases large photos down the center of the entire page, displaying scenes of interracial families, children, and multiracial sets of neighbors smiling and laughing together. In pictures and in text—one caption is titled, "multiracial haven," the article testifies that "the rest of society can learn some lessons from the Army about racial integration" given that the Census data show that "military bases . . . are among the more integrated communities."[81] The idyllic scenes of cross-racial personal relations make for a picture of progress engendered by interracial marriage and other close socializing born of "family ties," one of the other captions for a photo in the piece.[82] This sense of the nation becoming racial kin was echoed in many other articles.

Unlike the stories in Asian American articles, these family vignettes rarely included critical assessments of race, Whites, color privilege, or institutional racism. Rather, writers in the dominant press suggested that these teens and their families were qualitatively different in their approach to race than older generations. The focus on youth and their laid-back approach to multiracial identity reduced the problem of race and racism to one of generation; the new enlightened multiracial generation would replace an older generation still hung up on race. The following final quote, from biracial interviewee Lisa Lopez, sums up this belief: "It's more older people who try to categorize people [by race]."[83] Many articles cited findings from national surveys that teenagers are most likely to endorse interracial dating and marriages, and hypothesized that the result will be more interracial families, as in this quote from *Time* magazine:

> 2 out of every 10 babies born [in Sacramento] are multiracial. When those babies grow up and start marrying—a national survey shows more than 90 percent of today's teens approve of interracial marriage—the numbers will climb even higher.[84]

In these articles, race is framed as a function of generation and proximity to racial Others; the institutional and cultural roots of racism are not part of the picture. Operating in a historical vacuum, the future of race and racism projected in the mainstream press is one of increasing racial harmony as interracial couplings continue to increase. The enlightened will take over as the racially backward die out. Interracial marriage and multiracial children are, then, both a sign of the "declining significance of race," and a solution to the problem of race all in one. Conservative columnists and editorial boards took this logic to a particular policy extreme in the mainstream press, who used the desire of multiracial people to claim their entire heritage to the Census numbers to decry any and all government uses of racial data.

Conservative Champions of Miscegenation

The new census data provided another opportunity for conservatives to attack "racial preferences" and other elements of civil rights legislation. Their boldness coincided with a new administration that was less than enthusiastic about civil rights and other racial justice issues, and high-profile court cases against affirmative action policies.[85]

In a piece for the *National Review*, Clegg clearly articulated the neoconservative approach to multiracial identity in a hypothetical speech for George W. Bush to give on affirmative action. He advised the president to tell the nation that multiracial individuals are living proof that there are no pure races. As such, he argued, all government programs or policies that use race-based classifications or data are suspect because they

> pigeonhole people as if everyone were either pure black or white, Hispanic or non-Hispanic. The truth is, *as we learned in the latest census, not only is the American population increasingly multiracial and multiethnic, but so are many Americans as individuals.*[86]

He then scripted a passage for Bush to out his own family's interracial marriage (brother Jeb) and compared the Bush family to Tiger Woods's family, noting that intermarriage was true for "millions of Americans." Thus, he concluded, racial labeling—and "preferential treatment" based on such labels—is intrinsically wrong and has no place in public policy.

Similarly, the *Weekly Standard* editorialized that Census 2000's data revealed a trend "that threatens to make racial classification in the state [of California] anachronistic."[87] The paper went on to endorse Ward Connerly's Racial Privacy Initiative (RPI) as a vehicle to "hasten this process along and finally put an end to the mischief of racial quotas." Likewise, Jacoby blamed "minority interest groups" for clinging to a system of "narrow racial and ethnic pigeonholes" in order to sustain their benefits from "affirmative action largesse."[88] Their insistence that multiracial children choose only one race, he argued, holds our society back from its colorblind future. Even in news features, the notion that use of racial labels in any context is invalidated by the presence of multiracial Americans was widespread. In October 2003, *U.S. News and World Report* published a news feature on the RPI titled, "Beyond race, or beholden to it?" The piece is dominated by quotes from Ward Connerly and his allies, and ended with the rhetorical question, "Does measuring race perpetuate divisiveness—or provide the tools to end it?"[89] Given the opinions showcased in the majority of the piece, the former seems the preferred answer.

Perhaps the most inventive use of multiracial identity to support conservative arguments against race-based policies was in George F. Will's March 2002 column for *Newsweek*. Titled "Dropping the one-drop rule," Will's essay encapsulates what Houston J. Baker calls the "conservative nostalgic" version of the civil rights movement and Dr. Martin Luther King Jr's, vision of race relations. Invoking (and decontextualizing) the classic line from the "I Have A Dream" speech regarding skin color and character, Will excoriated civil rights groups that opposed the multiracial classification option and reimagined them as the keepers and enforcers of the one-drop rule. The rule has become, he wrote, a tool of "the institutionalized—fossilized, really—remnants of the civil rights movement." Indeed, he added, they are trying to keep people of color in line with a "retrograde" racial agenda.[90]

Will effectively equated the White supremacist creation and use of the one-drop rule to exclude, brutalize, and disfranchise people of color with the desire for racial solidarity, a solidarity some, for better or for worse, believe is based on a shared racial identity. This was, at best, an attempt to ally with those in the multiracial movement who believe all racial identification is suspect, and at worst a cynical redefinition of the one-drop rule that paid no attention to its original (and continued) use against people of color. To end the piece, Will predictably championed the RPI in the name of multiracial children for whom it was "morally reprehensible and . . . preposterous . . . to choose to 'be' the race of just one parent."[91] Similar to the antiracist White heroes[92] of contemporary films such as *Mississippi Burning* and *A Time to Kill*, Whites who cross the color line to marry—and those who champion their choices—are framed as the vanguard of improved race relations, erasing the century of activism and struggle of people of color to make the present-day ease of interracial marriage a possibililty. Thus, a new "positive" White subject—the intermarried White partner—is validated outside of history and without attention to the pain and anguish past, present, and future intermarried partners often face.

What George Will and his intellectual colleagues neglect to consider is that the browner and poorer children of interracial marriages (whom they allegedly champion in these articles) will not have any "racial privacy" as they negotiate the public sphere. While on school and government documents families and children may have a "choice" to articulate their racial identity as they see fit, those choices may only be relevant on the paper, filed in a cabinet for a few bureaucrats to see. In classrooms, on the bus, in parks and restaurants, these children and their families will still be subject to scrutiny, curiosity, and perhaps discrimination. They will not be asked to show their census forms or school forms: they will be identified visually using relevant racial schemata available to the viewer, and that identification will affect their interactions.

It is an odd idea, that race can be private—as if privacy vis-à-vis state records or the use of personalized racial labels were the vehicles to racial equality. In the United States, the only people who get racial "privacy" are White middle- and upper-class people. As Whiteness studies practitioners have articulated, one central feature of being White is not having to think about one's race on a daily basis or worry that one's race might be viewed negatively. Thus, most White people live in a world where their race doesn't (seem to) matter, for private or public agendas.[93] While this is a false sense of race-lessness, it seems to be an unrealistic (and perhaps undesirable) state of being for most people of color, mixed race or not. Race and ethnic identities are not just negative mind-states or instrumental characteristics that help people get "preferential treatment." The reductionist approach to racial and ethnic identity taken by neocons ignores the lived, often positive experiences and cultural grounding many people of color associate with their chosen group(s).

Race is also experienced in multiple sites and through various interactions, not just in the privacy of one's home or the halls of government bureaucracy. Elevating individual "choice" and "privacy" over all other aspects of racial identity, as found in social and political processes, pretends that race is merely a matter of cosmetics and record keeping. Similar to their faith in private moral strength and individual effort, they extract the social element of race from the discussion. If, they argue, individuals are not really one race, or if the anthropologists and geneticists are correct that race is not a salient feature of humankind, but a social construction, then government use of racial categories makes no sense, and is an encroachment on individual liberty. Forgotten is the long history of White-dominated society and White-dominated government impeding people of color from achieving liberty, and the continued struggle by people of different colors, classes, genders, and sexual orientations to fully realize the dream of complete citizenship.

Beyond these larger approaches to race, Will and his ilk conveniently forget that multiracial children will not necessarily be forced into choosing one parent over the other when filling out their forms. OMB regulations guide the selection of racial identities utilized on official forms for state agencies and employers. Furthermore, many multiracial groups have been successful getting school districts and health care agencies to provide multiracial options for families when they enroll their children. Why, one might wonder, don't the compassionate neocons advocate that all state and local governments provide a multiracial and/or check-all option as on Census 2000? This would eliminate the tragic "forced choice" problem, albeit it would leave affirmative action untouched. And, up to a certain age, it is *parents* who are filling out the forms. David Harris's research with multiracial youth reminds us that, as Generation M comes of age in 2010 and 2020, they may not fill out their forms the same way their parents did for Census 2000.[94] Depending on the context, multiracial individuals may choose different ways to identify themselves throughout their life course.

Dispatching Race

This comparison of African American, Asian American, and dominant news coverage reveals both hopeful and disturbing trends in media narratives about multiracial people. Perhaps the most promising developments came in the news media outlets for people of color. In the Black press, articles were not full of opinions and arguments framing multiracial people as self-hating or politically naïve, opening the door for more discussion of what Black identity may be becoming. African American writers also strayed from the zero-sum thinking that structured earlier predictions about the impact of the census changes, and turned to talk of coalition politics with Hispanics and including multiracial Blacks rather than rejecting their choice of multiracial identity. Although some commentators were still wary of multiracial identity and the use of Hispanic population statistics by opponents of civil rights, these pieces did not attribute as many negative qualities to either group as in prior reports.

Another stark contrast was that Asian American news writers were unique in their inclusion of White behavior and privilege as they assessed the opinions and impact of multiracial Asians after the census. Although critiques of Whiteness were implicit in many African American articles, only Asian American publications included explicit discussions and critiques of White privilege and White racism. In addition, Asian American publications provided space for Hapas to present their own feelings about their skin privilege and conflicted relationships with Whites. Both Asian American and African American sources asserted group-centered approaches to racial identity, promoted solidarity within and across racial groups, and continued to name institutional and interpersonal racism as major issues in need of political and social remedies.

These themes were largely absent in the dominant press. Indeed, the mainstream news media embraced multiracial identity as a solution to race relations in the twenty-first century. Framed as a triumph of tolerance and individual choice, multiracial identity was only problematic in terms of how the Census Bureau would square the numbers; Whiteness, institutional racism, and structural inequalities were not part of the story. Instead, as commentators speculated about the "blurring" of racial lines, they simultaneously reified them with discussions that echoed discourses of hybrid vigor and biological determinism: multiracial youth were portrayed as naturally more tolerant; demographic projections of increased intermarriage was equated with increased racial harmony in the United States. Thus, intermarriage and multiracial individuals were the cure to racial ills and the sign of the end of race problems in the United States. From the perspective of the mainstream press, multiracial identity is the natural end point of the centuries of struggle over race: now that we're marrying each other, we've crossed the final threshold of multiculturalism.

Of course, this development—framing multiracial people as harbingers of racial harmony rather than racial degradation—is evidence of some progress. Promoting tolerance and cross-racial intimacy at the dawn of the twenty-first century is much better than the hysteria over race mixing that ushered in the twentieth. In criticizing the picture painted by the dominant press, I do not mean to underemphasize the improvement for multiracial identity, particularly since not thirty years ago psychologists still assumed that to be biracial was to be forever confused about one's place in society. That the mainstream press is declaring a consensus that interracial marriage is a social good is no small change. But the manner in which this social good is articulated with the ideologies favored by conservatives is striking. The radical import of race mixing as envisioned by theorists of multiracial identity is that this identity will break down ideas of racial purity and White supremacy. Thus far, the mainstream press's celebration of multiracial identity has nothing to do with these progressive ideas. Multiracial people were presented as a new *minority*, not a new kind of White person. Furthermore, racial groups that are wary of the use of multiracial identity by the state are framed as retrograde and racist; as in the case of Maria Hylton, civil rights organizations that raised objections continued to be excoriated by conservative columnists.

The contrast between how African American and Asian American and dominant news organizations framed the Census Bureau's new counts of our country's racial and ethnic groups highlights the continued tension over what race means in the United States after the civil rights movement: Is race an individual issue, or a social and political issue? Is racism all in the mind of the individual, or are institutions still implicated in the continued inequalities between Whites and people of color? The dominant press tells the happy side of the story of multiracial identity, a story of individuals and private families achieving their right to choose their identity; left out of the story are the public implications of those choices and the glacial pace of integration in housing, schools, and other institutions. The other two sets of articles did address these issues, but were still left with gaps in how to approach the presence of multiracial people within their group. The Black press, although changing its negative stance on separate multiracial identification, did not get much farther than questions about how to respond to the results of the census and its implications for minority politics. The Asian American press probed the privileges of Whiteness through the experiences of Hapas, but did not reach far beyond the borders of the Asian American community to envision options for future political action. Thus, the presence of multiracial people in each set of publications evinced very different pictures of the state of American race relations. While the dominant press had an air of certainty about how multiracial people would affect society, the Asian and African American presses were not willing to predict wholesale improvements to race relations, providing experiences and evidence of continued inequalities and distrust of Whites' use of multiracial and Hispanic identity issues to drive wedges between people of color.

Conclusion

Dispatches from the Twenty-First Century Color Line

Conservatives changed the debate about race from an argument about how to best redress the economic and political injuries of racism to one that equates ending racism with eliminating racial reference within juridical discourse and public policy.

—Nikhil Pal Singh, *Black Is a Country*

Multiracialism does not lead to an invention of new human kinds but calls our attention to areas of overlap between different categories . . . [and] may challenge pernicious customs of differentially valuing human kinds in the following way: if a black person can be white and a white person black, then black and white persons cannot have different degrees of moral worth by virtue of being black or white.

—Laurie Shrage, "Ethnic Transgressions: Confessions of an Assimilated Jew"

At a time when Vin Diesel, Keanu Reeves, and Lenny Kravitz are the faces of pop culture cool, it's hard to remember that nary a generation ago the main symbols of multiracial identity were the "marginal man" and the "tragic mulatto," let alone that interracial relationships were either illegal or social suicide in most parts of the United States. Certainly, this shift in multiracial acceptance is cause for some celebration, albeit cautious celebration. Most people prefer to live in a society where a majority of Americans polled say they are not opposed to interracial marriage and legal barriers to it no longer exist. Many citizens enjoy the fruits of the legal victories of the civil rights movement that have made interracial romance a realistic possibility. But as multiracial celebrities and interracial families are touted as symbols of a new multicultural America of racial tolerance, what are media makers celebrating and what can we really say multiracial identity has brought us in terms of how we think about racial identity and public policy in the United States, and how the news media report race to the public?

The first three chapters of this book illustrated how news reports concerning multiracial people can easily be transformed into stories about Black/White biracial tensions. Before the press acknowledged the presence of the multiracial movement and/or the new label *multiracial*, the people of Black/White descent covered in these chapters were positioned as Black or non-White, but not multiracial. In the cases of Susie Phipps and Maria Hylton, mainstream journalists treated issues of race, racism, and racial labels as if they belonged to the past. Reporters and sources located the problem in arcane procedures of the state or in the minds of misguided Blacks and "politically correct" liberals. Only in the Malones' story did mainstream media begin to address more complex issues involved in how to classify people as Black, White, or otherwise. In addition, the Malone case prompted some journalists—particularly those who addressed African American opinions and experiences—to include and take seriously the claims of African Americans that race and racism still constrain the job market and affect their lives in subtle and non-subtle ways. This was also a case where a critique of Whiteness surfaced. The culpability of Whites in the Boston Fire Department made it harder to isolate African Americans as the problematic group in affirmative action, or as the group responsible for keeping race in the public eye. Thus, in the Malone case, White racial innocence was challenged implicitly, but a sense of a separate multiracial identity for "White-looking Black people" did not surface as an option, just as in the Phipps and Hylton cases. In all three cases, people of Black and White descent remained racial anomalies, awkwardly existing within a binary racial world.

In the last two chapters, which contrasted reports on the 2000 Census created by and for people of color with those of dominant media, differences in reporting reflect not only the policy preferences of each group; rather, we see opposing ideas about what race means in America. The writings of African American and Asian American journalists employed group-based frameworks of race to provide historicized analysis of present-day controversies. Rather than pushing race and racism into the past, writers of color used the racial past to reveal how history shapes the present. In the dominant media, however, the movement toward ever more privatized definitions of race continued. From the *New York Times* editorial that stated people such as Susie Phipps should be able to choose to be White if their "blood" is "51 percent White" to the *Washington Post's* quiz on how to correctly label "hybrids" with hip racial lingo, there is a push toward seeing multiracial identity as a mere matter of choice. These news discourses communicate a strong desire to put racism in the past, to minimize racial identity by confining the issue to descriptions of individual choices, be they naming one's own racial identity or choosing to consume others' identities. The exuberant discourses surrounding the multiracial population smacks of the same conservative nostalgia[1] that excises Martin Luther King Jr.'s famous line from the Mall—judged by the content of their character, not the color of their skin—from the context of his vigorous fight to make economic and social justice part of the national program of racial reform.[2]

As described earlier in this book, news media frames promote particular solutions to public problems. In the dominant media, multiracial people and interracial marriage are proposed as a solution to the problem of the color line. In doing so, media are implicitly endorsing particular models for understanding the role of race in our society, in the public sphere. Citizens, thus, should think of race as a slowly dying social category, a nineteenth-century anachronism that will soon have less influence in our lives than eye color. Celebrating the fashion of multiracial identities, they hail demographers' predictions of increases in interracial marriage as a portent of good racial things to come, namely, a nation deracialized by virtue of race mixing. Thus, all of our cultural, political, and historical differences will be negated, and we will become one nation, out from under the shadow of race.

This utopian—or I would say dystopian—vision of the impact of multiracial identity on the public is troublesome. It is still dependent on a myth of separate races; the only "positive" difference is the belief they can be joined through biological hybridity. However, this still leads us to asking biology—mating—to solve a problem that is political. Looking to Brazil, for example, we can surely see that majority mixed-race populations do not guarantee racial equality, or even uniformity of skin tone. Rather, a spectrum of peoples is arrayed on a light-to-dark hierarchy where lightness (if not Whiteness) is privileged. As multiracial identity is employed to reimagine and project an idealized multicultural nation, it is also prescribing how citizens should understand their own and others' racial identities in the public sphere, in public policy, and in private life. These discourses imagine how we citizens should "*do* race," how we should understand it and perform it in our own lives, and how to communicate our racial identity to our fellow Americans.

Theorist Robert Asen suggests that scholars reorient their "approaches to civic engagement from asking questions of what [citizens do] to asking questions of how" they do citizenship. He suggests we think of citizenship as consisting of "mode[s] of public engagement." Viewing citizenship as modalities, Asen asserts, helps us recognize citizenship as fluid and instructs us to look at the ways in which citizens engage each other, engage institutions, and produce communications. This theory of citizenship also recognizes that citizenship often entails risk, for in engaging other members of the public in, perhaps, creative or unapproved modes, one will risk rejection or even violence. Relatedly, this theory of "doing citizenship" sees engaged actors using discourse to draw lines; between public and private, for example, or between genders, races, or classes. As lines—of identification, perhaps—are drawn as citizens engage each other, "[s]ome participants will be better positioned to draw lines that better represent their interests."[3]

Using Asen's approach, I want to suggest that there are different modalities of *racial citizenship*, and that with their power to influence and set boundaries for public discourse, news media are major players in drawing lines between identity groups, and between acceptable ways of doing race, doing citizenship. For example, scholars have demonstrated how protestors are often framed as acting outside acceptable norms for public speech and citizen action. Likewise, others have demonstrated how "White," "male," "property-owner," and "citizen" have been yoked together from the founding of the country, when only White males were granted the rights and privileges of citizenship.[4] Being White in the public sphere means to do citizenship as an unmarked, raceless being. Being White in the eyes of the state has historically meant access to particular rights and privileges explicitly denied to other racial groups. To be Black or female in the public sphere has meant doing citizenship in a very risky manner: fighting for the right to name oneself a citizen in the face of legal, social, and economic barriers that denied that name.

Similarly, to be Asian American in the dominant public sphere has also been to be seen as an alien, noncitizen, to have to fight to be viewed as worthy of citizenship. As Lisa Lowe eloquently explains, immigration laws restricting or preventing particular Asian nationals from entering the country served to reinforce the connection between Whiteness, property, and citizenship.[5] In her work "Whiteness as Property," Cheryl Harris details how American property law structured a system that protected not only White property but implies Whiteness and its privileges to be "rights as legal property" to be protected by the state.[6] The connections between Whiteness, property, and citizenship are thrown into relief when those entities are denied to people of color. As Hong notes, Executive Order 9066, which forced Japanese Americans into internment camps, exposed the links as Japanese Americans' property was stolen by Whites with the permission of the state, and reparations were not to be had for decades. "Internment is thus arguably the most blatant demonstration that one must be white to have rights that are properly maintained and supported by the state. Indeed, it was the state itself that divested Japanese Americans of their property."[7] Thus, to be Black—or Asian or Native American or Latino—in the United States has often required a mode of citizenship engagement centered around risk, dissent, and creativity; and it has necessitated attention to the reality of race. If Singh is correct that the political lesson of the civil right movement is indeed that we must encounter and reencounter race as we attempt to reshape our society, then the invisibility and privileges of Whiteness are the polar opposites of the racial experiences of citizens of color. That is, in prosecuting their case to be recognized as citizens, people of color have developed creative modes of engagement that center race and racial identities rather than covering them up or pretending they don't matter.

In the past, multiracial identity has engendered varied modes of enacting citizenship; under the antebellum one-drop rule, mixed race people of any iota African descent were enslaved, noncitizens. In nineteenth-century New Orleans, creoles of color often enjoyed certain political, economic, and social privileges, and were able to engage in limited expressions of citizenship. These expressions, of course, were bounded by the whims and strategies of White patrons. The modality of passing allowed the Whitest-looking multiracials to experience the privileges of citizenship close to that of Whites; however, because passers were beset by the fear of being unveiled, passing was a very risky mode of racial citizenship.

Today, multiracial citizenship is articulated with ideals of multicultural harmony and tolerance, imagined alongside color-blind visions of raceless citizens. The multiracial citizen is often described as a bridge, linking disparate racialized sections of the public. In exchange for sublimating the untoward (read: colored) aspects of his or her racial heritage, the multiracial individual is being offered a new way to be part of We the People. In the next section of this chapter, I explore this dynamic by sketching out the idealized ways of "doing race" exemplified by mainstream media portrayals of famous multiracial men. In these sketches, I show how restrictive and restricting these modes of racial citizenship can be, and how they feed on assumptions that continue to relegate other people of color outside racial norms.

Doing Race in the Twenty-First Century: Tiger Woods and Barack Obama

Two multiracial figures for whom racial autobiography has become part and parcel of their public appeal are Tiger Woods and Barack Obama. It is notable that both are male, and both share some African heritage. Gender is instructive here as it reflects the continued bias to see men as representative of racial groups. I do not mean to replicate that bias, but to point out that these two men have become prominent vis-à-vis multiracial politics in a time when Black leadership is still gendered male and where the experiences and images of multiracial women are relegated mostly to entertainment media and/or exotic exceptionalism.[8] Whereas pundits have dubbed these men "All-American," or "Son of the United States," women of multiracial descent, such as Halle Berry or Mariah Carey, are not described as such; they are celebrated (and in some circles, denigrated) for attracting White audiences and White male desire, but not for representing America.[9] The bodies of multiracial women are still coded as vehicles for illicit sex, illegitimate births, and hushed histories of sexual conquest;[10] thus, it is rare to find biracial women described as exemplary American citizens, as people who can stand for or represent *all* (White) Americans.

In mainstream media discourses, Tiger Woods and Barack Obama have represented two modes of racial citizenship:

- Tiger Woods's multiracial identity prescribes a multicultural consumer as the ultimate racial citizen. To create a more perfect union, we are encouraged to see figures of multiracial descent such as Woods as vehicles for understanding and experiencing the Other, and seeing some similarity in the Other. Multiracial figures like Woods solve the problem of an ever-fragmenting public sphere/marketplace by allowing each and all to safely project or find oneself in multiculturalism, where citizens can experience difference through purchases and media consumption. Watching Tiger win (and buying his Nike products), we are the world, and Tiger is us all. Racial difference need not be confronted or understood, only consumed.

- Barack Obama's biography is re-created by pundits as a space to deal with race without talking about it. This multiracial figure is, similar to Woods, a bridge between cultures, a cipher to fill with one's own racial desires—particularly the desire to avoid racial conflict. Although I argue that his own autobiography contradicts many of the hopes thrust upon him, when he was anointed the right kind of Black politician for the twenty-first century, his multiracial identity and class position were used to make clear distinctions about how race should and should not be articulated in politics and policy. In this vision of multiracial citizenship, Blacks are positioned as perpetual antagonists to national unity via their insistence on speaking out against racial injustice and utilization of cultural signifiers of Blackness.

We Are Tiger Woods? Consuming the Other to Make the Nation

> It's also possible that multiracial individuals are more likely to inherit unusual combinations of traits. For example, Tiger Woods seems to combine the muscularity and masculine charisma of an African-American superstar with the self-discipline and focus of the finest Asian-American athlete.
>
> —Steve Sailer, President of the Human Biodiversity Institute
> http://www.isteve.com

Eldrick "Tiger" Woods is arguably the most famous multiracial person on the planet. Number one in the world golf rankings and beneficiary of the most lucrative endorsement contracts in sports, Woods's face is everywhere in the media and sports marketplace, often alongside those of his parents. Most recently, American Express has featured a loving portrait of Tiger embracing his Thai mother, Kulthilda. In a two-page classy black-and-white photo placed in top-selling national magazines, the picture with the slogan, "My life, my card," needs no explanation for the readers, for they know that this dark-skinned man hugging the lighter-skinned Asian woman is her son; we all already know the family history of the Woods clan, including Tiger's childhood term for his racial makeup, "Cablinasian."

Tiger's success as a spokesmodel for elite products and services (including luxury cars, platinum watches, and golf equipment) epitomizes the recent popularity of multiracial models in advertising. Prior to and since the 2000 Census, marketers recognized a new way to "do ethnicity" using ambiguous-looking multiracial models. And, since the Census data became available, advertisers are salivating over the potential multiracial youth market: 46 percent of people who chose more than one race are under eighteen, as compared to only 26 percent of the one-race population. This youthful profile, alongside the assumption that Generation Y is more tolerant of "mixing it up" as the mainstream press puts it, has made multiracial actors and models hot commodities. In a piece for American Demographics' *Forecast*, casting agents and advertising directors gushed over the popularity and utility of multiracial identity.

> Paula Sindlinger, a partner in Godlove & Sindlinger Casting in New York City, says . . . "The blended look says 'we're all in this together' and that 'the world's getting smaller . . .'" Al Ries . . . also endorses the use of multiracial casts to advertise mainstream products. Ethnic casts, he says, are effective at targeting only one segment. A practice that may disappear along with single-race segments—if the trend toward multirace continues.[11]

Thus, it seems, multiracial people can do double duty: they are acceptable to both "mainstream" and "ethnic" consumers. However, as implied by Mr. Ries's paraphrased comment, neither ethnic nor multiracial casts are "mainstream" (read: White). The appeal of the multiracial model or cast, according to these experts, is that they communicate "current, youthful, and urban" in a flash with their ambiguous skin tones, wavy hair, and facial features. Hints of their multiracial parentage are believed to be simultaneously exotic and enticing as well as reassuring, as demonstrated by the "we're all in this together" remark.

Tiger Woods is often mentioned as a figure destined to bring us together as a nation of consumer-citizens. Not only did ad industry and sports pundits announce that part of his appeal to Nike and other firms was that he could be marketed to Black, Asian, and White middle and upper-class consumers, but also the story of his family was cited as an inspirational example of racial progress. The sports audience was often conflated with the national public as columnists and commentators waxed rhapsodic over Woods's historic 1997 victory at the Masters Tournament. Journalists combined his Cablinasian heritage with his self-made athletic skills to shape a narrative of hope for a multicultural, harmonious future on and off the greens. Sports writer Jerelyn Eddings of *U.S. News & World Report* explained the Tiger phenomenon like this:

> That's why the success of a Tiger Woods or a Jackie Robinson continues to have meaning beyond the individual's achievement. When such moments bring Americans of all races together in celebration of excellence, the process of coming together is as important as the values that inspire it.[12]

Although many commentators have ridiculed his father, Earl's, declaration that Tiger is "qualified through his ethnicity to accomplish miracles" to heal a racially divided world, time and again, as with Michael Jordan, sportswriters and politicians wax rhapsodic about Woods's ability to "transcend race." Although there is scant evidence that Tiger Woods desires such a role to change either the White-dominated golf world or the course of racial politics, it is clear that he and other multiracial models are offered as symbols of national/racial unity via transcendence of race. This alleged transcendence, however, is not necessarily the model to which we should aspire when seeking ways to heal racial divides. Rather, "the rhetoric of transcendence is tied to notions of exceptionalism that appear to distance [celebrities] from the semiotic field that locates and positions other African American men," thereby erasing the particularities of race and power that shape both Tiger and the "other Blacks."[13]

Similarly, Woods's multiracial heritage and his mastery of an elite White sport—golf—further distance him from the "other" people of color. It is no mere coincidence that Woods has joined the three other men of color for whom, Dr. Ravi Dhar of Yale found, "the American public has broad, powerful associations: Bill Cosby, Colin Powell, and Michael Jordan."[14] According to Lauren Berlant, these men of African descent have become such familiar, likable figures for Whites because "these 'positive' icons of national minority represent both the minimum and the maximum of what the dominating cultures will sanction for circulation, exchange, and consumption." That is, the narratives crafted by and about these men adhere closely to the individualistic, patriarchal vision of the American Dream. Under the slogan, "Just Do It," itself a bootstrapping phrase, the icon of multiracial Tiger Woods works to personify and reinforce the myth of conquering race through hard work. But as D. L Andrews succinctly put it, figures such as Woods don't transcend race, they "displace racial codes onto other black bodies."[15] Race does not and cannot so simply disappear into the ether.

The celebration of Tiger Woods and other multiracial celebrities as symbols of national integration via consumer choice is problematic on another level: it ignores the racial inequalities that limit certain groups' participation in the consumer economy. To acquire the products and participate in the leisure activities Woods promotes presupposes income levels and social status out of reach of many Americans of any color. Beyond that, the labor system that produces these goods depends on low-wage Black, brown, and yellow female workers. The multiracial fantasy of consumptive citizenship erases the role of these citizens and would-be citizens of the United States. The sweatshops and factories where they work are a far cry from the idyllic golf courses and high-fiving multiracial school children who declare "I am Tiger Woods" in Nike's television commercials, which project an idealized vision of a White-dominated sporting world transformed by Tiger's mixed-race identity.

Another problem with the marketers' "we're all in this together" romanticized vision of multiracial identity is that it papers over the global and local politics that facilitate certain kinds of interracial relationships more than others. The Woods family is a perfect example of this phenomenon. Asian American women have the highest rates of out-marriage; the story of Earl and Kultilda Woods's marriage is not just a love story, but also a tale of the effects of the United States' military presence in Southeast Asia. Earl Woods spent two tours of duty in Viet Nam, and while stationed in Asia met Kultilda, who was working as a secretary at a U.S. Army base. Their meeting was not chance; the movement of Black males to Southeast Asia in the 1960s was not for leisure travel, but to fight in a war. Asian women served, and continue to serve, many roles in and around U.S. military bases.[16] Many became "war brides"; others were left behind with Amerasian children who were shamed for having American birth fathers. Retelling the Woods's story within the framework of American imperial and military might in the 1960s exposes a different set of reasons why Americans have "always been mixed" and why Asian-American mixing isn't so "new." As Lowe points out, the racialization and gendering of Asians as immigrants and imperial subjects in U.S. law and custom sets the stage for contact with specific Asian subgroups.[17] It would have been highly unlikely for Earl Woods to have met Kultilda as a Black man in the 1960s outside the parameters of military occupation and immigration policies that made his passage to Asia possible.

Can we imagine other ways of interpreting Tiger's and other multiracial models' images and labels in ways that challenge the current trend? Could his multiracial identity be more than an object of commercial exploitation? Raquel Salgado's reading of his chosen moniker, "Cablinasian," suggests an alternative. Salgado says Woods's declaration of his Cablinasian identity, and his visible parents, offers us "a transmodern narrative, an imaginative political statement . . . demonstrating the limitations of words and the absurdity of categories that try to locate identity."[18] However, she contends that such demonstrations might not succeed without deliberations and actions that strive to dismantle racial hierarchies. Particularly, she contends that multiracial individuals such as Woods should

> challenge orthodoxies, realize that self cannot be separated from other, and work collectively for change. But too often, especially in this country that is built on imagined individuality, we often see individual well-being as a condition opposed to collective action—as if one negates the possibility of the other.[19]

However, even if only for a moment, "Cablinasian" excites the imagination and provides a glimpse of a novel discourse of race beyond the language we currently use.

How could we extend this moment beyond the catch of breath, exhaling it into a national discussion that has been choked by the rhetoric of racial realism and the primacy of the individual? One vehicle suggested by Salgado's musings on "Cablinasian" is for multiracial individuals and families to resist media typecasting of them as exceptional or transcendent. Rather, they should seek to explain their choices in a context that does not divide them from "other people of color" or valorize their multiracial existence as a function of colorblindness. Although some multiracial people surely hew to the racial realist paradigm, many do not, as evidenced by the prominent discussions of race privilege in the Asian American press. And, while individuals and organizations cannot control the entire framing process, they can endeavor to shift the balance by providing information about and characterizations of their identities in ways that emphasize collectivity and rejection of racial hierarchy. They can dispute the notion that the fight for inclusion on the 2000 Census was not a fight to erase race from the national lexicon, but to expand that lexicon in a way that forces us to confront the realities of pigmentocracy and racial inequalities. This kind of presentation of multiracial identity frames interracial intimacy as a starting point of new conversations rather than the end of talk about race.

Guess Who's Coming to the Senate: Barack Obama, Not a "Stereotypical Black"

> "My moment was a focus group," recalls Obama's campaign manager, Jim Cauley. "The moderator . . . asked the older [white female] group, 'Who do each of these [candidates] remind you of?' for Dan Hynes, a woman said, 'Dan Quayle,' . . . And she looked at Barack and the lady said, 'Sidney Poitier.' At that moment I was like, 'Shit, this is real.'"
>
> —Noam Scheiber, "Barack Obama's Miraculous Campaign"

Once Barack Obama lit up the 2004 Democratic National Convention with a rousing keynote speech, the whole country was talking about the senatorial candidate from Illinois. From declaring him the first Black politician to have a real shot at the presidency to anointing him the "de facto leader of the Black community"[20] should he win his Senate seat, the press ushered Obama into the sphere of political celebrity with great enthusiasm. The immediate embrace of this self-described "skinny guy with big ears"—by voices on the Right and the Left—is unprecedented for a politician of African descent. However, within this consensus of hope and excitement for a candidate of color are troubling discourses of race that resonate with those generated by and about Woods. Journalists, pundits, voters, and fellow politicians reacted to Obama with elements of the racial realism and liberal resignation about race described in the Introduction. When contrasted with Obama's own descriptions of his identity and connections to Black communities, their assessments of his interracial background clearly miss important aspects of the candidate's sensibilities about race in the United States.

In the afterglow of the keynote speech, journalists and commentators rushed to explain to the public why Obama was attractive to both

White and Black voters. The merits of his rhetorical abilities are clear to anyone who has seen or read the now-famous speech; his dogged campaigning in all regions of Illinois clearly elevated his profile with rural and working-class Whites; and his connections to and endorsements from key Black politicians in Chicago and the Illinois legislature were crucial. But time and again, the press linked his popularity with Whites to his interracial—and implicitly, his middle-class—background. Scott Malcolmson of the *New York Times* wrote, "[S]ome political analysts have wondered whether white voters don't also find him attractive because while he is black, . . . *he is not black in the usual way.*"[21] The "usual way" being the tactics, mannerisms, and biographies of politicians such as Jesse Jackson or Al Sharpton, both of whom were compared unfavorably to Obama. For instance, the *Boston Globe* published a letter from reader Michael Johnson subtitled "It's time for Jackson to retire."

> [O]n the same day as [Obama's] unifying message, the Rev. Jesse Jackson was expressing his freedom of speech to further divide the races. Even if what Jackson says is the truth, his message almost always seems to come off as an attack on white people. . . . When Jackson speaks on race, the impressions many white people get is that he wants to raise black people up and tear white people down. Jackson will not get white people on his side by using that approach. . . . Obama's message was that we should all help each other, every race, to rise up![22]

In his letter, Johnson articulates a desire to assume a position of innocence in discussions of racial inequality. Whiteness theorists have emphasized that this desire has been an impediment to discussions of racial justice and equality.[23] Even if they recognize that racial inequalities still exist, the reluctance and refusal to acknowledge the historical and current role of white privilege in the maintenance of racial inequality continues to be a roadblock in discussions of race. Furthermore, the writer's letter suggested the idea that racial progress is a zero-sum game—that elevating the position of Blacks necessitates a lowering of Whites. His letter combines the Democrats' conventional wisdom that race loses white votes with the underlying fear of the loss of White privilege. Thus, any African American spokesperson or politician who talks about contemporary racism as a part of racial inequality is marked as someone trying to "bring down the whites."

Jonathan Tilove's article in the *New York Times* contained a similar assessment of Barack's appeal to Whites:

The old model of the black protest leader making demands no longer makes sense in an age tapped out and tired of race, Professor [Angela] Dillard said. Obama can argue for policies virtually indistinguishable from Sharpton's in cooler, nonracial terms, *while still affirming a message of racial identity and uplift in his very being.*[24]

If the age is "tired of race," we can certainly imagine that the fatigue of Whites may be very different than that of people of color. Whites may be tired of hearing demands for racial equality and power sharing; Black, Hispanic, and Asian Americans may be tired of having their demands for equality construed as "special interests" or met with indifference. Furthermore, it seems a very interesting trick, to talk about race-based policies in nonracial terms. The key to this ability, it seems from reporters and commentators, is "[t]he power of Obama's exotic background" as Noam Scheiber put it.[25] Emphasizing his parents interracial marriage, his father's status as an immigrant from Kenya, and Obama's elite education at Harvard, journalists and interviewees surmised that Obama is not "stereotypically Black," but rather, "transcends race."

> The son of a Kenyan immigrant and Kansas native, Obama is the product of a interracial marriage. His Ivy League pedigree . . . belies his humble upbringing. . . . But on Tuesday, *he was simply a son of the United States.* He was us, all of us. . . . Time and again, Obama offered a vision that transcended everything: race, creed, color, party politics, and social and economic strata.[26]

Interweaving his family story with lines from his speech calling for Americans to reach across the lines of Black and White, blue and red states, journalists made Obama a "son of the United States" who was the polar opposite of his Black predecessors. Class and parentage distance him from the alleged divisive old guard of Black leadership, as illustrated in this passage from Tilove's analysis:

> Sharpton and Obama could not be more different in style and biography. Obama, the son of a white mother and Kenyan father he barely knew, was the first black president of the Harvard Law Review. Sharpton, who counts James Brown the closest thing to a father figure, was an ordained preacher while still a small child. Sharpton practices the politics of controversy and polarization. Obama listens, reasons, and calms.[27]

If we recognize the stylistic and biographical elements arrayed in this quote as proxies for both race and class differences between Sharpton and Obama, it is clear that Obama's sophisticated middle-class education and diverse background is deemed superior to Sharpton's working-class origins in the Black church. Especially telling is the parallel Tilove draws between their fathers: Obama's is absent, yet elevated due to his immigrant status; Sharpton occupies the space of the fatherless Black child, and Tilove's reference to James Brown has a mocking tone. The social capital and speaking style Obama accrued through his Ivy League education—indicated here by his ability to "reason and calm" rather than polarize—brings him much closer to the white middle-class aesthetic for political speech than Sharpton. Thus, part of Barack Obama's appeal is that he is seemingly not like "other Blacks." Writers made it clear that Whites are "tired" of racial politics and Black political leaders who make explicit demands for remedies to racism.

While Obama's exceptionalism works to include him as a son of the United States of America, it simultaneously "support[s] and obscure[s] the powerful naturalization and centrality of the White category"[28] to his status as "All-American" and "presidential." The basis for comparisons between Sharpton and Obama are rooted in Anglo-American expectations for debate and decorum, in assumptions about how, when, and where race can be spoken of in public. Those black and brown leaders who do not display the "reasoning" style of Obama are not acceptable in the dominant public sphere. As the state and mass media recognize the demographic diversity of multiracial people like Obama, the privileged racial citizenship extended to them is still predicated on the continued denigration of other people of color. As such, this "positive" narrative about an interracial leader encourages people of color to "cover" the cultural and political traits that do not sit well with White majorities.[29] If one talks about race with its sharp edges and ugly past exposed, then one will be dismissed as an "old school" politician dealing in disunity. Thus, the narrative of interracial union promoted by these contrasting images of Obama and Jesse Jackson or Al Sharpton promotes a kinder, gentler assimilation ethic: bring us your difference, but only that which does not discomfit.

But the question remains, Can one talk about race without naming it and still solve the problems of race? The enthusiasm of the press for Obama's multiracial biography, like the hype surrounding multiracial models in the world of advertising, becomes a way of talking about race without talking about it. That is, speaking about multiracial individuals and trends provides a "race-specific technology" of discourse. I take the term *race-specific technology* from Dorothy Roberts's discussion of new race-specific pharmaceuticals that have recently entered the market.[30] Roberts argues that, as scientists have seesawed on the "biological realities" of race, these race-specific drugs may have opened the door for a "renewed acceptance of inherent racial differences" beyond the treatment of heart conditions or sickle cell anemia, partly because their emergence coincides with "intensified state surveillance of inner city communities: racial pro-filing, mass incarceration, welfare restructuring," and other policies that stigmatize particular racial groups. This return to discussions of the bio-logical origins of race in the medical sphere, she fears, will spread to other arenas to provide "a ready rationale for . . . disfranchisement of black citizens and complement colorblind policies based on the claim that rac-ism is no longer the cause of social equality."[31] Similarly, multiracial iden-tity provides a technology—individual couplings—that can be extolled in mainstream media. The "positive" discourse of race mixing provides a language whereby we are explicitly talking about race and society, but the focus on individuals, style, and reproduction pushes discussions of social, political, and economic racial realities backstage. As such, the circulation of these discourses of racial biography dovetails with the racial technolo-gies Roberts critiques, and furthers the racial project of colorblind policy that negatively impacts people of color. The "natural" progression toward interracial marriage becomes another aspect of the re-biologization of race; to eliminate racial disharmony, we must mate. People of color who do not participate in this genetic-level "integration" or engage in cover-ing their differences are left out of the national equation.

But before we leave the new senator's story, we should ask, does the press's imagination of Barack Obama's transcendent racial identity match his actual approach to and opinions of racial politics? Looking at Obama's political career, he is very close to many movers and shakers in Black Chicago as well as African American power brokers in the Illinois senate. Furthermore, in his autobiography, his record in the state house and his campaign materials, it is clear that Obama's policy agenda runs to the left of the political spectrum. Beyond his articulation of his family story in front of the DNC, Obama wrote in his autobiography about race and the often torturous process someone of African descent must go through in the United States due to the continued effects of racism in our country. In *Dreams from My Father*, Obama conveys with deep-seated affection— as well as criticism—his relationships with Black communities in Chicago when he was a community organizer. Although he ultimately does not agree with the nationalist platform and ideology of the Nation of Islam (NOI), a strong presence on the South Side, he eloquently testifies to the appeal of NOI to African Americans in the context of continued racial stratification and oppression. He testifies to the need for stronger Black political institutions and new Black political strategies, although not

organized around an essential definition of Blackness. He writes of Black
people not in terms of individualism, but collectivism. He calls for racial
cohesion, but does not collapse into an easy single sense of who Black
people are or must be:

> Black survival in this country had always been premised on a
> minimum of delusions. . . . The continuing struggle to align word
> with action, our heartfelt desires with a workable plan—didn't
> self-esteem finally depend on just this? It was that belief which
> had led me into organizing, and . . . which would lead me to
> conclude, perhaps for the final time, that notions of purity—of
> race or culture—could no more serve for the typical black
> American's self-esteem than it could for mine. Our sense of whole-
> ness would have to arise from something more fine than the
> bloodlines we'd inherited. It would have to find root in Mrs.
> Crenshaw's story and Mr. Marshall's story, in Ruby's story and
> Rafiq's; in all the messy, contradictory details of our experience.[32]

After this moment of clarity, the author describes taking Ruby to a play
featuring Black women telling their stories in song; he evokes the joy,
beauty, and release the audience and performers experience together as
Black men and women. He links his realization about race not to rejecting Blackness, but to embracing it in its collective contradictions. Obama's
descriptions of his experience and revelation resonate with Singh's description of the political and cultural genius that has emanated from the
Black public sphere in the long civil rights era. Singh reminds us that
Black activists and scholars have long strained "at both the borders of the
U.S. nation-state and the boundaries of its liberal creed" as they fought
the restrictions of racism within American democracy. Singh's framework
challenges the conservative conception of the civil rights movement as

> the moment when black people emerged (at long last) as indi-
> vidual subjects of capitalist-liberalism and as formal participants
> in democratic-nationalism. . . . What may be most remarkable
> about the long civil rights era is the emergence of black people
> as a distinct people and a public—and the concomitant develop-
> ment of race as a political space. There was no precedent for this
> in the liberal-democratic narrative of nationhood that explained
> how they needed to progress.[33]

In this light, we might want to reframe Obama's call for a new America,
his appeal to our better angels during the Democrats' convention, not

as a simple roll call for individuals, but a challenge to push the boundaries of America and American identity yet again. As he said in the speech, it is time to hold up the dream of America "against a harsh reality and see how we are measuring up" to it. That speech, when placed in the context of his career in Black politics and sense of Black identity, can be reread as an updated version of King's charge to America to make good on the bounced check of equality. Near the end of his speech, Obama invokes the value of being our brother's keeper as central to Americanness. This vision of nation as family is not consistent with bootstrapping and colorblindness; one must be able to see all aspects of her brothers and sisters in order to communicate well and help keep us all from harm.

Rethinking Options for Racial Citizenship

> What if the political lesson of the long civil rights era is that we advance equality only by continually passing through a politics of race and by refusing the notion of a 'beyond' race? . . . The historic denials of black voting rights, like today's racially coded withdrawals of social welfare provision . . . have disenfranchised and disempowered numerically far greater numbers of non-black citizens and residents. Conversely, protections granted under the Civil Rights Act of 1964 and affirmative action programs have protected and enhanced the life chances of broad majorities within the society . . .
>
> —Nikhil Pal Singh, *Black Is a County*

So what do these two men teach about the possibilities for multiracial identity in the news and public discourse? One lesson is, as others have written, to say that race is socially constructed cannot end the conversation; rather, social construction allows us to see how races are constructed in relation to one another, not in a vacuum. "Social and political power, as well as the implications in social terms, must be identified. There is no black without white, there is no white without black,"[34] and so on. To return to Stuart Hall's question—What identities are working this week?—this book testifies that the social construction of multiracial-identified individuals is occurring in relation to devalued constructions of Blacks and other people of color. Multiracial identity has been working for neoconservatives precisely because they have managed to cast multiracial identity in the mold of individual choice and detach it from the racial past. Multiracial identity works for Tiger Woods's commercial partners because his image collapses "multiculturalism into an easy pluralism that simply adds what it constructs as the Other without upsetting the fundamental precepts and paradigms of Western culture."[35]

We cannot celebrate the rise in interracial marriage as a simple indicator that the "last walls" of racism are tumbling down; rather, there are new cracks in the wall, but those flaws are not necessarily enough to bring the entire edifice down. Rather, the kind of discourse being formed in response to those cracks may be more likely to serve as mortar for those fissures. Discourses of individual choice, "best of both worlds," "colorblindness," and charges of obsessive "reverse racism" or intransigence on the part of other racial groups divert our attention away from the continued strength of racial thinking and entrenched racial inequalities in our society. The use of the multiracial movement's attack on the one-drop rule for conservative aims could silence many other critiques and necessary innovations that could spring from a serious meditation on the meanings of multiracial identities in a racially stratified nation. Look different, but don't act differently, is the message. Talk about your individual family's racial diversity, but not about how to achieve racial equality.

Salgado asserts that if the narrative of mixed-race theory "is embodied in the tension, conflicts, and deliberations that inhere in discursive genres like the personal essay," then mixed-race theory is about the fluctuating moments of connection between self and other, across the racial lines that have been constructed.[36] The mainstream media, and at times, alternative media sources for people of color, often present a set of limiting choices and limited connections as they incorporate multiracial identity into existing racial frameworks. In their dispatches, there is colorblindness and the end of race; monoracial rules that define and delimit racial affiliations; honorary Whiteness; exotic multicultural playmates; and silence. But insisting that multiracial-identified people augur colorblindness or should adhere to prior models of racial identity are both invalid propositions. The engagement of self and other in productive, ongoing tension—at interpersonal and social levels—can inspire an ongoing dialogue that could lead to new questions, new consensus, or more dissent. For us to form multiracial society, this tension is to be expected, and the forming of a more perfect racial union may be too much to ask in the short term. But for people to share in the moments of possibility opened by a critical grasp of multiracial identity is not so hard to imagine, I think. To open up an honest, perhaps uncomfortable exchange of thoughts about what race has been, is, and will be with more diverse voices would be, perhaps, what President Clinton's abortive attempt at a national conversation on race was supposed to be.

Hapa Asian Americans interviewed in Asian American magazines embodied and performed Salgado's vision of this self/other confrontation and dialogue when they critiqued White assumptions about their race and questioned the viability of part-White privilege. As they critiqued Whiteness, they simultaneously entered into dialogue with Asian communities that desire their silence, asserting a role in both White and Asian American politics and cultures. We see the contextualization of racial identity dramatized in the Census results as well: Puerto Rican Americans in New York were nearly three times as likely to consider themselves Black and of Hispanic origin than Puerto Ricans in Puerto Rico, who were more likely to describe themselves as White and Hispanic. Those who did so demonstrate not only their desire to choose both/and, but also reveal the continued relevance of and confrontations between the Black/White divide to their own lives.

In an earlier iteration of this project, I hesitantly threw out the statement that perhaps multiracial identity has ushered in the death of strategic essentialism. This concept has been batted about as a sort of compromise in a post–civil rights, postcolonial, postfeminist world where essential identities are rejected but still seem tactically necessary for women, people of color, gays and lesbians, and other marginalized social groups. Now I think I was too early to declare the end of this strategy, but I am also attracted to other theorists' alternative renderings of group identity and related interactions. The spatial metaphors of public spheres in particular draw my attention. If we imagine, as Arjun Appadurai has, that public spheres are made of scapes, or zones, we might reimagine the nation's projection of its identity as a zone, a zone of intersecting shifting planes of discourse and traffic of bodies. This zone in motion is a place where home is never guaranteed or completely safe from contradiction. What is home/nation, and who gets to claim and define membership is determined not only by the geography of this zone, but who moves in and out of the space. This set of intersecting zones—individuals, institutions, bodies, groups—that occupy and contest the space defines our sense of self, other, and nation.

Here I revisit the metaphor of the borderlands provided by Anzaldúa as exemplary of this zone: if multiracial people are, in and of themselves, products of intersection, then reading them as mobile subjects of multiple zones opens the door to discussion of what is happening in the moment of contact, or crossing, *now*. When we ask, *What identities are working today*, then, the first question we might want to ask is *Where are they and with whom are they colliding ? How long do they remain in contact? What are their shared struggles? Conflicts?* This line of questioning asks us to be particular, yes, and perhaps that raises the fear of ever-fragmenting identities and publics. However, when one looks at the intersection of more than one group, then one must think in relational terms, to look for overlap as well as disjuncture, to work in tandem in order to get a sense of depth that honors all participants. This conception of racial identities could spark discourse that brings our sense of race to a new plane of specificity while still striving to develop communities of resistance.

Multiracial identities need not be a starting point on the journey to "one America, one race" but rather the beginning of a very rigorous debate, a contentious discussion, an often painful hearing of memories and histories buried under the scrim of official national identity and history. What state recognition of multiracial identity could prompt is a demand to end the quest for a common culture, and an end to the fiction that race did not structure our country. In other words, I argue we should reject mainstream framing of multiracial identity as the *end* of race, and attempt to interject the idea that multiracial identity can help us discuss the meaning of race in a society that is caught between the legacy and familiarity of a binary racial order and the demographic realities of a spectrum of racial identities. To do this, we have to imagine new modes of citizenship and interaction and sociality that go beyond consumption and facile labeling. I don't really know what this will entail, or what it will look like, but I know it is not a laissez-faire multiculturalism where anything goes; we can't tell people of color that their only place in society is in a static, cultural museum for others to tour or poach from to augment their own identities. If multiracial individuals explode the options for systems of racial and ethnic identification, then we must always remember to ask: Are all of the people within the state and society able to exercise the same freedom of choice, of perusal, of learning about identity—or rejecting identities? Are all of those identity choices afforded the same privileges of association and citizenship, and if not why? If the emergence of multiracial-identified people does not prompt us to ask these questions and to imagine a world where we can answer affirmatively, then our discourse on racial identity is truly idle talk.

How to Do Race and the News?

Although many of the minority news media outlets and practitioners represented in these chapters provide some stunning and promising examples of how to utilize multiracial identity as a way to open discussions about white privilege, institutional racism, and the perils of colorblind ideology, the burden for reforming race reporting cannot fall solely on the shoulders of these small-circulation publications and their electronic counterparts. Due to the restricted scope of their circulation, it is unlikely that their frames will reach the majority White population. Furthermore, the "mainstream" media's lack of these frames and voices exemplifies the

problem of race in general circulation publications: White news producers and White readers still set the parameters for an unstated norm against
which people of color are measured. Thus, reforms within mainstream
news media outlets—as well as academies of journalism instruction—need
to occur.

Normalizing the Presence of Journalists of Color in Mainstream Newsrooms

Although some progress has been made in hiring more diverse staffs, the
people of color who do join the ranks of elite and mainstream newsrooms
are often under pressure to prove that they aren't "biased" toward their
racial identity groups. As Pamela Newkirk's[37] and Clint Wilson's[38] studies
of Black reporters revealed, African American reporters must often choose
between career advancement and reporting on stories near and dear to
their communities. They are often discouraged from investigating issues
that would shed a different light on Black communities, and are wary of
retaliation in the form of harassment or demotion. Nearly forty years
after the Kerner Commission condemned the mainstream news media's
coverage of Blacks, the American Society of Newspaper Editors (ASNE)
is nowhere near its own goal of having 30 percent of its workforce composed of people of color.[39] Given that people of color still do not work
in large numbers in dominant newsrooms—especially in editorial and
managerial positions—it is crucial to maintain and enhance the presence
of news media resources created by and/or for people of color. Because
these alternative news media often strive to provide alternative framing of
racial issues, dominant news media would do well to attend to the differences in coverage and evaluate their own practices to see where and how
more diversity of viewpoints on racial matters could be created. Of course,
there are very different stylistic and economic imperatives operating for
mainstream and ethnic news media. Most ethnic news media were created
primarily to make up for gaps and biases in mainstream news; they are
first and foremost devoted to delivering information to their constituencies in a manner consonant with those cultures. Thus, with their
community-centered imperatives, Asian and African American news publications take on racial news items and viewpoints we don't see in dominant news. In these newsrooms, Whiteness and White privilege do not
operate to stifle journalists of color. As Gwyneth Mellinger summarizes:

> Diversity in newsroom employment, then, is not primarily a prob-
> lem of economic inequity and class exploitation, as it would be in
> other workplace contexts, but an issue of cultural valuation and

> recognition as well; it is not just about who gets to be the boss
> but about who gets to mediate the messages that define racial
> reality within the dominant public sphere.[40]

While it may be crucial to maintain the presence of critical ethnic news media to continue to provide an alternative, it may be a heavy and unrealistic burden for these news outlets to spark wide-ranging conversations about race and transformations in dominant discourse on their own. Because minority audiences are smaller and valued less by advertisers, it is more difficult to sustain commercial media enterprises targeted at audiences of color. As Oscar Gandy notes in his overview of research on race and the market for ethnic audiences, current conditions make it difficult for Black-owned and/or oriented media to sustain news divisions due to lack of funds and commercial prejudices that favor lucrative entertainment media models.[41] Furthermore, given the influence of general audience news media, we cannot give a pass to the dominant news producers on racial issues. To say that race can only be done well (or at all) by racial minorities reinforces the myths that Whites are not affected by race and do not need to think about racial issues.

Changing Racial Narratives in the Mainstream News

A small number of journalism schools, private foundations, and professional organizations have been trying to address the interrelated issues of racial reporting and racial diversity in newsrooms. Most of their interventions currently focus on two goals: (1) increasing the number of journalists and editors of color in a variety of newsrooms, and (2) providing journalism students and practicing journalists with tools to improve the quality and quantity of race and ethnicity reporting. The former goal is usually pursued through mechanisms such as scholarships, internships, and seminars that provide students and up-and-coming journalists with opportunities to work with and learn from members of the profession. Other workplace-oriented programs invite seasoned journalists, managers, and editorial staff to participate in diversity seminars that provide guidance on how to seek and retain talented minority journalists. Predictably, many of these programs focus on socializing minority journalists into the existing newsroom culture; few concentrate on the ways in which newsroom cultures themselves need to change in order to truly integrate the "differences" minority journalists may bring. As such, many of these well-meaning programs may favor candidates who are willing to assimilate into the already-existing practices that mitigate against innovative reporting on racial issues.

A promising example of a program that directly confronts this dilemma is the Columbia Journalism School's "Let's Do It Better" awards and workshops. The central goal of the workshop is to encourage journalists, educators, and editors to view coverage of race and ethnicity "as an urgent journalistic duty." The program gives awards to journalists who produce exemplary articles and reports, which are judged by their candor about race and ethnicity, their creativity, and their attention to history and social factors that shape the issues and events being covered. These exemplars are then used as models for workshop participants to explore how race reporting can go beyond established norms. In the workshops, news "gatekeepers"—editors, journalism instructors, and journalists—are engaged in the process of improving race and ethnicity reporting, and are given tools to bring the lessons learned back to their classrooms and newsrooms. Importantly, this includes discussions of how to "improve the newsroom and classroom environment in which journalists and students of varying race and ethnicity function" so as to "deepen the multicultural dialogue and help retain talented young journalists in the profession."[42] While the workshops also provide advice about recruiting minority talent, they recognize that getting people in the door is just the beginning, and that changing the culture, not just the composition, of the newsroom is a necessary step in improving the overall quality of reporting on race and ethnicity.

Many scholars and critics of news media are quick to remind us, however, that market imperatives may work against integrating and transforming newsrooms. As summarized earlier, audiences of color are not highly valued by advertisers, particularly in the news industry. And, as competition between news providers increases across various media, and advertisers demand access to choice affluent segments of the audience, people of color and "their issues" may lose even more space to topics preferred by the desired audience. Even media outlets that are targeted at racial and ethnic minorities may not contain much, or any, news, as programming on BET (both before and after the Viacom takeover) suggests. However, I argue that the way in which media managers imagine the economically desirable audience and its news interests is linked to the dominant assumptions about race that make this market logic seem like common sense. If we conceptualize racial politics as a zero-sum game, or racial identity as an aspect only of the lives of people of color, not Whites, then it is hard to see race as anything but a "minority issue," not a "general market" interest.

I want to suggest that, in order to transform current practices of racial reporting and to curtail the negative impacts the dominant framing of race has on public discussion and opinion, journalists must endeavor to make clear how so-called minority issues impact the general public. Lani Guinier and Gerald Torres provide an extremely useful metaphor for us to discuss race across racial publics: the miner's canary.[43] In their book of the same title, these scholars explore how racial inequalities are indicative of broader social problems that, in fact, impact the majority of Americans, who will eventually pay hidden costs. That Whites and people of color share these problems can be seen best when one looks from the perspective of the canary in the coal mine. The canary, whose sensitivity to noxious gases tells all occupants of a mine that the environment is poisonous, will suffer first; if the miners and others see its suffering, the best course of action is to heed the warning and fix the problem rather than ignore the canary, blame it for getting sick, or tell the bird to shut up. Reports on racial controversies or specific racial groups should be similarly related to the condition of the general public. I recommend that we transport their canary metaphor for investigating and responding to racial inequality to discussions of how journalists craft discourses about race and ethnicity in both general- and specialty-market publications.

In their book, *The Black Image in the White Mind*, Robert Entman and Andrew Rojecki suggest that we need to see more news frames that support "racial comity" to encourage readers to see more commonalities between racialized groups than differences. Similarly, Amitai Etzioni reminds us that when one looks at poll results regarding "American virtues" such as hard work, Blacks, Whites, and Hispanics are closer in opinion than one would imagine given the prominence of racial discord in most reporting. I applaud these authors for calling on journalists and others to see and communicate how much closer we are to consensus on many political and cultural issues. But I am wary of the strategy of comity in the particular case of multiracial identity. More examples of people's commonalities are certainly needed to help break down color barriers, but looking at the current set of narratives involving multiracial people, frames of racial comity may also encourage racial amnesia. Certainly, the dominant articles analyzed in the previous two chapters reveal racial comity, but this agreement and comfort is built on "best of both worlds" mini-features that cast individual multiracial people as brave, special, and implicitly (or explicitly) better than other people of color in terms of their approach to racial identity. Racial comity, in these news reports, has been represented by profiles of interracial families "transcending race" and "bridging divides" to make relatives or neighbors see the light. Indeed, these stories are popular and circulate widely in the press, magazines, autobiographies, movies, and novels. But this thread of discourse can easily lead to colorblind conclusions that blind us to racial stratification.

What I would propose instead is the development of "racial cour-age" in addition to racial comity. By racial courage I mean producing reports that are complex but not esoteric; narratives that are not afraid to point out culpability or privilege; a narrative that tries to humanize par-ticipants not by playing to sympathy, but by taking a hard but nuanced look at how race is embedded in each person's life and what it means in broader context. This kind of reporting would acknowledge the influence of the past on not only current policies, but also on contemporary indi-viduals' abilities to traverse racial boundaries, claim particular names or cultural objects. Racial courage would delineate the consequences of both social- and individual-level racial or racist acts. It recognizes that Black and White are important polarities in the racial system, but we ignore the realities of Native American, Asian, Latino/a, and Arab American experi-ences to our peril. Reporters who approach race with courage would dis-cuss Whiteness as a social phenomenon that continues to exist as a benchmark for humanness. Racial courage would attempt to get away from simple quantifications of who suffers most and seek answers for the ques-tion: How might we, despite the fact that we are all implicated in the racial system, strive to work to end racism from our particular standpoint?

The kind of racial discussion I seek may seem impossible in a venue such as the commercial news media, yet some journalists and editors continue to reach for it. The "Let's Do It Better" awards have recognized eight classes of journalists who have covered race with courage. The *Akron-Beacon Journal's* year-long series on race relations, which grew into a public journalism project that involved and inspired the entire commu-nity to think about race is another example. The *New York Times* series "How Race Is Lived" also tried to provide a deeper and multifaceted portrait of race and racism in the United States. Individual newsrooms, such as Georgia's *Savannah Morning News*, have opened their doors to African Americans and rural Whites in their city, training them in jour-nalism and providing them with an outlet to write about their commu-nities for the newspaper. Specialty magazines that straddle academic, activist, and lay audiences, such as *Color Lines, Ms.,* and *Race, Gender and Class,* publish insightful, progressive depictions of race and power that deserve larger audiences than each of these publications currently reaches. Outside of these topical periodicals, however, one of the greatest ob-stacles to changing the way race is done in the news is the fact that news values privilege coverage of sporadic and sensational racial events.

The kind of racial courage that we need to see in the news can only be developed through sustained coverage of social issues that have racial components. Today, if, say, a rash of shootings happen in an inner city neighborhood, it may spark a few articles on the economic depression of the area and the lack of educational resources, but then the coverage will dwindle as the shooting stops. Instead, we need regular coverage of the hypersegregated areas that delves into the history of how the area came to be hypersegregated; of how years of benign neglect and suburbanization contribute to failing schools at least as much as overworked and underpaid parents. Coverage of the role of race in the disaster wrought by Hurricane Katrina was to some a welcome change; reporters from some news outlets attended to structural and historical causes of the unequal impact of the storm on New Orleans' Black population. But as the story dwindles into the middle and back pages of mainstream newspapers, it remains to be seen if reporters will continue to include analysis of racial inequalities as they document the rebuilding and resettling of New Orleans and the Gulf Coast.

Beyond the news, there are other genres that certainly invite and provoke discussions that move beyond racial binaries and happy-go-lucky predictions of easy racial intermarriage. Recent documentaries, autobiographies, and fictional movies spark (often heated) conversations about what race means today. Independent journalists on the Internet and bloggers are credited by many with ensuring that race was part of the Katrina story. Many spaces can generate productive reports and dialogue about race. However, as the medium that purports to provide the salient descriptions of events in the real world, and to provide the preeminent vehicle for public information for political discussion, dominant news media have a special responsibility. We spend a lot of time debating the realities of race, and the contributions of the news media to our thoughts and discussions could certainly be improved.

Final Dispatch

If our society's vision of race is to be truly transformed, this process cannot only occur through the glacial pace of one-marriage-at-a-time. And even if this slow pace were the only road, all families have secrets, pain, and hard times; the stories of idyllic unions across racial lines that make up the majority of the dominant media's current coverage of the 2000 Census, multiracial celebrities, and their racial aftereffects do not tell the whole story. They cannot be but a beginning to a larger, more contentious and difficult set of "family conversations" about what race and race relations have been and are becoming.

Think, for instance, about the "multiracial state" of Brazil, or the "mestizo" nation of Mexico, or the territory of Puerto Rico: all three have officially embraced race mixing as part of the national heritage, but all three also exhibit troubling patterns of racial discrimination and stereotyping that have left the darkest-complected members of the multiracial family at the bottom of the socioeconomic ladder. In Mexico, President Vincente Fox's recent insensitive racial remarks about Black workers and the issuance of a stamp showcasing Black minstrel cartoon characters are indicative of the continued conflicts over the role of African heritage in the "national family." Thus, officially sanctioning mestizo/mixed racial identities, even celebrating them, is no guarantor for racial equality. If, as they say in many Latin American countries, "money whitens," then Black-ness remains at the negative end of the color spectrum in most people's minds. The suppression and the return of the African influence in these nations demonstrates that the European/White elements of mixed heri-tage are still valued higher than Black contributions. The Cuban rejoin-der, "where are you hiding grandma," is used to put people in their place, remind them of their Afro and Indian roots when they insist upon em-phasizing only their "Spanish" lineage, an attempt to whitewash their history. Safely ensconced, allegedly, in only the most ancient roots of the family tree, Blackness (and often Indianness) is segmented off from the present day multiracial national persona.

This tension between public and private renderings of the racial/ethnic national family is also evident in a recent controversy over hon-oring participants in our national pastime, baseball. In the summer of 2005, fans were asked to vote for the "Latino Legends Team," spon-sored by Major League Baseball and Chevrolet. Two notable absences on the ballot were Reginald Martinez Jackson, aka Reggie Jackson, Mr. October, and Ted Williams, both of whom are already enshrined in the Baseball Hall of Fame. These great players were not included, accord-ing to the organizers, because they did not have a public connection to Latino identity or community. Similar to the Malone brothers, then, being Latino was predicated on both family ties and community visibil-ity. While some have said Jackson's middle name, prominently displayed on his Hall of Fame plaque, makes his Latino identity "public," others insist he is known as an African American player first and foremost, echoing the Latino law students' disqualification of Maria Hylton. Williams, most agree, did not do anything to acknowledge his Latino heritage while he lived, and by some accounts actively suppressed his mother's Mexican identity to avoid social embarrassment and discrimi-nation as he came up in the leagues.

Will the Latino Legends controversy lead to calls for Ted Williams, *American* hero, to be recognized as Ted Williams, *Latino American* hero? Are we ready to remember him that way, or can we? Until we can wrestle with the contradictions that make the second incarnation of Ted Williams seem foreign and the former normal, then we have not dealt with the continued contradictions of looking at our racial world with binary blinders. If we cannot reimagine these people with a full view and reckoning of their racial and ethnic stories and how our society and state helped shape them, we will never embrace both the pain of Williams's Latino family and the excellence of their son's accomplishments. We can never fully recognize the triumph in the story of Mildred and Richard Loving, whose famous suit against the State of Virginia legalized interracial marriage, until we speak to the years they spent living in anxiety and danger as they waited for the judiciary to make their decision. If we do not chart our way to a future reckoning with these aspects of our mixed-up racial past, we will never let grandma out of the closet, and we can never form a more perfect union if we try to do it on the backs of individual couples and families, blending in an ever-distant future.

Notes

Introduction

1. Many researchers in the social sciences have published work on the continued inequalities between Whites and people of color in these areas. Although all do not agree on the causal agents of these inequalities, they do not deny their existence. Some believe the nexus of race, class, and gender inequalities are reinforced by various "race-neutral" policies and practices, as well as the residual effects of centuries of domination of people of color; other scholars find fault with the cultural and psychological behaviors of people of color.

2. In *The Retreat from Race*, Dana Y. Takagi describes how the model minority concept emerged in the midst of urban uprisings of African Americans in the 1960s. The stereotype of Asians as nonconfrontational bolsters the idea that Asian Americans don't think or complain about racism. The model minority myth conveniently ignores stark differences between Asian American groups and their relative rates of economic and social success. Tuan documents how some Asian groups have been awarded "honorary white" status as model minorities. However, the flip side of this praise is the continued practice of portraying Asian Americans as "forever foreigners" in mainstream discourses. In these discourses, Asian Americans are portrayed as displacing "native-born" White Americans. Tuan, *Forever Foreigners*, 30–40.

3. Omi and Winant, *Racial Formation in the United States*.

4. Ibid., 55.

5. Ibid., 56.

6. Rhodes, "Fanning the Flames of Racial Discord," 97.

7. Entman, "Framing: Toward Clarification," 52.

8. Gandy, *Communication and Race*, 160.

9. Ibid., 172.

10. Iyengar, *Is Anyone Responsible?*

11. Gamson and Modigliani, "The Changing Culture of Affirmative Action."

12. Ettema, "Press Rites and Race Relations," 309–31.

13. Shah and Thornton, "Racial Ideology in US," 11; Chavez, *Covering Immigration*; Jacobs, *Race, Media, and the Crisis of Civil Society*.

14. See Squires, "Black Talk Radio," and Vogel, "Introduction" to *The Black Press*.

15. Flores and McPhail, "From Black and White to *Living Color*"; Squires and Brouwer, "In/Discernible Bodies: The Politics of Passing."

16. See Oscar Gandy's discussion in "Privatization and Identity."

17. See Rhodes's essay on the Black Panthers in the news, "Fanning the Flames of Racial Discord."

18. Some theorists complicate the role of news media in the movement (see essays in Ward, ed., *Media, Culture, and the African American Freedom Struggle*). Others assert that the focus on Southern racism allowed Whites in the North to claim "racial innocence." See Lassiter, "Suburban Origins of 'Color-blind' Conservatism."

19. These are all terms used by different people of mixed race. "Multiracial" has become the most popular due the 2000 Census; "Metis" is for Afro-French-Canadians; "Cablinasian" is Tiger Woods's personal label; and "Hapa" is a term for people of Asian/Pacific Islander descent.

20. Brown, et al., *Whitewashing Race*.

21. See for example Bonilla-Silva, "The New Racism"; Omi and Winant, *Racial Formation*; Piliawsky, "Racial Equality in the United States," esp. 135–43.

22. Dates and Barlow, *Split Image*; Dines and Humez, *Gender, Race, and Class in Media*; Gray, *Watching Race*; Hunt, *Screening the Los Angeles Riots*; Jhally and Lewis, *Enlightened Racism*; Entman and Rojecki, *The Black Image*.

23. See Shah and Thornton, *Newspaper Coverage of Interethnic Conflict*, and Jacobs, *Race, Media, and Crisis*, for comparison between ethnic and mainstream coverage of racial crises.

24. See Valentino, Hutchings, and White, "Cues that Matter," and Mendelberg, *The Race Card*.

25. See Gilens, *Why Americans Hate Welfare* for a study of the media linkage between blacks and welfare; Dixon and Linz, "Overrepresentation," for discussion of images of Black criminality.

26. Entman and Rojecki, *The Black Image*.

27. Entman and Rojecki discuss the lack of frames that support racial comity in *The Black Image*, as do Shah and Thornton, *News Coverage*.

28. Reicher, "The Context of Social Identity," 935.

29. See, for example, discussions online at *Interracial Voice*, an e-publication for multiracial identified people: http://www.webcom.com/~intvoice/point22.html. In this stream, participants debate the "claim 'em if they're famous" trend of publicizing celebrities as multiracial.

30. See Gitlin, *The Whole World is Watching*; Rhodes, "Fanning the Flames."

31. There is literal identity entrepreneurship happening in the world of entertainment and advertising media where multiracial stars and models are seen as valued commodities for their "crossover" appeal to audiences of different races, particularly whites. See Hunter, *Race, Gender*; Streeter, "The Hazards of Visibility"; and Bost, *Mulattas and Mestizas*.

32. Some conceptualize White resistance to civil rights reform and racial equality in phases. The first phase, "massive resistance," featured White violence against Blacks and resistance to federal enforcement of integration. The second phase is "white flight." In this phase, Whites argue against housing and school integration on the "color-blind" basis of personal choice and property rights. For example, they resisted busing plans and housing laws both by moving away from school districts adjacent to Black populations and fought court battles to preserve their "freedom of choice" to put their children in the (all-White) school of their choice. Thus, the language of personal and private freedoms replaced the language of white supremacy to replicate segregated conditions. See Lassiter, "Suburban Origins"; Formisano, *Boston Against Busing*; Cruse, *White Flight*.

33. Steinberg, "The Liberal Retreat from Race," 22. See Roediger, "White Workers, New Democrats," for a discussion of Democrats' dis-ease with race in electoral politics.

34. Johnson said, "So, unless we work to strengthen the family . . . all the rest: schools, playgrounds, public assistance and private concern will never be enough to cut completely the circle of despair and deprivation" of the black poor. Steinberg, 22.

35. Ibid., 26.

36. Steinberg and others often single out William Julius Wilson as an important figure for the Democrats' retreat from race. His books *The Declining Significance of Race* and *The Truly Disadvantaged* are deemed exemplars of the liberal turn away from race. In his defense, Wilson and others emphasize that he never meant to suggest that racism was no longer an impediment to African Americans. See Wilson, "Race, Class, and Urban Poverty." Similarly, in "The Continuing Significance of Race," Marshall notes that when Wilson's most famous book was published, "[t]he title received more attention than the argument. . . . [A]nalysts too hastily concluded that race was no longer a major factor in U.S. politics," 611.

37. Political scientists interested in how politicians and media elites frame public policy issues have experimented with "race-explicit" and "race-neutral" poll questions. See for example Sniderman, et al., "Beyond Race," 35–55. Their experiments suggest that self-described liberal Whites are more likely to support programs that will assist Blacks when race is eliminated from poll questions and when the race of policy beneficiaries is qualified with a "universalistic" frame.

38. See Guinier and Torres, *The Miner's Canary*.

39. Glaeser and Vigdor, *Racial Segregation in the 2000 Census*, 8.

40. See Sunstein, *Free Markets*, esp. chap. 6, "Why Markets Don't Stop Discrimination," for a vigorous discussion of how commercial markets can easily promote and reinforce racism and segregation.

41. See Massey and Denton, *American Apartheid*.

42. Dickerson, "Untangling Race/Gender Economic Inequality."

43. Wilson, *When Work Disappears*; Kirschenman and Neckerman, " 'We'd Love to Hire Them.' "

44. Wilson, *When Work Disappears*, 112. See esp. chapter 5.

45. See chapter 5 of Brown et al., *Whitewashing Race*, for summaries and discussions of research on racial inequalities and employment.

46. Here I follow Brown et al.'s definition of racial realism.

47. Brown et al., *Whitewashing Race*, 7–9.

48. See Brown et al., *Whitewashing Race*, 15–17, and Bonilla-Silva, "The New Racism."

49. Steinberg, "The Liberal Retreat from Race." See P. Williams, *The Alchemy of Race and Rights* for a critique of "color-blind" legal theories that impede understanding of racial inequalities.

50. Brown et al., *Whitewashing Race*, 163.

51. Brown et al. conceptualize White dominance as a result of a history of accumulation of economic, political, and social capital that excluded Blacks and other people of color. The flip side of this accumulation is the *disaccumulation* experienced by people of color, because Whites prevented them—through law, social norms, and violence—from gaining footholds in the marketplace and government. Thus, centuries of disaccumulation of resources left communities and individuals of color resource-poor, while generations of Whites enjoy the fruits of the state-sponsored privileges of their forebears. See 22–25; 231–32.

52. Kousser, *Colorblind Injustice*; P. Williams, *The Alchemy of Race and Rights*.

53. Calhoun, "Introduction."

54. See Strauss and Corbin, *Basics of Qualitative Research*; Lincoln and Guba, *Naturalistic Inquiry*.

55. Lindlof and Taylor, *Qualitative Communication Research Methods*, 218.

56. See chaps. 4 and 7 of Miles and Huberman, *Qualitative Data Analysis*; Altheide, *Qualitative Media Analysis*.

57. I wanted to study Latino/a press reactions as well, but could find no English-language Latino news coverage of the controversy.

58. Neuendorf, *Content Analysis Guidebook*.

Chapter One. "Hybrid Degenerates" to "Multiracial Families"

1. The science of hybrid degeneracy grew with skewed applications of Darwin's theory of evolution. See Comas, "Racial Myths."

2. The increase in mixed-race studies across various fields is stunning. In history and social sciences, one can read work on the legal definitions of miscegenation and race mixing and their effects (see Davis, *Who Is Black*; Kennedy, *Interracial Intimacies*; Scales-Trent, *Notes of a White Black Woman*; Williams-Leon and Nakashima, eds., *The Sum of Our Parts*); literary and media analysis of passing and miscegenation texts (see Bennett, *The Passing Figure*; Boeckmann, *A Question of Character*; Sollors, *Neither Black Nor White*; Wald, *Crossing the Line*); close readings of particular cases of passing or miscegenation (see Carlson, " 'You Know It' "; Ginsberg, ed., *Passing and the Fictions of Identity*); and numerous autobiographical narratives (McBride, *Color of Water*; Taylor-Haizlip, *Sweeter the Juice*).

There is a growing collection of work focused on the new multiracial identity and/or the effects from the Census Bureau change (Perlman and Waters, eds., *New Race Question*; Spickard, *Mixed Blood*).

3. See, recently, Glazer, "Reflections on Race."

4. Readers should consult the referenced authors for many more details on these issues.

5. E.g., Castle, "Biological and Social Consequences"; Davenport, "Race Crossing."

6. By yoking Darwin's theory to racist explanations of social inequality, "progress in biology was misused to provide superficially scientific and simple solutions to allay scruples on points of human conduct." Comas, "Racial Myths," 17–18.

7. Ibid., 21.

8. See Lipsitz, *Possessive Investment*; Lowe, "The International within the National."

9. See Roberts, *Killing the Black Body*; P. Williams, *Alchemy of Race and Rights*.

10. According to Sollors, in the years prior to the Civil War, for example, Edward Love's *The History of Jamaica*, written in 1774, enjoyed a revival. Love's "research" declared that mulattoes were inferior human stock, unable to breed. In 1840, Josiah Clark Nott used Love's theory to interpret Census data that showed a decrease in the mulatto population. Nott used "the mulatto sterility hypothesis" to explain the drop. Sollors, *Neither Black Nor White*, 128–30.

11. Nakashima, "An Invisible Monster," 166.

12. Menchaca describes how the Treaty of Guadalupe-Hidalgo, ratified by the United States in 1848, granted U.S. citizenship to Mexicans living in the newly annexed territories. However, as these new American states created their own constitutions, they disregarded the treaty's provisions and incorporated racial definitions of citizenship. Menchaca, *Recovering History*.

13. Menchaca relates how mobs of Whites, aided by the legal system, chased out African Americans and *afromestizos* who had previously enjoyed freedoms under Mexican law.

14. Grant, *Passing of the Great Race*.

15. Quoted in Davis, *Who Is Black?*, 13.

16. Many of these laws were not repealed until 1965.

17. In Palumbo-Liu, *Asian/American*, 27.

18. Wilson, "Blood Quantum," 122–23.

19. Baird-Olson, "Colonization, Cultural Imperialism," 195–97. Wilson also documents cases in "Blood Quantum" where mixed-bloods who led antigovernment resistance were labeled by the government as degenerates. See also Lawrence, "Gender, Race, and the Regulation of Native Identity."

20. Furedi, "How Sociology Imagined."

21. Furedi quotes Anson Phelps-Stokes's reminder to his colleagues in 1946 that their reports "should avoid giving the impression that 'we favor intermarriage.'" Furedi, 37.

22. Nakashima, "Invisible Monster."

23. Furedi, 33.

24. Some anthropologists were inspired by the diversity and racial mixing in the Hawaiian Islands. A variation on the melting pot theme, these scientists predicted that the Hawaiians might be a prototype of a "new American," tolerant of racial and ethnic differences. They proposed that Hawaiians were predisposed to tolerance and acceptance of different racial groups. See Gulick, *Mixing the Races in Hawaii*. See Edles, " 'Race,' 'Ethnicity,' and 'Culture' in Hawai'i" for critique of assumptions about Hawaiian racial identities.

25. Recently, there has been a surge in literature concerning the use of the mulatto figure by African American authors. Many of these scholars emphasize that mulatto characters in these works are employed to critique racism, sexism, and class conflicts, and often to lampoon whiteness, e.g., DeVere Brody, "Clare Kendry" and Boeckmann, *A Question of Character*.

26. After the Census of 1910, the federal government eliminated terms such as "mulatto" from their official list of racial categories.

27. Dixon, *The Clansman*.

28. Griffith, *Birth of a Nation*.

29. Boeckmann argues that in *The Clansman*, the mulatto politician Silas Lynch exemplifies the contamination of the soul that occurs when even the slightest bit of Black blood mixes with White. Thus, Dixon goes beyond the visibility of race to explore its invisible aspects. Boeckmann, 85.

30. See Sollors, *Neither Black Nor White*, esp. chapter 5.

31. Sollors provides an exhaustive catalogue of novels, plays, and novellas published from the 1850s to the 1950s where the sign of the bluish tinge is used. Sollors, *Neither Black*, 145, 156.

32. Bost, *Mulattos and Mestizas*.

33. See Lewis and Ardizzone, *Love on Trial*; Kennedy, *Interracial Intimacies*.

34. To discern the "truth" of her blackness, Alice Rhinelander was ordered to disrobe from the waist up before the members of the jury. Carlson, " 'You Know It When.' "

35. Lewis and Ardizzonne, 92.

36. The trials of Jack Johnson also served to keep in circulation fears of Black sexuality and miscegenation. See G. Ward, *Unforgivable Blackness*; Kennedy, *Interracial Intimacies*.

37. Nakashima, "An Invisible Monster," 167.

38. Nakashima, "Servants of Culture," 37–38.

39. Written as a story in 1900 and adapted for the stage in the United States, composer Giacomo Puccini discovered the tragedy of a young geisha after the successful play traveled to London.

40. Cited in Nakashima, "An Invisible Monster," 167.

41. Nakashima, "Servants of Culture," 39.

42. Palumbo-Liu, *Asian/American*, 34.

43. Hearne, "Cross-Heart People."

44. Ibid., 181.

45. Hearne also mentions that central "White" male characters themselves are part Indian or gain Native American assets via romance with an Indian woman, later replaced by a White bride.

46. Nakashima cites Stedman's research on images of Native Americans, which found that "curiously enough, fiction writers generally saw more difficulties in being part Indian than being all Indian." Nakashima, "An Invisible Monster," 172.

47. In slave narratives and newspapers, the horrors of sexual exploitation were part of the antislavery discourse. See Andrews, "Introduction," 88; Foreman, "The Spoken and the Silenced"; Blassingame, ed., *Slave Testimony*.

48. Giddings, *When and Where I Enter*. 29.

49. Wells, *Selected Works*, 20–22.

50. By 1920, both the *Pittsburgh Courier* and the *Chicago Defender* posted paid circulation in excess of two hundred thousand. See Hogan, *A Black National News Service* and Finkle, *Forum*, who both suggest multiplying official circulation numbers by three or four—and in the case of the *Defender*, five—to get a better estimate of how many Blacks got the information in these papers. So between 1920–1940, we can estimate that around five million Blacks were getting information from the Black papers via subscriptions or sharing with others. This would mean nearly half of the black population was exposed to the Black press.

51. Some credit the *Defender* with accelerating the Great Migration. See Vogel, ed., *The Black Press*; Wolseley, *The Black Press, USA*.

52. *Chicago Defender*, "The Negro of Conquest."

53. The *Defender* ran a three-part serial in December of 1920 titled "From Under the Yoke" by Leslie M. Rogers, which concerned the family of a mulatto girl who was raped by a white man.

54. *Chicago Defender*. "Race Woman Defends Honor."

55. Kerlin, *Voice of the Negro*.

56. Ibid.

57. Ibid.

58. These examples come from an ongoing analysis of *Chicago Defender* and *New York Age* reports on interracial dating and sex from 1918–1924, as well as Kerlin's collection of articles and excerpts from 1919.

59. *Chicago Defender*, "Bob Anderson Slain."

60. E.g., *Chicago Defender*, "Says Chauffeur Stole His Wife's Heart."

61. E.g., *Chicago Defender*, "The Japanese Question" and "Races Cannot Intermarry."

62. *Chicago Defender*, "Stirring up a Hornet's Nest."

63. *Wisconsin Weekly Blade*, in Kerlin, 113–14.

64. *Chicago Defender*, "Southern Afro-American Girl" (my italics).

65. See Bost, *Mulattas and Mestizas*, and Zackodnik, *The Mulatta*.

66. I did not find a single instance of ridicule of a Black man or male mulatto in this way.

67. Daniel, *More Than Black*; Davis. *Who Is Black?*

68. *Chicago Whip* (my italics).

69. Hauke, "The 'Passing' of Elsie Roxborough."

70. Ibid., 158–60.

71. Ernest Lehman wrote in his autobiography that he "had no idea that Mona was 'passing.' She told me one reason she liked me: I reminded her of Arthur Miller." In Hauke, 165–66.

72. Ibid., 163.

73. Ibid., 166.

74. Fabi, *Passing and the Rise.*

75. Boeckmann, *A Question of Character.*

76. DeVere, "Clare Kendry's 'True' Colors."

77. Berlant, "National Brands/National Body."

78. Wald, *Crossing the Line.*

79. Ibid., 130.

80. Ibid., 131.

81. See chapter 2.

82. See for example Barbara Savage's history of radio programs aimed at Blacks during World War II, *Broadcasting Freedom.*

83. Wald, *Crossing the Line.*

84. Ibid., 84–85.

85. Ibid., 110.

86. *Slaying the Dragon.*

87. Courtney, *Hollywood Fantasies.*

88. Means-Coleman, *African American Viewers*, 83–89. See also Bodroghkozy. " 'Is This What You Mean by Color TV?' "

89. Ward, *Just My Soul, 111.*

90. Ibid., 108.

91. *Brown v. Board of Education.*

92. Patterson, *Brown v. Board,* 87.

93. Ibid.

94. At the time, sixteen states still had antimiscegenation laws on the books.

95. This is not to say that representations of multiracial families were completely absent in mass media. *The Jeffersons*, for example, is notable for its inclusion of a Black female/White male couple and their son, who were often the butt of jokes told by the protagonist, George Jefferson.

96. Root, ed., *The Multiracial Experience.*

97. See Root, ed., *The Multiracial Experience,* esp. *Part III: What of the Children?*

98. Brown and Douglass, "Evolution of Multiracial Organizations," 113.

99. Dozier, "Race, It's No Longer."

100. Daniel, *More Than Black.*

101. E.g., *Zebrahead, Jungle Fever.*

102. See chapter 6.

103. Williams, "From Civil Rights to Multiracial," 89.

104. DaCosta, "Multiracial Identity," 69.

105. The articles printed in African American–owned newspapers analyzed in chapters 1, 4, and 5 clearly articulated the view that multiracial people are naïve and/or selfish.

106. Dalmage, "Mama, Are You Brown?" 90–91.

107. For example, in his written testimony in 1997, Professor G. Reginald Daniel, a member of AMEA and author of works on multiracial identity, advocated for a multiracial option by concluding that "changes in current data collection methods would be another logical step in the progression of civil rights—not to mention human rights—and help deconstruct the very means by which racist ideology and racial privilege are enforced in the United States, which is the notion of racial 'purity.' " This testimony was referenced in congressional hearings by the coordinator of law and civil rights issues for AMEA. Fernandez, Written Testimony. Sociologist Mary C. Waters also testified that "[t]he political debate about this issue has tended to concentrate on the counts and identities of African Americans. . . . All of the statistical and demographic research however points to this change having the biggest effect on American Indians, Alaskan Natives, and Asian and Pacific Islanders. . . . Law makers and government statisticians should pay particular attention to how these groups will be affected and should probably make a special effort to make sure they are consulted." Waters, Testimony.

108. For commentary on Graham and Project RACE, see Spencer, "Census 2000"; Brown and Douglass, "Evolution." For Graham's own take on the check-all option, see Graham, Testimony.

109. DaCosta, "Multiracial Identity," 72.

Chapter Two. The In/discernible Body of Susie Phipps

1. Schlangenstein, "Appeal Filed."

2. This law was prompted by the actions of a private lawyer. The state of Louisiana considered his client 1/128th black, and refused to grant his child a birth certificate with the racial designation white. The lawyer worked with his political contacts and persuaded the legislature to change the law to say one thirty-second ancestry made one black. Trillin, "American Chronicles," 62–78.

3. This case could be seen as a precursor to Ward Connerly's recent attempt to eliminate state racial records.

4. Trillin mentions one story in the French press about Phipps titled, "En Louisiane, le Sang N'Est Jamais Rouge" (In Louisiana, Blood is not Always Red).

5. Concerning our choice of representative texts, we recognize that the writings of interracial people rather than Blacks might have been warranted. However, we chose the Black press because multiracial people did not have many media resources or exposure at the time. More importantly, Phipps did not seek a multiracial identity, but rather opposed herself to a Black one.

6. Analysis includes newspaper and magazine articles published from 1982 to 1986.

7. Ginsberg, "Introduction," 8.

8. Moon, "Inter-Class Travel," 215–40.

9. Sloop, "Discipling in the Transgendered," 165–89.

10. Robinson, "It Takes One to Know One."

11. Carlson, " 'You Know It When You See It,' " 111–28.; Hasian and Nakayama, "The Fictions of Racialized Identities," 182–95.

12. Hasian and Nakayama, 184.

13. E.g., Lule, "The Rape of Mike Tyson," 176–95; Parisi, "The *New York Times* Looks at One Block," 236–54.; Sloop, "Disciplining the Transgendered," 165–89.

14. E.g., Flores and McPhail, "From Black and White to *Living Color*," 106–22.

15. E.g., Squires, "Black Talk Radio"; Shah and Thornton, *Newspaper Coverage of Interethnic Conflict*.

16. Jaynes, "Suit on Race Recalls Lines."

17. Ibid.

18. Demaret, "Raised White," 155–56.

19. Herron, Wright and Douglas, "Louisiana Drops Racial Fractions."

20. *New York Times*, "A Little Local Color."

21. Trillin, "American Chronicles," 62.

22. Jaynes, "Suit on Race Recalls Lines."

23. Schlangenstein, "Appeal Filed."

24. *New York Times*, "A Little Local Color."

25. Demaret, "Raised White," 155–56.

26. Gabler, *Life the Movie*.

27. *Messina v. Ciaccio*, Court of Appeal of Louisiana, Fourth Circuit. 290 So. 2d 339: 1974 and *Thomas v. Louisiana State Board of Health*, Court of Appeal of Louisiana, Fourth Circuit. 278 So. 2d: 1973.

28. DeMers, "Written Arguments Attack Racial Classification Law."

29. Schlangenstein, "Appeal Filed."

30. Debenport, "Lawyer Says."

31. Marcus, "Louisiana Repeals Black Blood Law."

32. Plume, "Woman Loses Bid."

33. Trillin, "American Chronicles," 66.

34. Jaynes, "Suit on Race Recalls Lines."

35. *New York Times*, "Slave Descendant Fights."

36. Trillin, "American Chronicles," 73.

37. Daniel, *More than Black?*

38. Furedi, "How Sociology Imagined Mixed Race"; Nakashima, "An Invisible Monster."

39. Trillin, "American Chronicles," 73.

40. Jaynes, "Suit on Race Recalls Lines."

41. Hills, "State's 1-32nd 'Negro Blood' Law Valid."

42. Demaret, "Raised White," 156.

43. Debenport, "Round Two."

44. *Time Magazine*, "Color Bind," 17.
45. Marcus, "Louisiana Repeals Black Blood Law."
46. Trillin, "American Chronicles," 68.
47. Trillin's discussion of passing to improve one's class status did not include a comparison with Latin American nations and cultures, where one can marry into higher status with a light partner.
48. Trillin, "American Chronicles," 78.
49. *New York Times*, "Black and White."
50. *Jet Magazine*, "Ex-College Prexy," 23.
51. Ibid.
52. *Jet Magazine*, "La. Repeals," 42; *Jet Magazine*, "La. Woman," 5.
53. E.g., *Jet Magazine*, Woman Resumes Fight," 39.
54. *Jet Magazine*, "Louisiana Court."
55. *Ebony*, " 'What Makes You Black?' " 118.
56. Root, ed. *The Multiracial Experience*.
57. *Ebony*, " 'What Makes You Black?' " 116.
58. Ibid.
59. Gilliam, "Black/White."
60. Wald, *Crossing the Line*.
61. Gilliam, "Black/White."
62. Smart-Grosvenor, "Obsessed with 'Racial Purity,' " 28–30.
63. *Ebony*, " 'What Makes You Black?' " 116.
64. Smart-Grosvenor, "Obsessed with 'Racial Purity,' " 28–30.
65. Ibid., 30 (my italics).
66. *Jet Magazine*, "Louisiana Woman Losing," 36.
67. Nakayama and Krizek, "Whiteness: A Strategic Rhetoric."
68. Hurtado, "The Trickster's Play."
69. Fuss, *Essentially Speaking*.
70. Sloop and Ono, "The Critique of Vernacular Discourse"; Flores and McPhail, "From Black and White."
71. Tilove, "Racial Identity in the U.S."

Chapter Three. "Not as Black as the Next Guy"

1. See Brown et al., *Whitewashing Race*; Oliver and Shapiro, *Black Wealth, White Wealth*; and Wilson, *The Truly Disadvantaged* for how the Black middle class expanded in the 1970 and '80s while large portions of the Black population continued to lag behind.
2. Richey, "Hiring Programs."
3. L. Williams, "Justices Hear Quota Cases."
4. J. Williams, "Quotas are a dead issue."
5. Lehmann, "Taking Affirmative Action Apart," 34–51 (my italics).
6. Brown et al., *Whitewashing Race*; Oliver and Shapiro, *Black Wealth, White Wealth*.

7. Ignatiev, *How the Irish Became White*; Lipsitz, *The Possessive Investment in Whiteness*; Roediger, *Colored White*.

8. Shome, "Outing Whiteness."

9. Brooks and Rada, "Constructing Race," 113–56.

10. Ibid., 147–48.

11. Ibid., 368.

12. Carlson, " 'You Know It When' "; Hasian and Nakayama, "The Fictions of Racialized Identities."

13. Madison, "Legitimation Crisis and Containment."

14. Shome, "Outing Whiteness," 369.

15. Projansky and Ono, "Strategic Whiteness."

16. Omi and Winant, *Racial Formation*.

17. Clawson, Strine, and Waltenburg, "Framing Supreme Court Decisions," 784.

18. Gamson and Modigliani, "The Changing Culture," 137–77.

19. Ibid., 148.

20. Entman, "Manufacturing Discord," 32–51.

21. Ibid., 35.

22. Clawson et al., "Framing Supreme Court Decisions," 784–810.

23. Ibid., 793.

24. Messer-Davidow, "Manufacturing the Attack," 68.

25. See Gamson, "Ambivalences about Affirmative Action," and Entman and Rojecki, *The Black Image in the White Mind*, esp. chap. 7.

26. Kinder and Sanders, *Divided by Color*; Entman and Rojecki, *The Black Image*.

27. Steele, *Content of Our Character*.

28. Notably, Jennifer Gratz, who sued the University of Michigan for allegedly denying her admission because she is White, assists Connerly's efforts to eliminate state racial records.

29. Unlike the Susie Phipps case, I am not as concerned with taking the Malones' statements at face value. Rather, I agree with the prosecutors of their case that they only claimed black status to advance their careers. Unlike Phipps, the Malones did not attach any public or personal meaning to their chosen identity.

30. Hernandez, "Wife Defends Ex-Firefighter."

31. I searched for articles on the Malones using keywords such as "Malones," "firefighters," "affirmative action," and "fraud." I found no mention of the case in Black or Latino news.

32. My search was done through available library database materials. It may be the case that small, local newsletters or pamphlets that do not get archived in library systems covered the case.

33. *Boston Globe*, "The Hiring Fraud Mystery."

34. Diesenhouse, "Boston Case Raises Questions."

35. Hernandez, "Wife Defends Ex-Firefighter."

36. Ibid.

37. Barnicle, "A Break from the Real World."

38. Canellos, "Race Fraud Triggers Memories."

39. MacNeil/Lehrer, "Racism in America."

40. Canellos, "Race Fraud Triggers Memories."

41. Disenhouse, "Boston Case Raises Questions."

42. Jackson, "Malones Open Old Wounds."

43. Ibid.

44. Hernanadez and Ellement, "Two Fight Firing."

45. Disenhouse, "Boston Case Raises Questions."

46. Disenhouse, "In Affirmative Action."

47. Hernandez, "SJC Considers Firefighters' Claim."

48. Hernandez, "Wife Defends Ex-Firefighter."

49. Disenhouse, "Boston Case Raises Questions."

50. Osgood, "New Brothers in the Family."

51. Marantz and Hernandez, "Defining Race."

52. Ibid.

53. At the time of the Malone case, many states still had or had only recently gotten rid of statutes like Louisiana's one thirty-second law. Native Americans' tribal status is also bound to blood percentages.

54. Marantz and Hernandez, "Defining Race."

55. Ibid.

56. Jackson, "Malones Open Old Wounds."

57. Barnicle, "A Break."

58. Hernandez and Ellement, "Two Fight Firing."

59. Hernandez, "Firemen Who Claimed."

60. Jackson, "Malones Open Old Wounds."

61. Bella English is a White American reporter. In an e-mail exchange with her, she told me that she did not believe the Malones' story, and went to their hometown to demonstrate that Whites there don't tolerate Blacks.

62. English, "Color Coordinated."

63. Osgood, "New Brothers."

64. Jackson, "Malones Open Old Wounds."

65. Clawson et al., "Framing Supreme Court Decisions."

66. Jackson, "Malones Open Old Wounds." I also corresponded via e-mail with Jackson to make sure I was reading his implication correctly. He confirmed that he was alluding to *Plessy*.

67. Wen, "Schools on Look Out."

68. Shome, "Outing Whiteness"; Madison, "Legitimation Crisis."

69. Hernandez, "Wife Defends Ex-Firefighter."

70. Waters, *Ethnic Options.*

71. Williams, "Rush Limbaugh's Inner Black Child."

Chapter Four. Descended from Whom?

1. I follow the work of scholars who conceptualize blackness as the product of cultural, historical, and political contexts. The charge of inauthenticity is

leveled to discredit people of African descent in a manner that essentializes racial identity rather than attending to the subtle differences and changing circumstances that shape identifications with blackness.

2. See Morrison, ed., *Race-ing Justice*; Wilson, *Inventing Black-on-Black Violence*. A recent iteration of the debates over the so-called "Black underclass" coalesced around Bill Cosby's remarks regarding their alleged unwillingness to "hold up their end of the bargain." For an extended meditation on the meaning of Cosby's allegation, see Dyson, *Is Bill Cosby Right?*

3. Gray, *Watching Race*.

4. Zook, *Color by Fox*, 2.

5. Wilson, *Inventing Black-on-Black Violence*.

6. Ibid., 131.

7. Gilens, *Why Americans Hate Welfare*.

8. Following Gray, *Watching Race*.

9. Zook, *Color by Fox*, 2–3.

10. Gibbs, *Race and Justice*; Cooding-Williams, *Reading Rodney King*; Schuetz and Lilley, eds., *The O. J. Simpson Trials: Rhetoric, Media, and the Law*; Morrison, *Race-ing Justice*.

11. One cannot help but notice the level of hyperbole in this quote.

12. Leland and Samuels, "The New Generation Gap," 53.

13. Lubiano, "Like Being Mugged," 64–75.

14. Morgenthau, "What Color Is Black?" 62–63.

15. Piper, "Passing for White," 234–69.

16. Morgenthau, "What Color Is Black?" 62.

17. Ibid., 64.

18. Ibid., 65.

19. Baynes, "Who Is Black Enough," 208. Baynes's article on the Hylton case is not part of the analysis presented here; his work on the case was published in a law journal, not a popular press outlet. I use his piece as an authoritative account of the case, due to the quality and depth of information he collected on the case, such as the original memo written by Joyce Hughes.

20. Secter, "Black Prof."

21. Baynes, "Who Is Black Enough," 209.

22. Ibid., 225–27.

23. Ibid., 210.

24. Ibid., 227.

25. These elements were reprinted in Sege, "Not Black Enough" and Baynes, "Who Is Black."

26. I searched radio and television transcript databases, but found no mention of Hughes in those resources. Attempts to get local Chicago TV news coverage of the case were unsuccessful.

27. Charges of political correctness, identity politics, or "playing the race card" have become commonplace in the post–civil rights era. "P.C." is attacked as censorship, preventing people from speaking their minds freely in discussions of race, gender, class, and other controversial topics.

28. *Chicago Tribune*. Editorial, December 14, 1994.

29. Sege, "Not Black Enough?"; Preston, "Battle to Keep"; Greenburg, Crawford, and O'Brien, "Race Issue."

30. "News and Views," 20.

31. Preston, "Battle to Keep."

32. Root, Ed. *Racially Mixed People in America.*

33. By 1995, groups such as AMEA and Project RACE had been in the news a number of times.

34. Sege, "Not Black Enough?"

35. Secter, "Black Prof."

36. "News and Views," 20.

37. Kirkpatrick, "Rule of Law."

38. Sege, "Not Black Enough?"

39. *Boston Globe*, "Academic Blacklisting."

40. Preston, "Battle to Keep."

41. Byrne, "McCarthy's Evil Spirit."

42. Sege, "Not Black Enough?"

43. Kirkpatrick, "Rule of Law."

44. *Boston Globe*, "Academic Blacklisting."

45. See Morrison, ed. *Race-ing Justice*, for essays on how Clarence Thomas and his supporters portrayed him as an innocent minority within a minority.

46. Some observers have argued that Loury's recent move to Brown University also signals his move away from many of his past positions against affirmative action and other race-based policies. See Krugman, "Glen Loury's Round Trip." However, at the time of the Hylton case, Loury was squarely in the camp of those who espoused color blindness.

47. McPherson, "The Loudest Silence."

48. Bennett, Letter to the editor.

49. Baynes, "Who Is Black Enough, 222–23.

50. Byrne, "McCarthy's Evil Spirit."

51. For an excellent set of essays on the role of affirmative action, race, class, and gender in the university, see Post and Rogin, eds., *Race and Representation.*

52. Edwards, "The Journey," 944–78.

53. *Chicago Tribune*. Editorial, December 14, 1994.

54. Sege, "Not Black Enough?"; Kirkpatrick, "Rule of Law"; Greenburg, Crawford, and O'Brien, "Race Issue."

55. *Chicago Tribune*. Editorial, December 14, 1994.

56. *Boston Globe*, "Academic Blacklisting."

57. "News and Views," 20.

58. Kirkpatrick, "Rule of Law."

59. Preston, "Battle to Keep."

60. Baynes, "Who Is Black Enough," 224.

61. Ibid., 225. See Brouwer and Squires, "Public Intellectuals," 201–13, and Lubiano, "Like Being Mugged," 64–75, on demands for Black intellectuals to be "relevant" to their communities in addition to being productive scholars within academe.

62. Dillard, "How the New Black Elite."
63. See Messer Davidow, "Manufacturing the Attack."
64. Ibid., 55.
65. Giroux, "Racial Politics," 304. As scholar George Lipsitz pointed out, focusing on Black "reverse racist" behavior is a strategy that stretches back to at least the film *Birth of a Nation*. Lipsitz, personal communication, December 24, 2005.
66. Daniel, "Multiracial Identity." Hanchard, " 'Black Cinderella?' "
67. Hanchard, " 'Black Cinderella?' " 169–89.
68. Ibid., 169.
69. Ibid., 182.
70. Russell, Wilson, and Hall, *The Color Complex*.
71. Herring, Keith, and Horton, *Skin/Deep*.
72. Rimer and Arenson, "Top Colleges."
73. Ibid.
74. The debate over slavery reparations has included discussion of how to identify descendants of slaves given the amount of race mixing and the lack of clear records.
75. Alexander, "Can You Be BLACK."
76. Piper, "Passing for White."

Chapter Five. Counting Race, Counting Controversy

1. See Anderson and Fienberg, *Who Counts?*; Perlmann and Waters, *The New Race Question*.
2. Peterson, "A Politically Correct Solution," 3.
3. Calhoun, *Social Theory and the Politics of Identity*.
4. As noted earlier, the Census Bureau previously used categories such as "mulatto."
5. This research only includes English-language Asian American periodicals.
6. E.g., Hoyt, "Reporting Race: Diversity Fatigue?"
7. See Daniel, "Multiracial Identity in Global Perspective."
8. The results are presented with Asian American newspapers and magazines leading, followed by analysis of the dominant press and the Black press. I do not want to duplicate a bias born of ordering, where the first element of a comparison is seen as a norm or baseline; I want to de-center dominant narratives of race by using the statements of people of color to initiate the chapter. By giving Asian American newspapers the first word and African American periodicals the last word, I hope to center views on race that are often cast as merely "alternatives."
9. Wong, "YellowPearls."
10. *AsianWeek*, "Count on It," 4.
11. Colety, "Census 2000: Interracial-marriage."
12. Takahashi, "Checking off the Future."
13. Wu, "Washington Journal."
14. Winfrey, "Magazine Publisher, Editor."

15. *AsianWeek*, "Count on It," 4.
16. Lavilla, "Hapa Issues."
17. Soo, Lavilla, and Dang. "Finally, It's History."
18. Ayuyang, "Her Job Really Counts."
19. Swamy, "All Is Not Well."
20. Williams, "Racial Seduction," 18.
21. Leland and Beals, "In Living Colors," 59.
22. Moon, "Amerasia Journal."
23. Lavilla, "Hapa Issues," 11.
24. Writers for dominant publications rarely have their racial identity revealed to their reading public. In contrast, most readers of African American and Asian American publications assume that the writers, editors, and owners are members of the same racial/ethnic group. Although at least a few of the journalists who wrote stories on the multiracial category controversy were people of color, they did not identify themselves as such.
25. Skerry, *Counting on the Census?*
26. Entman and Rojecki, *The Black Image.*
27. Autman, "Mixed Race Categories for Census."
28. Schemo, "Despite Opinions on Census."
29. Younge, "Multiracial Citizens Divided."
30. E.g., Bivens, "Report Discounts"; Fletcher, "Census Change Could Have Little Effect."
31. Mathews, "Beyond Other."
32. Brand-Williams. "Census Change Stirs."
33. See Funderberg, "Boxed In"; Johnson, "In Mixed Race Kids"; Spencer, "Just What We Don't Need."
34. See Autman, "Mixed Race Categories for Census"; Brand-Williams, "Census Change Stirs"; Marriot, "Multiracial Americans Ready"; Younge. "Multiracial Citizens Divided"; Fletcher, "Census Change Could Have Little Effect."
35. Vobjeda, "Census Expands Options."
36. Autman, "Mixed Race Categories for Census."
37. Matthews, "Beyond Other."
38. Ibid.
39. Ball, "We're Doing It Again."
40. Tilles, "Multiracial Category Becomes Law."
41. *Washington Afro American*, "Census—The Multiracial Threat,"
42. Aubry, "Urban Perspective."
43. Norment, "Am I Black, White, or In between?"
44. Quoted in Frisby, "Black, White, or Other?"
45. See Herring, Keith, and Horton, *Skin/Deep*; Russell, Wilson, and Hall, *The Color Complex.*
46. Herring, Keith, and Horton, *Skin/Deep*; Keenan. "Skin Tones and Physical Features."
47. Smith, "Higher Education Expresses Concerns," 14.
48. Norment, "Am I Black, White, or In between?"

49. *Philadelphia Tribune*, "Multiracial Census Listing."
50. Lowery, " 'Tiger' on Course."
51. Eason, "Biracial Classifications: History Forgotten?"
52. Norment, "Am I Black, White, or In between?"
53. *Los Angeles Sentinel*, "Colin Powell."
54. Shah and Thornton, *Newspaper Coverage of Interethnic Conflict*.

Chapter Six. After the Census

1. Although data collection began after May 2000, only one article was found from 2000.
2. Takagi, *The Retreat from Race*.
3. See Ono and Sloop's *Shifting Borders* and Chavez's *Covering Immigration* for how immigration rhetoric and media representations rely upon stereotypes about Latino immigrants.
4. Kong, "Number Crunch," 38.
5. O'Sullivan, "Asian-American Affairs."
6. Ibid.
7. *Little India*, "Most Indian State."
8. Lieser, "Hapa Issues Forum Celebrates."
9. Ibid.
10. Yuen, "HapAmerica."
11. Ng, "Who Am I?"
12. Ibid., 12.
13. Winfrey, "Mixmaster Matt."
14. *Little India*, "Mix and Match."
15. Kao, "2050: The Face of Race."
16. Streeter, "The Hazards of Visibility."
17. It is also notable that these public service advertisements mimicked so clearly Nike's "I am Tiger Woods" ads, which featured children of all colors on golf courses. These spots serve as a "kind and gentle" reminder that for decades people of color were not welcome on golf courses, but communicate to viewers that since Tiger, everyone can achieve their golf dreams.
18. *A Magazine*, "The Pursuit of Hapa-ness."
19. Ibid.
20. Ibid.
21. Yuen, "HapAmerica."
22. Ibid., 18.
23. Yamaguchi, "He's Got the Look."
24. Kao, "2050: The Face of Race."
25. Ibid.
26. Lieser, "Hapa Issues Forum Celebrates."
27. O'Sullivan, "Asian-American Affairs."
28. Ibid.
29. Yamaguchi, "He's Got the Look."
30. Winfrey, "Mixmaster Matt."

31. Ibid.

32. Streeter, "The Hazards of Visibility."

33. This trend continues, most recently crystallized in news coverage of the first Latino mayor of Los Angeles, Antonio Villaraigosa (e.g., *Newsweek*, "Latino Power").

34. *Washington Informer*, "New Census Race."

35. Toler, "No Major Changes."

36. Roach, "When Academia Meets Activism."

37. Hughes, "Multi-racial Category."

38. Stefanik, "Mixed Race Experience Examined."

39. To be sure, Blackness is not and never has been a static entity; however, in the language of popular politics, solidarity has been a major theme in Black rhetoric. Exposing "dirty laundry" of intraracial disputes or cultural differences is normally frowned upon.

40. *Jet*, "How Census Results Could Redefine," 4.

41. Ibid.

42. Bean, "No Longer Black."

43. Hubbard, "Multiracial Category."

44. Ibid., 5.

45. *Tri-State Defender*, "What Does Being African American Mean."

46. Ibid.

47. Ibid.

48. Interracial dating is also implied as a contributor to the "Black male shortage."

49. Anderson, "Biracial Profiling."

50. Hubbard, "Multiracial Category."

51. *Jet*, "How Census Could Redefine."

52. Marable, "Along the Color Line."

53. Hubbard, "Multiracial Category."

54. The chart on the Hispanic power theme is not entirely accurate as a gauge of dominant publications' interest in the issue. Because the stories used in the analysis had to include mentions of the "multiracial" population, this set of articles does not reflect the great interest in the Hispanic population count in the mainstream news. Indeed, we did a Lexis Nexis search to see how many articles in daily U.S. newspapers had lead paragraphs with the terms *Hispanic*, *Census*, and *African Americans*, and found more than eight hundred articles, but very few also contained the term *multiracial Americans*.

55. Strausberg, "Rep. Jackson Seeks."

56. Hubbard, "Multiracial Category."

57. Walters, "From the Desk: The Census."

58. Alonso-Zaldivar, "Black or Latino."

59. Ibid.

60. Kane, "Woods Has to Do More."

61. See Wynter, *American Skin*, for a history of how American advertising became multiethnic.

62. La Ferla, "Generation E.A."

63. Pawlowski, "The Blending of 'American Skin.'"
64. Kotkin and Tseng, "Happy to Mix It All Up."
65. Ibid.
66. Aduroja, "It's All About the Box Office."
67. Ibid.
68. Movies such as *Save the Last Dance*, *Crazy/Beautiful*, and *O* all featured White teen actresses with Black or Latino actors as love interests. *Times-Picayune*, "Teen Movies."
69. Jones, "Mixing and Matching."
70. See Roman, "Denying (White) Racial Privilege" and hooks, "Madonna," for critiques of White appropriation of racial Others' culture for pleasure and economic benefits.
71. All praise (and apologies) to Prince for the inspiration for the title of this section.
72. Large, "Multiracial and Tearing Down."
73. *Omaha World-Herald*, "Iowan's Racial Makeup."
74. Florio, "Kids Top Racial Chart."
75. Ibid.
76. Belsie, "Profile Rises for Multiracial People."
77. *Pittsburgh Post-Gazette*, "Melting Pot, Mixing Bowl."
78. Ibid.
79. Rey, "Blurring the Lines."
80. Page, "Acceptance Amid the Diversity."
81. Ibid.
82. This reinforces a popular narrative that the armed forces have "led" America in desegregation because the military was able to use its disciplinary hierarchy to enforce integration.
83. Rey, "Blurring the Lines."
84. Stodghill and Bower, "Where Everyone's a Minority."
85. The Bush administration was early on viewed as an enemy to African Americans, due in part to the Florida recount controversy, where disproportionate numbers of African Americans were prevented from voting.
86. Clegg, "Words for the President," (my italics).
87. *Weekly Standard*, "Choosing Colorblindness."
88. Jacoby, "Rise of the Blended American."
89. Shea, "Beyond Race or Beholden to It?"
90. Will, "Dropping the 'One-Drop' Rule," 64.
91. Ibid.
92. See Madison, "Legitimation Crisis and Containment."
93. See Frankenberg, *White Women, Race Matters*.
94. Harris, "Does It Matter How We Measure?"

Conclusion

1. Houston Baker Jr. coined the term *conservative nostalgia* in "Critical Memory."

2. See Turner, "The Dangers of Misappropriation."

3. Asen, "A Discourse Theory," 199.

4. Harris, "Whiteness as Property." P. Williams, *Alchemy of Race and Rights*.

5. Lowe, "The International Within the National."

6. Harris, "Whiteness as Property."

7. Hong, "Something Forgotten," 298.

8. See Streeter, "Hazards of Visibility"; Bost, *Mulattas and Mestizas*.

9. For example, Patricia Hill Collins notes in *Black Sexual Politics* how Halle Berry is able to "work her *Blackness*" (my italics) in her varied Hollywood film roles. She is light-skinned and "projects a kind of beauty that is not purely Black" and has been cast as an object of desire in roles that White or Latina actresses could also play (194–95).

10. See Bost, *Mulattas and Mestizas*; Zackodnik, *The Mulatta and the Politics of Race*.

11. Whelan, "Casting Tiger Woods."

12. Eddings, "Tiger's Triumph," 8.

13. Cole, "Nike's America/America's Michael Jordan," 91.

14. Quoted in Bamberger, "Mining Woods," 27.

15. Andrews, "The Fact(s) of Michael Jordan's Blackness," 128.

16. See Enloe, *Bananas, Beaches, and Bases*.

17. Lowe, "The International Within the National."

18. Salgado, "Misceg-narrations," 48.

19. Ibid., 50.

20. Scheiber, "Barack Obama's Miraculous Campaign."

21. Malcolmson, "Obama's Speech," (my italics).

22. Johnson, "Let's Hear More From Obama," D12.

23. See Fine, Weis, Pruitt and Burns, Eds., *Off White*; L. Williams, *The Constraint of Race*; Frankenberg, *White Women, Race Matters*.

24. Tilove, "New Star Emerges," (my italics).

25. Scheiber, "Barack Obama's Miraculous Campaign," 26.

26. Hooper, "Speaker's Words Felt." (my italics).

27. Tilove.

28. Lowe, "The International Within the National," 32.

29. I take the term *to cover* from Kenji Yoshino's book, *Covering: The Hidden Assault On Our Civil Rights*. Yoshino claims there are overt and covert pressures on minority groups to "tone down" or not display cultural and behavioral differences in public settings. The pressure to "cover," he argues, masks important realms of discrimination and limits our ability to safely express our authentic selves. Yoshino identifies an "assimilationist bias" in American law and society wherein traits that are "mutable"—such as language or hairstyles—are not seen as realms of discrimination like "immutable traits"—such as skin color or gender.

30. Roberts, "A World Without Race," 33–34.

31. Roberts, 33.

32. Obama, *Dreams From My Father*, 204.

33. Singh, *Black Is A Country*, 214–15.

34. Powell, "The Colorblind Multiracial Dilemma," 158.

35. duCille, *Skin Trade*, 270.
36. Salgado, 53–54.
37. Newkirk, *Within the Veil*.
38. Wilson, *Black Journalists in Paradox*.
39. Mellinger, "Counting Color," 129–51.
40. Ibid., 145.
41. Gandy, *Communication and Race*.
42. "Let's Do It Better!" http://www.jrn.columbia.edu/events/race/about.asp.
43. Guinier and Torres, *The Miner's Canary*.

Bibliography

Books, Films, Journals

Alexander, Elizabeth. "'Can You Be BLACK and Look at This?': Reading the Rodney King Video(s)." In *The Black Public Sphere*, eds. The Black Public Sphere Collective, 81–98. Chicago: University of Chicago Press, 1995.

Altheide, David. *Qualitative Media Analysis.* Thousand Oaks, CA: Sage, 1996.

Anderson, Margo J., and Steven E. Fienberg. *Who Counts? The Politics of Census-Taking in Contemporary America.* New York: Sage, 2001.

Andrews, David L. "The Fact(s) of Michael Jordan's Blackness: Excavating a Floating Racial Signifier." *Sociology of Sport Journal*, 12, (1996): 125–58.

Andrews, William L. "Introduction." *Six Women's Slave Narratives.* New York: Oxford University Press, 1988.

Asen, Robert. "A Discourse Theory of Citizenship." *Quarterly Journal of Speech*, 90, (2004): 189–211.

Baird-Olson, Karen. "Colonization, Cultural Imperialism, and the Social Construction of American Indian Mixed-Blood Identity." In *New Faces in a Changing America: Multiracial Identity in the 21ˢᵗ Century*, eds. Loretta I. Winters and Herman L. DuBose, 194–221. Thousand Oaks, CA: Sage, 2003.

Baynes, Leonard M. "Who is Black Enough for You? An Analysis of Northwestern University Law School's Struggle over Minority Faculty Hiring," *Michigan Journal of Race and Law* 2, no. 2 (1997): 205–33.

Bennett, Juda. *The Passing Figure: Racial Confusion in Modern American Literature.* New York: Peter Lang, 1996.

Berlant, Lauren. "National Brands/National Body: Imitation of Life," in *The Phantom Public Sphere*, edited by Bruce Robbins, 173–208 (Minneapolis: University of Minnesota Press, 1993).

Blassingame, John W., ed. *Slave Testimony: Two Centuries of Letters, Speeches, Interviews, and Autobiographies.* Baton Rouge: Louisiana State University Press, 1977.

Bodroghkozy, Aniko. "'Is This What You Mean by Color TV?': Race, Gender, and Conflicted Meanings in NBC's *Julia.*" In *Gender, Race, and Class in Media: A Text Reader* (1st edition) eds. Gail Dines and Jean M. Humez. Thousand Oaks, CA: Sage, 1995.

Boeckmann, Cathy. *A Question of Character: Scientific Racism and the Genres of American Fiction, 1892–1912*. Tuscaloosa: University of Alabama Press, 2000.

Bonilla-Silva, Eduardo. "The New Racism: Racial Structure in the United States, 1960s–1990s," In *Race, Ethnicity and Nationality in the United States: Toward the Twenty-First Century*, ed. Paul Wong, 55–101. Boulder: Westview, 1999.

Bost, Suzanne. *Mulattas and Mestizas: Representing Mixed Identities in the Americas, 1850–2000*. Athens and London: University of Georgia Press, 2002.

Brooks, Dwight and James Rada. Constructing Race in Black and Whiteness: Media Coverage of Public Support for President Clinton. *Journalism and Communication Monographs* 4, no. 3 (2002): 113–56.

Brouwer, Daniel C. and Catherine Squires. "Public Intellectuals, Public Life, and the University." *Argumentation and Advocacy* 39 (2003): 201–213.

Brown, Michael K., Martin Carnoy, Elliot Currie, Troy Duster, David B. Oppenheimer, Marjorie M. Shultz, and David Wellman. *Whitewashing Race: The Myth of a Color-Blind Society*. Berkeley: University of California Press, 2004.

Brown, Nancy G. and Romona E. Douglass. "Evolution of Multiracial Organizations: Where We Have Been and Where We Are Going." In *New Faces in a Changing America*, eds. Winters and DuBose, 111–124.

Calhoun, Craig. "Introduction." *Social Theory and The Politics of Identity*. Oxford: Blackwell, 1994.

Carlson, A. Cheree. " 'You Know It When You See It': The Rhetorical Hierarchy of Race and Gender in *Rhinelander v. Rhinelander.*" *Quarterly Journal of Speech* 85(1999): 111–128.

Castle, W. E. "Biological and Social Consequences of Race-Crossing." *American Journal of Physical Anthropology* 9 1926: 145–56.

Chavez, Leo. *Covering Immigration: Popular Images and the Politics of the Nation*. Berkeley: University of California Press, 2001.

Clawson, Rosalee A., Harry C Strine IV, and Eric N Waltenburg. "Framing Supreme Court Decisions: The Mainstream Versus The Black Press." *Journal of Black Studies* 33, no. 6 (2003): 784–810.

Cole, C. L. "Nike's America/America's Michael Jordan." In *Michael Jordan, Inc.: Corporate Sport, Media, Culture and Late Modern America*, ed. David L. Andrews, 65-106.

Colker, Ruth. *Hybrid: Bisexuals, Multiracials, and Other Misfits under American Law*. New York: New York University Press, 1996.

Collins, Patricia H. *Black Feminist Thought: Knowledge, Consciousness, and the Politics of Empowerment*. New York: Routledge, 2000.

———. *Black Sexual Politics: African Americans, Gender, and the New Racism*. New York: Routledge, 2004.

Comas, Juan. "Racial Myths." In *The Race Question in Modern Science*. United Nations Educational, Scientific and Cultural Organization, Publication no. 891, 1951.

Cooding-Williams, Robert, ed. *Reading Rodney King, Reading Urban Uprising*. New York: Routledge, 1993.

Courtney, Susan. *Hollywood Fantasies of Miscegenation: Spectacular Narratives of Gender and Race, 1903–1967*. Princeton: Princeton University Press, 2005.

Cruse, Kevin M. *White Flight: Atlanta and the Making of Modern Conservatism*. Princeton: Princeton University Press, 2005.

DaCosta, Kimberly M. "Multiracial Identity: From Personal Problem to Public Issue." In *New Faces in a Changing America*, eds. Winters and DuBose, 68–84. 2003.

Dalmage, Heather M. "'Mama, Are You Brown?' Multiracial Families and the Color of Love." In *Skin Deep: How Race and Complexion Matter in the "Color Blind" Era*, eds. Cedric Herring, Verna Keith and Hayward D. Horton, 82–98. Urbana and Chicago: University of Illinois Press, 2004.

Daniel, G. Reginald. "Multiracial Identity in Global Perspective: The United States, Brazil, and South Africa." In *New Faces in a Changing America*, eds. Winters and DuBose, 247–286. 2003.

———. *More Than Black? Multiracial Identity and the New Racial Order*. Philadephia: Temple University Press, 2002.

Danielsen, Dan, and Karen Engle, eds. *After Identity: A Reader in Law and Culture*. New York: Routledge, 1995.

Dates, Janette L. and William Barlow, eds. *Split Image: African Americans in the Mass Media*. Washington, DC: Howard University Press, 1993.

Davenport, C. B. "Race Crossing in Jamaica." *Science* 72, no. 1872 (1930): 501–502.

Davis, F. James. *Who is Black? One Nation's Definition*. University Park: Pennsylvania State University Press, 1991.

Delgado, Richard, and Jean Stefancic. *Critical Race Theory: The Cutting Edge*. Philadelphia: Temple University Press, 2000.

DeVere Brody, Jennifer. "Clare Kendry's 'True' Colors: Race and Class Conflict in Nella Larsen's *Passing*." *Callaloo* 15, no. 4 (1992): 1053–65.

Dickerson, Niki T. "Untangling Race/Gender Economic Inequality: The Case of Black Women and Men. *African American Research Perspectives*, 8 (2002): 125–30.

Dillard, Angela. "How the New Black Elite Peddles Conservatism." *New Labor Forum* 13, no. 1 (2004): 31–38.

Dines, Gail & Humez, Jean. *Gender, Race, and Class in Media: A Text-Reader* (2nd ed.). Thousand Oaks: Sage, 2003.

Dixon, Thomas. *The Clansman: A Historical Romance of the Ku Klux Klan*. New York: Grosset and Dunlap, 1915.

Dixon, Travis L. and Daneil Linz. "Overrepresentation and Underrepresentation of African Americans and Latinos as Lawbreakers on Television News," *Journal of Communication* 50, no. 2 (1999): 131–54.

Du Cille, Ann. *Skin Trade*. Cambridge: Harvard University Press, 1996.

Dyson, Michael E. *Is Bill Cosby Right, or Has the Black Middle Class Lost Its Mind?* New York: Basic Civitas, 2005.

Edles, Laura D. " 'Race,' 'Ethnicity' and 'Culture' in Hawai'i: The Myth of the Model Minority State." In *New Faces in a Changing America*, eds. Winters and DuBose, 222–46. 2003.

Edwards, Harry. "The Journey from Brown v. Board of Education to Grutter v. Bollinger: From Racial Assimilation to Diversity." *Michigan Law Review* 102 (2004): 944–78.

Edwards, Justin D. *Gothic Passages: Racial Ambiguity and the American Gothic.* Iowa City: Iowa University Press, 2003.

Enloe, Cynthia. *Bananas, Beaches and Bases: Making Feminist Sense of International Politics.* Berkeley: University of California Press, 1990.

Entman, Robert M. "Framing: Toward Clarification of a Fractured Paradigm," *Journal of Communication* 43 (1993): 51–58.

———. "Manufacturing Discord: Media in The Affirmative Action Debate." *Press/Politics* 2 (1997): 32–51.

Entman, Robert M. and Carole V. Bell, "The Media's Place in the Denial of Race: Blocking Presidential Attempts to Alter the Public Sphere." Presented at the 2005 conference of the International communication Association, New York, May 30, 2005.

Ettema, James. "Press Rites and Race Relations," *Critical Studies in Media Communication* 7 (1990): 309–31.

Entman, Robert M. and Andrew Rojecki. *The Black Image in the White Mind: Media and Race in America.* Chicago: University of Chicago Press, 2000.

Fabi, M. Giulia. *Passing and the Rise of the African American Novel.* Urbana: University of Illinois Press, 2001.

Fernandez, Carlos. Written Testimony, House Government Reform and Oversight Management, Information and Technology Census 2000 Racial Identification, July 27, 1997.

Finkle, Lee. *Forum for Protest: The Black Press During World War II.* Rutherford: Fairleigh Dickinson University Press, 1975.

Flores, Lisa A., and Mark L. McPhail. "From Black and White to *Living Color:* A Dialogic Exposition into The Social (Re)Construction of Race, Gender, and Crime," *Critical Studies in Mass Communication* 14(1997): 106–22.

Foreman, P. Gabrielle. "The Spoken and the Silenced in *Incidents in the Life of a Slave Girl* and *Our Nig.*" *Callaloo* 13 (1990): 313–24.

Formisano, Robert P. *Boston Against Busing: Race, Class, and Ethnicity in the 1960s and 1970s.* Chapel Hill and London: University of North Carolina Press, 1991.

Frankenberg, Ruth. *White Women, Race Matters: The Social Construction of Whiteness.* Minneapolis: University of Minnesota Press, 1993.

Funderberg, Lise. *Black White Other: Biracial Americans Talk about Race and Identity.* New York: William Morrow, 1994.

Furedi, Frank. "How Sociology Imagined Mixed-Race." In *Rethinking 'Mixed Race,'* eds David Parker and Miri Song, 17–29. London: Pluto Press, 2001.

Fuss, Diana. *Essentially Speaking: Feminism, Nature and Difference.* New York: Routledge, 1989.

Gabler, Neal. *Life the Movie: How Entertainment Conquered Reality.* New York: Knopf, 1998.

Gamson, William A. "Ambivalences about Affirmative Action." *Society* 6 (1992): 41–45.

Gamson, William A. and Andre Modigliani. "The Changing Culture of Affirmative Action." *Research in Political Sociology*. 3 (1987):137–77.

Gandy, Oscar H. "Privatization and Identity: The Formation of a Racial Class." In *Media in the Age of Marketization* eds. Janet Wasko and Graham Murdock (eds). Creskill, NJ: Hampton Press, forthcoming.

———. *Communication and Race: A Structural Perspective*. London: Oxford University Press, 1993.

Gibbs, Jewelle Taylor. *Race and Justice: Rodney King and O. J. Simpson in a House Divided*. San Francisco: Jossey-Bass, 1996.

Giddings, Paula. *When and Where I Enter: The Impact of Black Women on Race and Sex in America*. New York: William Morrow, 1984.

Gilens, Martin. *Why Americans Hate Welfare: Race, Media and the Politics of Anti-poverty Policy*. Chicago: University of Chicago Press, 1999.

Ginsberg, Elaine K. "Introduction: The Politics of Passing." In *Passing and The Fictions of Identity*.

Ginsberg, Elaine K., ed. *Passing and The Fictions of Identity*. Durham: Duke University Press, 1996.

Giroux, Henry A. "Racial Politics and the Pedagogy of Whiteness." In *Whiteness: A Critical Reader*, ed. Mike Hill, 294–315. New York: New York University Press, 1997.

Gitlin, Todd. *The Whole World Is Watching: Mass Media and the Making and Unmaking of the New Left*. Berkeley: University of California Press, 1980

———. "The Rise of 'Identity Politics': An Examination and a Critique," *Dissent* 40 (1993): 172–77.

Glaeser, Edward L. and Jacob L. Vigdor. Racial Segregation in the 2000 Census: Promising News, 8. Washington, D.C. : The Brookings Institution, 2001.

Glazer, Nathan. "Reflections on Race, Hispanicity, and Ancestry in the U.S. Census." In *The New Race Question: How the Census Counts Multiracial Individuals*, eds. Joel Perlman and Mary C. Waters, 318–26. New York: Sage, 2002.

Graham, Susan. Testimony, House Government Reform and Oversight Management, Information and Technology Census 2000 Racial Identification, July 25, 1997.

Grant, Madison. *The Passing of The Great Race; or, The Racial Basis of European-History*. New York: C. Scribner's Sons, 1921.

Gray, Herman. *Watching Race: Television and the Struggle for "Blackness."* Minneapolis: University of Minnesota Press, 1995.

Guinier, Lani, and Gerald Torres. *The Miner's Canary: Enlisting Race, Resisting Power, Transforming Democracy*. Cambridge: Harvard University Press, 2002.

Gulick, Sidney L. *Mixing the Races in Hawaii: A Study of the Coming Neo-Hawaiian American Race*. Honolulu: The Hawaiian Board Book Rooms, 1937.

Hall, Stuart. "Subjects in History: Making Diasporic Identities." In *The House that Race Built*, ed. Wahneema Lubiano, 289–300. New York: Vintage Books, 1998.

Hanchard, Michael. "'Black Cinderella?': Race and the Public Sphere in Brazil." In *The Black Public Sphere*, 169–89.

Haney López, Ian F. *White by Law: The Legal Construction of Race*. New York: New York University Press, 1996.

Harris, Cheryl I. "Whiteness As Property." *Harvard Law Review*, 106 (June 1993): 1707–91.

Harris, David. "Does It Matter How We Measure? Racial Classification and the Characteristics of Multiracial Youth." In *The New Race Question*, eds. J. Perlmann and M. C. Waters, 62–101.

Hasian, Marouf, and Thomas Nakayama. "The Fictions of Racialized Identities." In *Judgment Calls: Rhetoric, Politics, and Indeterminacy*, eds. John M. Sloop and James P. McDaniel, 182–95. Boulder: Westview, 1998.

Hauke, Kathleen A. "The 'Passing' of Elsie Roxborough." *Michigan Quarterly Review* 23 no. 2 (1984): 155–70.

Hearne, Joanna. "The Cross-Heart People: Race and Inheritance in the Silent Western." *Journal of Popular Film and Television* 30 no. 4 (Winter 2003): 181–196.

Herring, Cedric, Verna Keith and Hayward Derrick Horton, eds. *Skin/Deep: How Race and Complexion Matter in the "Color-Blind" Era*. Chicago: University of Illinois Press, 2004.

Hogan, Lawrence D. *A Black National News Service: The Associated Negro Press and Claude Barnett, 1919–1945*. London: Associated University Presses, 1984.

Hong, Grace Kyungwon. "Something Forgotten Which Should Have Been Remembered: Private Property and Cross-Racial Solidarity in the Work of Hisaye Yamamoto." *American Literature* 71 (June 1999): 291–310.

hooks, bell. *Ain't I a Woman: Black Women and Feminism*. Boston: South End Press, 1981.

———. "Madonna." *Black Looks: Race and Representation*, 157–164. Boston: South End Press, 1992.

Horton, Merrill. "Blackness, Betrayal, and Childhood: Race and Identity in Nella Larsen's *Passing*." *CLA Journal* 39 (1994): 31–45.

Hoyt, Mike. "Reporting Race: Diversity Fatigue? Here's a Tonic." *Columbia Journalism Review*. (September/October, 1999): 20–24.

Hunt, Darnell. *Screening the Los Angeles Riots: Race, Seeing and Resistance*. Cambridge: Cambridge University Press, 1997.

Hurtado, Aida. "The Trickster's Play: Whiteness in the Subordination and Liberation Process." In *Race, Ethnicity, and Citizenship: A Reader*, ed. Rodolfo D. Torres, 225–244.

Ignatiev, Noel. *How the Irish Became White*. New York: Routledge, 1996.

Iyengar, Shanto. *Is Anyone Responsible? How Television Frames Political Issues*. Chicago: University of Chicago Press, 1991.

Jacobs, Ronald. *Race, Media, and the Crisis of Civil Society: From Watts to Rodney King*. Cambridge: Cambridge University Press, 2000.

Jhally, Sut and Justin Lewis. *Enlightened Racism: The Cosby Show, Audiences, and the Myth of the American Dream*. Boulder: Westview, 1992.

Keenan, Kevin L. "Skin Tones and Physical Features of Blacks in Magazine Advertisements." *Journalism & Mass Communication Quarterly* 73 no. 4 (1996): 905–12.

Kennedy, Randall. *Interracial Intimacies: Sex Marriage, Identity and Adoption*. New York: Pantheon, 2003.

Kerlin, Robert T. *The Voice of the Negro, 1919*. New York: E. P. Dutton, 1920.

Kinder, Donald, and Lynn Sanders. *Divided by Color: Racial Politics and Democratic Ideals*. Chicago: University of Chicago Press, 1996.

Kirschenman, Joleen and Kathryn Neckerman. " 'We'd Love to Hire Them, But . . .' The Meaning of Race for Employers." In *The Urban Underclass*, eds. Christopher Jencks and Paul E. Peterson, 203–34. Washington, D.C. Brookings Institution, 1991.

Kousser, Morgan. *Colorblind Injustice: Minority Voting Rights and the Undoing of the Second Reconstruction*. Chapel Hill: University of North Carolina Press, 1999.

Krugman, Paul. "Glenn Loury's Round Trip: The Travails and Temptations of a Black Intellectual." *Slate*, May 15, 1998. http://www.slate.com/id/1934/.

Kwan, SanSan, and Kenneth Speirs, eds. *Mixing it Up: Multiracial Subjects*. Austin: University of Texas Press, 2004.

Lassiter, Matthew D. "The Suburban Origins of 'Color-Blind' Conservatism: Middle-Class Consciousness in the Charlotte Busing Crisis," *Journal of Urban History* 30 no. 4 (2004): 549–82.

Lawrence, Bonita. "Gender, Race and the Regulation of Native Identity in Canada and the United States: An Overview." *Hypatia* 18 no. 2 (Spring 2003): 3–31.

Lehmann, Nicholas. "Taking Affirmative Action Apart." In *Affirmative Action: Social Justice or Reverse Discrimination?*, eds. Francis J. Beckwith and Todd E. Jones, 34–51. Amherst: New York: Prometheus Books, 1997.

Lewis, Earl, and Heidi Ardizzone. *Love on Trial: An American Scandal in Black and White*. New York: Norton, 2001.

Lincoln, Yvonna S. and Egon G. Guba, *Naturalistic Inquiry*. Beverly Hills, CA: Sage, 1985.

Lindlof, Thomas R. and Bryan C. Taylor. *Qualitative Communication Research Methods*, second edition. Thousand Oaks, CA: Sage Publications, 2002.

Lipsitz, George. *The Possessive Investment in Whiteness: How White People Profit from Identity Politics*. Philadelphia: Temple University Press, 1998.

———. Personal e-mail communication to author, December 24, 2005.

Lowe, Lisa. "The International within the National: American Studies and the Asian American Critique." *Cultural Critique* 40 (Autumn 1998): 29–47.

Lubiano, Wahneema. "Like Being Mugged by a Metaphor: Multiculturalism and State Narratives." In *Mapping Multiculturalism*, eds. Avery F. Gordon and Christopher Newfield, 64–75. Minneapolis: University of Minnesota Press, 1996.

Lule, Jack. "The Rape of Mike Tyson: Race, the Press, and Symbolic Types." *Critical Studies in Mass Communication* 12 (1995): 176–95.

McBride, James. *The Color of Water: A Black Man's Tribute to His White Mother*. New York: Riverhead Books, 1996.

McPherson, Lionel. "The Loudest Silence Ever Heard: Black Conservatives and Media." *Extra!* July/August 1992. http://www.fair.org/index.php?page=1488.

Madison, Kelly. "Legitimation Crisis and Containment: The 'Anti-Racist-White-Hero' Film." *Critical Studies in Media Communication* 16 (1999): 399–417.

Marshall, Dale R. "The Continuing Significance of Race: The Transformation of American Politics." *American Political Science Review* 84 no. 2 (June 1990): 611–16.

Massey, Douglas S., and Nancy J. Denton. *American Apartheid: Segregation and the Making of the Underclass.* Cambridge: Harvard University Press, 1993.

Means-Coleman, Robin R. *African American Viewers and the Black Situation Comedy: Situating Racial Humor.* New York: Garland, 2000.

Mellinger, Gwyneth. "Counting Color: Ambivalence and Contradiction in the American Society of Newspaper Editors' Discourse of Diversity." *Journal of Communication Inquiry* 27 (2003): 129–51.

Menchaca, Martha. *Recovering History, Constructing Race: The Indian, Black and White Roots of Mexican Americans.* Austin: University of Texas Press, 2001.

Mendelberg, Tali. *The Race Card: Campaign Strategy, Implicit Messages, and the Norm of Equality.* Princeton: Princeton University Press, 2001.

Messer-Davidow, Ellen. "Manufacturing the Attack on Liberalized Higher Education." *Social Text* 36 (1993): 40–80.

Miles, Matthew B. and A. Michael Huberman. *Qualitative Data Analysis: An Expanded Sourcebook*, second edition. Thousand Oaks, CA: Sage Publications, 1994.

Moon, Dreama G. "Inter-Class Travel, Cultural Adaptation, and 'Passing' as Disjunctive Intercultural Practice," *International and Intercultural Communication Annual* 23 (2000): 215–40.

Morris, Aldon. "Political Consciousness and Collective Action." In *Frontiers in Social Movement Theory* eds. Aldon Morris and Carol McClurg Mueller, 351–73. New Haven: Yale University Press, 1992.

Morrison, Toni, ed. *Race-ing Justice, En-Gendering Power: Essays on Anita Hill, Clarence Thomas, and the Social Construction of Reality.* New York: Pantheon Books, 1992.

Nakashima, Cynthia L. "An Invisible Monster: The Creation and Denial of Mixed-Race People in America." In *Racially Mixed People in America*, ed. Maria P. P. Root, 162–78. Thousand Oaks: Sage, 1992.

———. "Servants of Culture: The Symbolic Role of Mixed-Race Asians in American Discourse." In *The Sum of Our Parts: Mixed-Race Asian Americans*, ch. 3, eds. Teresa Williams-Leon and Cynthia L. Nakashima. Philadelphia: Temple University, 2001.

Nakayama, Thomas, and Krizek, Robert L. "Whiteness: A Strategic Rhetoric." *Quarterly Journal of Speech* 81 no. 3 (1995): 291–310.

Nakayama, Thomas K. "Show/Down Time: 'Race,' Gender, Sexuality, and Popular Culture." *Critical Studies in Mass Communication* 11(1994): 162–79.

Neuendorf, Kimberly A. *The Content Analysis Guidebook.* Thousand Oaks, CA: Sage, 2002.

Newkirk, Pamela. *Within the Veil: Black Journalists, White Media.* New York: New York University Press, 2000.

Obama, Barack. *Dreams from My Father: A Story of Race and Inheritance.* New York: Three Rivers Press, 1995, 2004.

Oliver, Melvin L. and Thomas Shapiro. *Black Wealth, White Wealth: A New Perspective on Racial Inequality.* New York: Routledge, 1997.

Omi, Michael, and Howard Winant. *Racial Formation in the United States: From the 1960s to the 1990s,* second edition. New York: Routledge, 1994.

Ono, Kent A., and John M. Sloop. "The Critique of Vernacular Discourse." *Communication Monographs,* 62 (1995): 19–46.

———. *Shifting Borders: Rhetoric, Immigration, and California's Proposition 187.* Philadelphia: Temple University Press, 2002.

Palumbo-Liu, David. *Asian/American: Historical Crossings of a Racial Frontier.* Stanford: Stanford University Press, 1999.

Parisi, Peter. "The *New York Times* Looks at One Block in Harlem: Narratives of Race in Journalism." *Critical Studies in Mass Communication* 15(1998): 236–54.

Patterson, Anita H. *From Emerson to King: Democracy, Race, and the Politics of Protest.* New York: Oxford University Press, 1997.

Patterson, James T. *Brown v. Board of Education: A Civil Rights Milestone and its Troubled Legacy.* Oxford: Oxford University Press, 2002.

Payne, Charles. *I've Got the Light of Freedom: The Organizing Tradition and the Mississippi Freedom Struggle.* Berkeley: University of California Press, 1995.

Peer, Limor, and James S. Ettema. "The Mayor's Race: Campaign Coverage and The Discourse of Race in America's Three Largest Cities." *Critical Studies in Mass Communication* 15 (1998): 255–78.

Perlman, Joel and Mary C. Waters, eds. *The New Race Question: How the Census Counts Multiracial Individuals.* New York: Sage, 2002.

Peterson, Paul E. "A Politically Correct Solution to Racial Classification." In *Classifying by Race,* ed. Paul E. Peterson, 3–20. Princeton: Princeton University Press, 1995.

Piliawsky, Monte. "Racial Equality in the United States: From Institutionalized Racism to 'Respectable' Racism," *Phylon,* 45 no. 2 (1984): 135–43.

Piper, Adrian. "Passing for White, Passing for Black." In *Passing and the Fictions of Identity,* ed. E. K. Ginsberg, 234–69.

Post, Robert, and Michael Rogin, eds. *Race and Representation: Affirmative Action.* New York: Zone Books, 1998.

powell, john a. "The Colorblind Multiracial Dilemma: Racial Categories Reconsidered," in *Race, Identity and Citizenship,* ed. R. D. Torres, 141–57.

Projansky, Sarah, and Kent A. Ono. "Strategic Whiteness as Cinematic Racial Politics." In *Whiteness: The Communication of Social Identity,* eds. Thomas K. Nakayama and Judith Martin, 149–74. Newbury Park: Sage, 1999.

Reicher, Stephen. "The Context of Social Identity: Domination, Resistance, and Change." *Political Psychology* 25 no. 6 (2004): 921–45.

Rhodes, Jane. "Fanning the Flames of Racial Discord: The National Press and the Black Panther Party," *Harvard International Journal of Press/Politics,* 4 (1999): 95–118.

Roberts, Dorothy. *Killing the Black Body: Race, Reproduction, and the Meaning of Liberty.* New York: Vintage Books, 1997.

———. "A World Without Race: But Does Black Nationalism Have to Go Too?" *Boston Review*, May/June 2006, 33–34.

Robinson, Amy. "It Takes One to Know One: Passing and Communities of Common Interest." *Critical Inquiry* 20 (1994): 715–736.

Roediger, David. *The Wages of Whiteness: Race and the Making of the American Working Class.* New York: Verso Books, 1991.

———. *Colored White: Transcending the Racial Past.* Berkeley: University of California Press, 2002.

———. "White Workers, New Democrats, and Affirmative Action." In *The House That Race Built*, ed. W. Lubiano, 48–65. 1997.

Roman, Leslie G. "Denying (White) Racial Privilege: Redemption Discourses and the Uses of Fantasy." In *Off White: Readings on Race, Power, and Society*, eds. Michelle Fine, Lois Weis, Linda Powell Pruitt and April Burns, 270–82. New York: Routledge, 1997.

Root, Maria P. P., ed. *Racially Mixed People in America.* Newbury Park: Sage, 1992.

———. *The Multiracial Experience: Racial Borders as The New Frontier.* Thousand Oaks: Sage, 1996.

Russell, Kathy, Midge Wilson, and Ronald Hall. *The Color Complex: The Politics of Skin Color Among African Americans.* New York: Anchor Books, 1993.

Salgado, Raquel Scherr. "Misceg-narrations." In *Mixing It Up: Multiracial Subjects*, eds. SanSan Kwan and Kenneth Speirs, 31–70. Austin: University of Texas Press.

Savage, Barbara P. *Broadcasting Freedom: Radio, War, and the Politics of Race, 1938–1948.* Chapel Hill: University of North Carolina Press, 1999.

Scales-Trent, Judy. *Notes of a White Black Woman: Race, Color, and Community.* University Park: Pennsylvania State University Press, 1995.

Schuetz, Janice, and Lin S. Lilley, eds. *The O. J. Simpson Trials: Rhetoric, Media and the Law.* Carbondale: Southern Illinois University Press, 1999.

Shah, Hemant and Michael C. Thornton. "Racial Ideology in U.S. Mainstream News Magazine Coverage of Black-Latino Interaction." *Critical Studies in Mass Communication* 11 (1994): 141–62.

———. *Newspaper Coverage of Interethnic Conflict: Competing Visions of America.* Thousand Oaks, CA: Sage Publications, 2004.

Sheehy, John. "The Mirror and The Veil: The Passing Novel and The Quest for American Racial Identity." *African American Review* 33 (1999): 401–15.

Shome, Raka. "Outing Whiteness." *Critical Studies in Media Communication* 17 (2000): 366–71.

Siegle, Reva B. "The Racial Rhetorics of Colorblind Constitutionalism: The Case of *Hopwood v. Texas.*" In *Race and Representation: Affirmative Action*, eds. Michael Rogin and Robert Post, 182–95. New York: Zone Books, 1998.

Singh, Nikhil P. *Black Is A Country: Race and the Unfinished Struggle for Democracy.* Cambridge: Harvard University Press, 2004.

Skerry, Peter. *Counting on the Census? Race, Group Identity, and the Evasion of Politics*. Washington, D. C.: Brookings Institution, 2000.

Slaying the Dragon. VHS. San Francisco: National Asian American Telecommunications Association, 1987.

Sloop, John M. "Disciplining The Transgendered: Brandon Teena, Public Representation, and Normativity." *Western Journal of Communication* 64 (2000): 165–89.

Sniderman, Paul M., Edward G. Carmines, Geoffrey C. Layman, and Michael Carter. "Beyond Race: Social Justice as a Race-Neutral Ideal," *American Journal of Political Science* 40 no. 1 (1996): 35–55.

Sollors, Werner. *Neither Black nor White yet Both: Thematic Explorations of Interracial Literature*. New York: Oxford University Press, 1997.

Spencer, Jon M. *The New Colored People: The Mixed-Race Movement in America*. New York: New York University Press, 1997.

Spencer, Rainier. "Census 2000: Assessments in Significance." In *New Faces in a Changing America*, eds. Winters and DuBose, 99–109.

Spickard, Paul R. "The Boom in Biracial Autobiography in the USA." In *Rethinking Mixed Race* eds. D. Parker and M. Song.

———. *Mixed Blood: Intermarriage and Ethnic Identity in Twentieth-Century America*. Madison: University of Wisconsin Press, 1989.

Squires, Catherine R. "Black Talk Radio: Defining Community Needs and Identity." *Harvard International Journal of Press/Politics* 5 (2000): 73–95.

Squires, Catherine, and Daniel C. Brouwer, "In/Discernible Bodies: The Politics of Passing in Mainstream and Marginal Media." *Critical Studies in Mass Communication* 19 (2002): 283–310.

Steele, Shelby. *The Content of Our Character: A New Vision of Race in America*. New York: Harper Perennial, 1991.

Strauss, Anselm, and Julia Corbin, *Basics of Qualitative Research: Grounded Theory Procedures and Techniques*. Newbury Park: Sage, 1990.

Steinberg, Stephen. "The Liberal Retreat from Race during the Post-Civil Rights Era." In *The House That Race Built*, ed. W. Lubiano, 13–47.

Streeter, Carolyn. "The Hazards of Visibility: 'Biracial' Women, Media Images and Narratives of Identity," In *New Faces in a Changing America*, eds. DuBose and Winters, 301–322.

Sunstein, Cass. *Free Markets and Social Justice*. London: Oxford University Press, 1999.

Takagi, Dana Y. *The Retreat from Race: Asian-American Admissions and Racial Politics*. New Brunswick: Rutgers University Press, 1992.

Taylor-Haizlip, Shirlee. *The Sweeter the Juice: A Family Memoir in Black and White*. New York: Touchstone, 1994.

"The Black Press: Soldiers Without Swords." VHS. Directed by Stanley Nelson, 1998. California Newsreel, San Francisco, CA.

Tuan, Mia. *Forever Foreigners or Honorary Whites? The Asian Ethnic Experience Today*. New Brunswick, NJ: Rutgers University Press, 1998.

Turner, Ronald. "The Dangers of Misappropriation: Misusing Martin Luther King Jr.'s Legacy to Prove the Colorblind Thesis." *Michigan Journal of Race & Law* 2 no. 1 (1996): 101–30.

Tyler, Carole-Anne. "Passing: Narcissism, Identity, and Difference." *Differences* 6, 1994: 212–48.

Valentino, Nicholas, Vincent Hutchings, and Ismail White. "Cues That Matter: How Political Ads Prime Racial Attitudes During Campaigns." *American Political Science Review* 96 (March 2002): 75–90.

Vogel, Todd. "Introduction." *The Black Press: New Literary and Historical Essays.* New Brunswick, NJ: Rutgers University Press, 2001.

Wald, Gayle. *Crossing the Line: Racial Passing in U.S. Literature and Popular Culture.* Durham: Duke University Press, 2000.

Ward, Brian. *Just My Soul Responding: Rhythm and Blues, Black Consciousness, and Race Relations.* Berkeley: University of California Press, 1998.

Ward, Brian, ed. *Media, Culture, and the African American Freedom Struggle.* Gainesville, FL: University Press of Florida, 2001.

Ward, Geoffrey C. *Unforgivable Blackness: The Rise and Fall of Jack Johnson.* New York: Knopf, 2004.

Warner, Michael. "The Mass Public and the Mass Subject." In *Habermas and The Public Sphere,* ed. Craig Calhoun, 377–401. Cambridge: MIT Press, 1992.

Waters, Mary C. *Ethnic Options: Choosing Identities in America.* Berkeley: University of California Press, 1990.

———. Testimony, House Government Reform and Oversight Management, Information and Technology Census 2000 Racial Identification, July 25, 1997.

Wells, Ida B. *The Selected Works of Ida B. Wells-Barnett.* Compiled with an introduction by Trudier Harris. New York: Oxford University Press, 1991.

———. "Lynching, Our National Crime." Speech given to the NAACP's founding conference, 1909. Reprinted in *The Rhetoric of Struggle: Public Address by African American Women,* ed. Robbie Jean Walker. New York: Garland, 1992.

———. *Southern Horrors and Other Writings: The Anti-Lynching Campaign of Ida B. Wells, 1892–1900.* With an introduction by Jacqueline Jones Royster, ed. Boston: Bedford Books, 1997.

Wiegman, Robyn. *American Anatomies: Theorizing Race and Gender.* Durham: Duke University Press, 1995.

Williams, Kim M. "From Civil Rights to Multiracial Movement." In *New Faces in a Changing America,* eds. Winters and DuBose, 85–98.

Williams, Linda Faye. *The Constraint of Race: Legacies of White Skin Privilege in America.* University Park: Penn State University Press, 2003.

Williams, Patricia J. *The Alchemy of Race and Rights: Diary of a Law Professor.* Cambridge, MA: Harvard University Press, 1991.

———. "Rush Limbaugh's Inner Black Child." *Nation.* October 27, 2003.

Williams-Leon, Teresa, and Cynthia L. Nakashima, eds. *The Sum of Our Parts: Mixed-Heritage Asian Americans.* Philadelphia: Temple University Press, 2001.

Wilson, Clint III. *Black Journalists in Paradox: Historical Perspectives and Current Dilemmas.* New York: Greenwood Press, 1991.

Wilson, David. *Inventing Black-on-Black Violence: Discourse, Space, and Representation.* Syracuse: Syracuse University Press, 2005.

Wilson, T. P. "Blood Quantum: Native American Mixed Bloods." In *Racially Mixed People in America,* ed. M. P. P. Root, 108–25.

Wilson, William J. *The Truly Disadvantaged: The Inner City, The Underclass, and Public Policy.* Chicago: University of Chicago Press, 1987.

———. *When Work Disappears: The World of the New Urban Poor.* New York: Alfred A. Knopf, 1996.

———. "Race, Class and Urban Poverty: A Rejoinder." *Ethnic and Racial Studies* 26 no. 2 (2003): 1096–14.

Wolseley, Roland E. *The Black Press, U.S.A.* 2nd ed. Ames: Iowa State University Press, 1990.

Wong, Paul, ed. *Race, Ethnicity and Nationality in the United States: Toward the Twenty-First Century.* Boulder: Westview, 1999.

Wynter, Leon E. *American Skin: Pop Culture, Big Business and the End of White America.* New York: Crown, 2002.

Yoshino, Kenji. *Covering: The Hidden Assault on Our Civil Rights.* New York: Random House, 2006.

Zackodnik, Teresa C. *The Mulatta and the Politics of Race.* Jackson: University of Mississippi Press, 2004.

Zook, Kristal Brent. *Color by Fox: The Fox Network and the Revolution in Black Television.* New York: Oxford University Press, 1999.

Newspaper and Magazine Articles

A Magazine. "The Pursuit of Hapa-ness." July 31, 2001, 34.

Aduroja, Grace. "It's All About the Box Office if Interracial Couples Are Cast." *San Diego Union-Tribune,* July 21, 2001, E5.

Alonso-Zaldivar, Ricardo. "Black or Latino: It's a Matter of Fearing Bias on Racial Lines." *New York Beacon,* March 26, 2003, 4.

Anderson, James. "Biracial Profiling." *Savoy,* September 2003, 30.

AsianWeek. "Count on It." January 14, 1998, 4.

Aubry, Larry. "Urban Perspective: Census, Multiracial Count is Problematic." *Los Angeles Sentinel,* February 16, 2000.

———. "Urban Perspective: Unfortunately, Ex-UC Regent Ward Connerly is at It Again." *Los Angeles Sentinel,* May 9, 2001.

———. "Urban Perspective: Does Initiative Process Make a Difference to Non-Whites?" *Los Angeles Sentinel,* November 5, 2001.

Autman, Samuel. "Mixed Race Categories for Census." *San Diego Tribune,* March 12, 2000.

Ayuyang, Rachelle Q. "Her Job Really Counts." *Filipinas Magazine,* May 30, 1998, 15.

Ball, H. G. "We're Doing It Again." *Norfolk Journal and Guide,* June 25, 1997.

Bamberger, Michael. "Mining Woods for Gold: Is Tiger Worth $100 Million to Nike? You Bet He Is." *Sports Illustrated*, September 25, 2000, 27.

Barnicle, Mike. "A Break from the Real World." *Boston Globe*, September 29, 1988, Metro section, 29.

Bean, Linda. "No Longer Black, White, Brown: Census Paints Race in New Shades." *Tennessee Tribune*, April 4, 2001.

Belsie, Laurent. "Profile Rises for Multiracial People." *Christian Science Monitor*, July 17, 2001.

Bennett, Robert W. Letter to the Editor, *Wall Street Journal*, February 2, 1995.

Bivens, L. "Report Discounts 'Multiracial' Listing Fears." *Washington Post*, May 16, 1997.

Boston Globe. "The Hiring Fraud Mystery." October 20, 1988, editorial.

———. "Academic Blacklisting." February 10, 1995.

Brand-Williams, Oralandar. "Census Change Stirs Mixed-Race Debate." *Detroit News*, January 5, 1998.

Byrne, Dennis. "McCarthy's Evil Spirit Haunts NU," *Chicago Sun-Times*, December 13, 1994.

Canellos, Peter S. Race fraud triggers memories of discord. *Boston Globe*, November 1, 1988, 15.

Clegg, Roger. "Words for the President." *National Review*, June 7, 2001.

———. "Census 2000: Interracial-Marriage Growth Creates Need for Broader Category." *Northwest Asian Weekly*, February 27, 1998.

Chicago Defender, "Must Not Insult Women of The Race," April 3, 1915.

———. "The Negro of Conquest," March 13, 1915.

———. "Races Cannot Intermarry," January 16, 1915.

———. "Race Woman Defends Honor," May 20, 1916.

———. "Bob Anderson Slain by Sweetheart," November 20, 1920.

———. "The Japanese Question," October 23, 1920.

———. "Stirring up a Hornet's Nest," November 13, 1920.

Chicago Tribune. Editorial, December 14, 1994.

Colety, Mark. "Census 2000: Asian or Pacific Islander? New Census Seeks Specifics on Race." *Northwest Asian Weekly*, March 6, 1998, 5.

Debenport, Ellen. "Round Two in 'Black Blood' Appeal." *United Press International*, November 13, 1984, Tuesday AM cycle.

———. "Lawyer Says State Law Steeped In Slavery," *New Orleans Times-Picayune*, November 14, 1984.

Demaret, Kent. "Raised White, a Louisiana Belle Challenges Race Records That Call Her 'Colored.' " *People*, December 6, 1982, 155–56.

DeMers, John. "Written Arguments Attack Racial Classification Law." *United Press International*, February 4, 1983, Friday AM cycle.

Diesenhouse, Susan. "Boston Case Raises Questions on Misuse of Affirmative Action." *New York Times*, October 9, 1988, A54.

———. In Affirmative Action, A Question of Truth in Labeling. *New York Times*, December 11, 1988, D26.

Dozier, Lee. "Race: It's No Longer a Matter of Black and White," *Tampa Tribune*, Nov. 29 1995, Baylife, 1.

Eason, Oscar Jr. "Biracial Classifications: History Forgotten?" *The New Pittsburgh Courier*, August 30, 1997.

Ebony. "What Makes You black?" January 1983, 115–18.

Eddings, Jerelyn. "Tiger's Triumph, America's Gain." *U. S. News and World Report*, April 28, 1997, 8.

English, Bella. "Color Coordinated." *Boston Globe*, October 12, 1988, 21.

Fletcher, Michael A. "Census Change Could Have Little Effect." *Washington Post*, May 16, 1997.

Florio, Gwen. "Kids Top Racial Chart: Multiple Choices on Census Forms Reflect Diversity." *Denver Post*, July 4, 2001.

Frisby, Michael K. "Black, White or Other?" *Emerge*, January 1996, 48–54.

Funderberg, Lise. "Boxed In." *New York Times*, July 10, 1996.

Gilliam, Dorothy. "Black/White." *Washington Post*, October 2, 1982.

Greenburg, Jan C., Bill Crawford, and John O'Brien. "Race Issue Sparks Hiring Controversy at NU Law School." *Chicago Tribune*, December 13, 1994.

Hernandez, Peggy. "Wife Defends Ex-Firefighter." *Boston Globe*, November 4, 1988, 21.

———. "Many Chances to Dispute Malones: Firefighters' Minority Status Unchallenged for 10 Years." *Boston Globe*, November 7, 1988, 1.

———. "No Minority Job Screens Done Before '84, City Says." *Boston Globe*, January 18, 1989, 19.

———. "City Still Awaits School Report on Minority Misrepresentation." *Boston Globe*, January 22, 1989, 36.

———. "2 Boston Firefighters, Probed for Minority Claim, Resign." *Boston Globe*, May 17, 1989, 29.

———. "SJC Considers Firefighters' Claim of Unfair Hearing in Minority Hiring Case." *Boston Globe*, May 25, 1989, 36.

———. "Prober Backs 7 Of 11 Firefighters in Ethnic Claims." *Boston Globe*, May 31, 1989, 17.

———. "Firemen Who Claimed to Be Black Lose Appeal." *Boston Globe*, July 26, 1989, 13.

Hernandez, Peggy, and John Ellement. "Two Fight Firing over Disputed Claim They Are Black." *Boston Globe*, September 29, 1988, 29.

———. "Race Fraud Probe Seeks Answers from 5 Firefighters." *Boston Globe*, October 13, 1988, 1.

Herron, Caroline, Michael Wright, and Carlyle Douglas. "Louisiana Drops Racial Fractions," *New York Times*, June 26, 1983.

Hills, Regina J. "State's 1-32nd 'Negro Blood' Law Valid," *United Press International*, May 18, 1983, Wednesday AM Cycle.

Hooper, Ernest. "Speaker's Words Felt by Every American." *St. Petersberg Times*, July 29, 2004, 3B.

Hubbard, Lee. "Multiracial Category on Census Raises Questions." *Indianapolis Recorder*, April 20, 2001.

Hughes, Bill. "Multi-racial Category Will Increase Further." *Oakland Post*, June 24, 2001.

Jackson, Derrick Z. Malones open old wounds. *Boston Globe*, October 7, 1988, 27.

Jacoby, Jeff. "Rise of the Blended American." *Boston Globe*, July 9, 2001.

Jaynes, Gregory. "Suit on Race Recalls Lines Drawn under Slavery," *New York Times* September 30, 1982.

Jet Magazine, "Sues to Change Classification of Her Race from Black to White," October 4, 1982, 6.

———. "Ex-College Prexy Calls Louisiana's Race Statute Unscientific and Biased," December 20, 1982, 23.

———. "La. Woman Seeking Repeal of 'Black Blood' Loses Case," June 6, 1983, 5.

———. "La. Repeals Mathematical Black Blood Classification," July 25, 1983, 42.

———. "Woman Resumes Fight over Race on Birth Certificate," December 10, 1984, 39.

———. "Louisiana Court Upholds Race on Birth Certificates," January 13, 1986, 5.

———. "Louisiana Woman Losing Her Bid to Be Categorized as White," January 12, 1987, 36.

———. "How Census Results Could Redefine American's Definition of Black." April 2, 2001, 4–10.

Johnson, Josh. "In Mixed Race Kids, America Sees Black." *Los Angeles Times*, August 16, 1997, M32.

Johnson, Michael. "Let's Hear More from Obama: It's Time for Jackson to Retire." *Boston Globe*, August 1, 2004, D12.

Jones, Vanessa E. "Mixing and Matching: Interracial Romances, Once Hollywood Taboo, are Creating Sparks on the Big Screen." *Boston Globe*, November 12, 2002.

Kane, Eugene. "Woods Has to Do More to Reach Mount Olympus." *Milwaukee Journal Sentinel*, July 25, 2000.

Kao, Grace. "2050: The Face of Race." *A Magazine*, January 21, 2001, 58.

Kirkpatrick, Melanie. "Rule of Law: Not Black Enough for This Law School," *Wall Street Journal*, January 11, 1995.

Kong, Deborah. "Number Crunch: Wondering How to Make Sense of Census 2000 and How It Will Affect You? Here's a Rundown." *A Magazine*, January 31, 2002, 38.

Kotkin, Joel, and Thomas Tseng. "Happy to Mix It All Up." *Washington Post*, June 8, 2003.

La Ferla, Ruth. "Generation E.A.: Ethnically Ambiguous." *New York Times*, December 28, 2003.

Large, Jerry. "Multiracial and Tearing Down Old Hierarchy." *Seattle Times*, August 17, 2003.

Lavilla, Stacy. "Hapa Issues Move into the Spotlight." *AsianWeek*, June 10, 1998, 11.

Leland, John, and Gregory Beals. "In Living Colors." *Newsweek*, May 5, 1997, 58–60.

Leland, John and Allison Samuels. "The New Generation Gap," *Newsweek*, March 17, 1997, 52–60.

Lieser, Ethen. "Hapa Issues Forum Celebrates 10th Anniversary." *AsianWeek*, July 31, 2002, 15.

Little India. "Most Indian State." March 31, 2001, 4.

———. "Mix and Match." May 31, 2002, 4.

Los Angeles Sentinel. "Colin Powell: 'Racism still serious problem in America.' " May 7, 1997.

Lowery, Joseph E. "'Tiger' on Course, 'Cub' in Jungle: The Remarkable Young Man, Eldrick 'Tiger' Woods." *Muslim Journal,* June 6, 1997, 21.

Malcolmson, Scott L. "Obama's Speech Says Much about Race Politics." *New York Times,* August 1, 2004, D3.

Marable, Manning. "Along the Color Line: The Death of Affirmative Action." *The Westside Gazette,* July 15, 2004.

Marantz, Steve, and Peggy Hernandez. "Defining race a sensitive, elusive task; Boston's hiring probe brings system under fire." *Boston Globe,* October 23, 1988, 33.

Marcus, Frances F. "Louisiana Repeals Black Blood Law." *New York Times,* July 6, 1983.

Marriot, Michel. "Multiracial Americans Ready to Claim Their Identity." *New York Times,* July 20, 1996.

Mathews, Linda. "Beyond 'Other:' More Than Identity Rides on A New Racial Category." *New York Times,* July 6, 1996, A1.

Moon, Su. "Amerasia Journal vol. 23 no. 1: 'No Passing Zone.' " *Yolk,* March 31, 1998, 61.

Morgenthau, Tom. "What Color is Black?" *Newsweek,* February 13, 1995, 62–65.

Newsweek. "Latino Power: L.A.'s New Hispanic Mayor-and How Hispanics Will Change American Politics." May 30, 2005.

New York Times. "A Little Local Color," September 19, 1982, E19.

———. "Black and White," September 26, 1982, Editorial Desk, 18.

———. "Slave Descendant Fights Race Listing," September 15, 1982, A16.

"News and Views: 'Not All with Dark Skins Are Black': Definition of Who is 'Black' Plagues Northwestern School of Law." *Journal of Blacks in Higher Education,* March 31, 1995, 20.

Ng, Janet. "Who Am I? Navigating the Interethnic Mix: Growing Up Multicultural in America." *AsianWeek,* June 20, 2001, 12.

Norment, Lynn. "Am I Black, White, or In between?" *Ebony,* August 1995, 108–116.

Omaha World-Herald. "Iowan's Racial Makeup, Ages, Detailed by Census." July 11, 2001.

Osgood, Viola. "New Brothers in the Family." *Boston Globe,* October 13, 1988, 19.

O'Sullivan, Taro. "Asian-American Affairs: Where Did All the White People Go?" *The Asian American Reporter,* July 10, 2001, 6.

Page, Lisa F. "Acceptance Amid the Diversity." *Washington Post,* July 16, 2002.

Pawlowski, Jay. "The Blending of 'American Skin.' " *Rocky Mountain News,* August 9, 2002.

Philadelphia Tribune. "Multiracial Census Listing Would Do More Harm Than Good." May 30, 1997.

Pittsburgh Post-Gazette. "Melting Pot, Mixing Bowl: Acceptance is Accelerating, Changing the Face of America." November 12, 2002.

Plume, Janet. "Woman Loses Bid To Change Racial Status." *United Press International*, October 18, 1985, AM cycle.

Preston, Rohan. "Battle to Keep a Black Professor Leaves Bruised Egos and Reputations." *New York Times*, March 8, 1995.

Rey, Jay. "Blurring the Lines of Racial Identity." *Buffalo News*, January 28, 2002.

Rimer, Sara and Karen W. Arenson. "Top Colleges Take More Blacks, but Which Ones?" *New York Times*, June 24, 2001.

Roach, Ronald. "When Academia Meets Activism: Harvard's Color Lines Conference Draws Nearly 1,000 Participants to Share New Insights, Data on the Nation's Agenda on Race." *Black Issues in Higher Education*, September 25, 2003, 36–39.

Scheiber, Noam. "Barack Obama's Miraculous Campaign: Race Against History." *New Republic*, May 31, 2004, 21–26.

Schemo, Diana J. "Despite Options on Census, Many to Check 'Black' Only." *New York Times*, February 12, 2000.

Schlangenstein, Mary. "Appeal Filed on Blood Law." United Press International, AM cycle, May 20, 1983.

Secter, Bob. "Black Prof Fails Political Test" *Chicago Sun-Times*, December 11, 1994.

Sege, Irene. "Not Black Enough? Law Professor Heads to BU after Furor at Northwestern over Her Racial Identity." *Boston Globe*, February 9, 1995.

Shea, Rachel H. "Beyond Race or Beholden to It?" *US News and World Report*, October 6, 2003.

Smart-Grosvenor, Venita. "Obsessed With 'Racial Purity.' *Ms. Magazine*, June 1983, 28–30.

Smith, Starita. "Higher Education Expresses Concerns with Multiple Choice Census." *Black Issues in Higher Education*, November 27, 1997, 14.

Soo, Julie, Stacy Lavilla, and Janet Dang. "Finally, It's History." *AsianWeek*, January, 13, 1999, 11.

Spencer, Jon M. "Just What We Don't Need." *Washington Post*, January 22, 1997.

Stefanik, Donna. "Mixed Race Experience Examined: National Conference Explores What It Is to be a Multiracial American." *The Skanner*, April 9, 2003.

Stodghill, R. and A. Bower. "Where Everyone's a Minority: Welcome to Sacramento, America's Most Integrated City." *Time Magazine*, September 2, 2002, 26–28.

Strausberg, Chinta. "Re. Jackson Seeks Black/Hispanic Agenda for Power." *Chicago Defender*, March 10, 2001, 3.

Swamy, Prakash M. "All Is Not Well With Recent Immigrants." *News-India Times*, April 23, 1999, 8.

Takahashi, Corey. "Checking off the Future." *A. Magazine*, March 31, 1998, 31.

Tilles, Mark. "Multiracial Category Becomes Law." *Michigan Chronicle*, September 26, 1995.

Tilove, Jonathan. "Racial Identity in U.S. Is Mix of Politics, Fashion, and Genetics. *Houston Chronicle*, April 26, 1992.

———. "New Star Emerges on Democratic Scene: Obama Speech Marks Race-Politics Watershed." *Times-Picayune* (New Orleans), July 28, 2004, 1.

Time Magazine. "Color Bind: Louisiana Reforms, Sort of." July 18, 1983.

Times-Picayune. "Teen Movies Embracing Interracial Couples." July 27, 2001.

Toler, Sonya M. "No Major Changes in Proposed District Lines." *New Pittsburgh Courier,* November 3, 2002.

Trillin, Calvin. "American Chronicles: Black or White." *The New Yorker,* April 14, 1986.

Tri-State Defender. "What Does Being African American Mean and Who Said So?" January 7, 2004.

Vobejda, Barbara. "Census Expands Options." *Washington Post,* October 30, 1997.

Walters, Ron. "From the Desk: The Census, Multiracial Confusion." *Washington Informer,* March 21, 2001, 13.

Washington Afro American. "Census—The Multiracial Threat." July 19, 1997.

Washington Informer. "New Census Race IDs Will Change Programs, Say Rights Leaders, Gov't." March 28, 2001, 4.

Weekly Standard. "Choosing Colorblindness." 7 no. 24 (2002): 3.

Whelan, David. "Casting Tiger Woods." *Forecast,* May 7, 2001, 1–4.

Will, George F. "Dropping the 'One-Drop' Rule." *Newsweek,* March 25, 2002, 64.

Williams, Juan. "Quotas Are A Dead Issue, Rights Panel Chairman Says." *Washington Post,* January 30, 1985, A2.

Williams, Lena. "Justices Hear Quota Cases from New York and Ohio." *New York Times,* February 26, 1986, A20.

Williams, Teresa Kay. "Racial Seduction: America's Gaze on Hapa Men." *Yolk,* March 31, 1998, 18.

Winfrey, Yayoi Lena. "Magazine Publisher, Editor—and Only 20 Years Old." *Northwest Asian Weekly,* August 6, 1999, 1.

———. "Mixmaster Matt: Yayoi Lena Winfrey Talks to MAVIN Magazine Founder Matt Kelley about Hapa Issues and Living la Vida Mestiza." *A Magazine,* July 31, 2001, 38.

Wong, Bill. "Yellow Pearls: A Multiracial Meeting of Minds." *AsianWeek,* July 9, 1998.

Wu, Frank. "Washington Journal: The Cusp of a New Era." *AsianWeek,* January 7, 1998, 19.

Yamaguchi, Jeffrey. "He's Got the Look: Michael Riego Updates the Jordache Brand for 2001." *A Magazine,* July 31, 2001, 26.

Younge, Gary. "Multiracial Citizens Divided." *Washington Post,* July 19, 1996.

Yuen, Jennifer. "HapAmerica." *AsianWeek,* May 21, 2003, 18.

Index

253